NICHECRAFT

NICHECRAFT

USING YOUR SPECIALNESS TO FOCUS
YOUR BUSINESS, CORNER YOUR
MARKET, AND MAKE CUSTOMERS
SEEK YOU OUT

DR. LYNDA FALKENSTEIN

HarperBusiness
A Division of HarperCollinsPublishers

HarperCollins books may be purchased for educational, business or sales promotional use. For information please write: Special Markets Department, HarperCollins Publishers, Inc., 10 East 53rd Street, New York, NY 10022.

FIRST EDITION

Designed by C. Linda Dingler

Library of Congress Cataloging-in-Publication Data

Falkenstein, Lynda.
    Nichecraft : using your specialness to focus your business, corner your market, and make customers seek you out / by Lynda Falkenstein. — 1st ed.
        p.   cm.
    ISBN 0-88730-801-5
    1. Success in business. 2. Market segmentation. 3. Customer services.
I. Title.
HF5386.F24   1996
658.8—dc20   96-10716

96 97 98 99 00 ❖/RRD 10 9 8 7 6 5 4 3 2

To my very special *parents,*
with love

Acknowledgments

In concluding this all-new edition of *Nichecraft: Using Your Specialness to Focus Your Business, Corner Your Market, and Make Customers Seek You Out*, I recognize the invaluable roles played by many extraordinary individuals—people without whom neither earliest nor current editions would exist. As in *Nichecraft's* first edition, I wish to acknowledge all my clients and other special people who by their example have served as a continuous reminder to me that good niches can be infinitely more than the stuff of dreams; they can also be transformed into straightforward intentional realities. I thank them for never settling for less than they originally intended to achieve. Most of all, I thank them for adhering to their vision. They are models for us all.

This newest edition owes special thanks to the scores of people who have taken time from their busy lives to communicate with me after reading my basic self-published *Nichecraft*. Your letters from every corner of America and from every walk of life and business have helped me understand even more the power and importance of creating the focus that works for each of us. By asking questions about the process, you caused me to refine my own thinking. You stretched my sense of possibility. Most of all, you helped me understand and believe in *Nichecraft's* potential. Thank you for giving the book and concept lives of their own.

Additionally, I want to extend my deepest gratitude to the many people who have believed sufficiently in *Nichecraft* to have invested their own time, energies, and professional commitments to its success. I especially acknowledge my superb editor, Suzanne Oaks, not only for her confidence in the product but especially for her gifted skills in ensuring this book about focus was, indeed, focused.

And finally, though not least, I want to acknowledge and thank my husband and friend, Michael Falkenstein, for his patience, support, and sense of humor as I took extended leave from the real world for the cerebral bubble called writing.

CONTENTS

6 THE GUARANTEE OF SUCCESS: NO PLAN B   208

7 THE CRAFT IN SUMMARY   245

NICHECRAFT

Introduction

Eliminating the competition (without bloodshed), distinguishing your business from everyone else's, and getting the right customers clamoring for your product or service *in any economy* are the most basic requirements for business success today. Whether you are running a small "Mom and Pop" operation or are CEO of a major corporation, the rule applies: You can no longer simply compete against anyone in a similar field. Not if you want to win, that is. The fact is, you win by being perceived as special, singular, unique, one of a kind. You must create a niche that you own, that nobody can steal or take from you, and that achieves your goals. And that's what this book is about—helping you define and achieve the kind of focus that assures your business success regardless of the headlines or ups and downs in the economy.

Enter the extraordinary world of niches and nichecrafting. I offer you fair warning, however. You are entering a world which at first blush may seem filled with contradictions and ambiguities. You will be told, for example, to "think small to get big," to "focus steadfastly and stay the course but be flexible," to be "authentic but match what you want to sell with what your customer wants to buy." As you continue your journey through *Nichecraft,* you will come to understand why these are not contradictions but instead critical features of *good nichecrafting.* Most of all, you will learn how to *do* them. What you will find out very soon is that this book is definitely not the theory of making niches. You will have nothing less than a practical 9-step blueprint* for achieving the focus that works for you and your business.

Our sojourn will take you the entire trip, from dispelling myths that get in the way of making effective niches to recognizing niches when you see them to creating entire product lines around the focus you commit to. You will also be challenged to consider the best ways of getting the word out to those who need and want what you have to offer. Additionally you will think about the life cycle of the niches you invent and the ultimate need to re-niche, preventing your business from going the way of dinosaurs. You will come to think of *good* niches as resembling healthy human beings who must grow and adapt to shifting environments if they are to survive. And perhaps the most delicate subject of the entire book, you will examine your feelings about risk and assess its implications for your business's long-term success.

I have been told by many that the trip I take you on here is at the very least an unorthodox one. The truth is, I consider that observation the highest compliment because it is totally consistent with the theme of this book; that is, ordinary business-as-usual doesn't work anymore. We must get out of our boxes, be nimble, creative, and of course, be niched. To ensure that you get the most out of your *Nichecraft* experience, I offer two tips or previews of what's to come. The first concerns our definition of this thing we call a niche. Is it a thing? A state of being? A place? A product? A target audience? A marketing system? The answer is "could be" on all counts. The critical element in our quest for a good niche is that it be perceived as *special, singular, unique, one of a kind.*

The second tip I share with you concerns the 9-step process you will be embarking upon. It is important to emphasize that while you will become competent in using each of the steps, you may not always follow the order in which they are presented. For example, you may find as you get started that you have Steps 1 and 2 well under control and are ready to jump right into Step 3. It's also entirely possible that you cannot

---

*See page 45 for an illustration of the entire 9-step system.

complete some earlier steps until you have information about later ones. Ultimately you will have all 9 steps defined and in your grasp. And this brings us to what is perhaps the greatest lesson of all I have been reminded of since writing my first *Nichecraft* manuscript several years ago. That is, we are engaged here in a *process* and not a pat answer. If you expect to get a niche overnight, this is not the book for you. If, on the other hand, you have a vision grounded in a sense of possibility, a commitment to the ultimate goal of defining a narrow but very deep business niche, along with a willingness to work with a friendly guide, dive in.

1

A NICHE IS BORN

NICHE:
Special, unique, one of a kind
CRAFT:
Skill, profession, art

You always knew you'd be in business someday. Not just *any* business, but your *own* highly successful one. In your heart you've probably thought of yourself as a closet entrepreneur or businessperson all your life. Your basic training most likely began when you were just a kid with a paper route, a seasonal lemonade stand, or a summer sales job to buy your first car. Maybe you worked in your parents' store or waited tables in someone else's restaurant. Later, as you realized your interest in business was more than a passing fancy, you may have taken business courses in college. You might even have gotten a fancy biz degree that officially verified your competence in the intricacies and nuances of this thing called business. So it was that business and you were an inevitable pair. Like hand in glove.

The New Rules

Whether you took the plunge years ago and have already built a company bringing you pride and profits or are just now

5

heeding the urge to strike out on your own or whether you are part of a large organization and charged with making it even more profitable, you know one thing for sure: whatever business you operate today, it's going to have to play by entirely different rules than in earlier years—if it is to prosper and grow, much less be successful! You are painfully aware of how the kingpin standards of yesteryear have all but vanished before your eyes.

You know which rules I mean. The ones saying if you worked hard, had a good product, gave great customer service, had experience and reasonable prices, were honest, demonstrated "excellence," and above all, were sufficiently customer-centered and genuinely loved what you did, you most certainly would be successful.

So much for history! Today these features are standards instead of exceptions to the rule. By themselves, they certainly don't guarantee success. There is no little irony, in fact, in that alone, these features are quite ordinary. Minimum standards, if you will. And today's world has no room for the ordinary. The fittest—whether people, services, tangible products, or organizations—must do more than simply stand out in a crowd if they wish to thrive in today's topsy-turvy, ever-changing times. They must be perceived as nothing less than *Special*. One of a kind. Unique. Being the only game in town is not an option or luxury. It's a basic prerequisite for winning. Regardless of what size your business is, regardless of what your widget or service may be, regardless of where your business is located or who your customers are, it is the single most important thing separating winners from losers, which are here today and gone tomorrow.

And the reason is that competition as you knew it, as your parents knew it, and maybe even as your own children knew it, is *dead. Gone. No more*. No longer can you win by competing against someone in a similar field or industry. In today's business world you win by being perceived as *Special*. By being distinguished from everyone else. By being so tightly focused that the right people seek you out. By being perceived as indispensable. By understanding that small can be very beautiful and that narrow can be extraordinarily deep and profitable. In short, you win by being "niched."

In the nineties, it's survival of the nichest!

But we are not talking about making just *any* niche. The point of all this is to make a *good* one—one that takes you and your business where you want to go—one that helps achieve your life's goals and ambitions—one that is the engine for your business—one that can nourish and grow multiple profit centers—one that ensures you prosperity in any economy—one that evolves before it wears out and disappears. And of course, we're talking about the kind of niche that has a customer at the other end. But most of all, it's one that puts and keeps you in charge of the ship. That keeps tail from wagging dog. And in fact, it is a constant reminder of which is which.

The "good niche" distinction is extremely important when you consider all the people we know who have made disastrous niches for themselves. Niches that some of my clients have colorfully described as "a niche from hell." Their lives or businesses went in directions they never intended. Their niche drove them, instead of the other way around. In some cases it got so out of control it bore little if any resemblance to their original concept. And like lawless genes, a niche without controls on it can produce horrific consequences. In other words, good niches have direction, and that direction is you.

SEARS: A NICHE DISASTER

Stark evidence abounds of what happens when businesses are either ignorant of or refuse to play by the new rules of success. Sears is a classic example. For decades nothing less than an American institution, this once-giant in retailing nearly fell apart after what in retrospect looks like an all-out effort to self-destruct, to eliminate whatever niche it had in the consumer's pocketbook. If you're over 30, Sears was probably synonymous in your mind with reliability, home-related products such as tools and appliances, and perhaps catalog and mail-order sales. Though probably not an exciting one, your image of what Sears stood for was probably nonetheless pretty clear; that is, until the company joined the acquisition bandwagon of the mid-seventies and eighties. All of a sudden you heard about the "Sears Financial Network." It had purchased Dean Witter, adding blue-chip stocks to its inventory. How convenient! You could augment your investment portfolio and walk just a few feet more to get your Roto-Rooter! And then Coldwell Banker joined the Sears family. Pretty soon even the most loyal customers didn't know what the company was up to or what it stood for. Worse yet, it lost sight of its core so much that even Sears didn't know what it stood for anymore.

Sears committed the ultimate sin. By acting on the assumption that big was better, it kept adding to its menu and literally killed what was once a powerful niche. Its downward spiral leveled off in the early nineties when the company began to shed its earlier acquisitions and undertook a massive overhaul of its merchandising, hoping to restore its niche and once again be taken seriously in the contemporary retail world.

OTHER NEAR-DEATH EXPERIENCES

Foolish though it was, Sears had a lot of company doing exactly the same things it was doing. Another familiar company that retrieved its niche from the brink of disaster was Paramount, formerly known as Gulf and Western Industries. Once a sprawling, directionless organization, the company was rescued from imminent bankruptcy in 1983. After a decade of tighter and tighter focus on the publishing and entertainment business, Paramount was sold to Viacom for $10 billion. Its huge sale price was testimony to the value of focus, focus, focus. Viacom's challenge will be to keep their own eyes on the prize—to keep their own focus on that which made the new Paramount successful and profitable. Time will tell us if they are truly wiser than the Gulf and Western leadership, people who never understood that narrow and deep are synonyms for big and profitable.

Indeed, the late eighties and early nineties saw scores of other corporate giants falling by the wayside one by one, their demise resulting from far more than faltering national or global economies. Like rank amateurs, banks, airlines, newspapers, manufacturing companies—the list continues ad nauseam—added and added, making themselves bigger while naively thinking themselves better and on their way to more success. And then all of a sudden we became familiar with a new jargon. Divestiture. Spin-off. Back to our core. You and I recognize these terms as euphemisms for in-over-their-heads.

Lest there be any misunderstanding that this self-destructive behavior is uniquely American, we have only to look at another more recent niche fiasco, this one accomplished by none other than Sony Corporation. Also falling prey to the merger and acquisition frenzy of earlier years, Sony proudly added huge movie studios, including Columbia and Tristar Pictures, to its list of holdings in 1990. It's reasonable to assume that by mid-1995, when it announced a staggering $3.2 billion loss, company officials must finally have realized it's one thing to make television sets but a whole different show to produce the movies shown on them.

Never to be upstaged, Mitsubishi Estate accomplished perhaps the most notorious niche mess of all by announcing its intent to default on nothing less than an American icon, Rockefeller Plaza. Bigger, but definitely not smarter, Mitsubishi Estate, Sony, and Sears did exactly what "small business" people are often criticized for doing. They got so far afield of their strengths, they sometimes didn't even know what they were. They chose the "cash in the door" route—creating short-term gains and huge long-term losses.

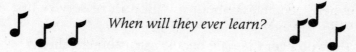

When will they ever learn?

Understanding the Game Plan: NicheThink Begins

The moral of these near-death niche stories and the underlying theme of this entire book is that niching is not an option, regardless of the size or nature of your enterprise. Whether you're working with an established "mature" company, a young start-up firm, or one somewhere in the middle, the issue remains the same. If you are serious about business success well beyond the hobby stage—success that generates healthy profits and predictable growth—making a good niche must be an integral part of your game plan.

It's entirely possible you've already come to this conclusion yourself. If that's the case, you've probably also figured out that saying you want to niche your business and actually doing it are two entirely different things! What you know for certain is that this critical feature of any successful business isn't going to pop out of the air ready-made with a nice big bow around it. Magic, good thoughts, and luck don't produce niches, or at least not good ones. Instead of referring to *finding* niches, or going on a niche hunt, smart businesspeople talk about what they are doing to *craft* them. They also know that the most ordinary-sounding and most important questions smart businesspeople ask cannot be fully answered until this "niche thing" is addressed. Questions such as:

1. How do I figure out what kind of widget to sell?
2. How can I ensure someone else wants my widget and it won't be destined for white-elephant status?
3. How do I get the right message out to the right people about my widget so that it doesn't become the world's best-kept secret?
4. How do I create a business that is truly recession-proof, where people ask about my product or service first and price second?
5. How do I get the *right* people as customers/clients?
6. How do I protect my product or service from the knock-off artists lying in wait for me to be successful so they can steal my precious idea or widget?
7. How do I create a business that is flexible, maybe even portable if I move or travel frequently?
8. How can I distinguish my product or service from all the others out there claiming to be excellent with good track records and superior customer service and all the other virtues quality businesses are supposed to possess?

9. How can I grow a business that doesn't become obsolete?
10. How can I turn my existing skills and knowledge into a successful business?
11. How can I develop a business with a single focus and multiple profit centers each generating important revenue of its own?
12. How do I know if my temperament and personality are suited to the life of business and entrepreneurship?
13. How can I create a business that lets me do what I love and pays me well at the same time?
14. What about making a business plan, capitalization, and other nitty-gritty issues I need to know about?
15. And above all, how can I create a business that enhances the quality of my life and the quantity of my income at the same time??!!

The reason for emphasizing *good* niching—achieving just the right focus—so heavily at this early stage is simple: How well you do with that piece directly influences your success with every other aspect of your enterprise. Flunk niche and your dream business doesn't happen or suffers an early demise. The rest of this book then is devoted to helping you answer questions such as those we just listed. To ensure your niche is also well cared for, all these important matters will be addressed within the framework of a straightforward 9-step process for achieving focus. The kind that eliminates competition (without bloodshed), that takes you where you where you want to go, that is intentional, and that someone else wants! The process is called *nichecraft*. It is your game plan for winning in any time and any economy. Build your business using its logical 9 steps and you'll wonder why you waited so long to get started.

You've made the commitment. The game is on. Before you can play, however, much needs to be done. Foremost on your list is knowing more fully what this whole business of niching is about and especially how nichecraft can help your business develop to its maximum. This chapter is devoted to helping you recognize niches when you see them, know how they are relevant to your business success, and most importantly, understand the basic 9-step process you will use to transform your dream to reality.

Characteristics of a Niche

As your first step in understanding the idea of *niche*, I want you to think about the word *love*. Yes, that's what I said—love! Aside from the fact that they are both short, the words *love* and *niche* have a lot in common. For one thing, each is too big an idea to be accurately or fairly explained by a single word or phrase. By the same token, you don't need a formal definition of love to know when it's not present. The same goes with a niche. Oftentimes it's most conspicuous by its absence.

We have already seen that huge organizations are not immune to lack of focus. Unfortunately, small to mid-size businesses are no less vulnerable. A visit with just a few of the scores of nice but nicheless people I've met demonstrates this point and gives us vital clues about our subject and goal, the *good* niche.

DOING WHAT I LOVE, BUT NOT MAKING ANY MONEY AT IT!

Mark and I met a few years ago shortly after he was referred to me through another client. In his mid-30s, he had been a stockbroker for nearly a full year. Before entering the securities industry he sold high-grade plastic to manufacturers around the United States. Though the plastic business satisfied his financial requirements, Mark yearned for what he perceived as a "professional environment"—a secretary, a place to go to work other than his basement home office, a reason to dress well every day, all the trappings of a pinstriped environment! Thus, when the opportunity was presented to him to join one of the nation's largest stock brokerages, he jumped at the chance. His new employer's training program appeared to be the best in the business, and Mark's expectations for his success were at their highest.

By the time he came to my office, the honeymoon had been over for about three months, the amount of time since his formal training had ended. His guaranteed salary was over and it was straight commission from now on. Mark was definitely on his own. Unfortunately, nothing was happening.

"I don't know what's wrong," he said, a frustrated and perplexed look on his face. "I passed all the tests with high scores. I've studied all our products—and they are good ones. I've done my homework, all the things the company says to do. I just can't get enough business! And the business I do get, well, it's hardly the right kind. . .

"The irony is," he went on with a kind of wry expression, "this is the first time I've ever had a job I can say I really love! I guess this is another case where love alone isn't enough!"

"I agree with you," I said. "It's important, but definitely not enough. Tell me, Mark, what do you do to try to find clients?"

"Well, I have made up all the lists the company suggested—friends, acquaintances, people I've done business with in the past—everything."

"Then what do you do?"

"I sit down and call x number every day, just like we were told."

"Doesn't sound as if you like that part very much," I observed.

Feeling Like a Beggar

"It isn't that I don't like it, which I don't. The fact is, it doesn't work. As I said, the little bit of business I get is far from the right business. Actually, I feel like a beggar, cold-calling people who don't even know me. And here I wanted to enter a profession so that my self-image would be raised. In truth, I feel worse every day. Like I'm digging a bigger and bigger hole." As he talked, frustration showed on his face, and I could feel the pain of someone working very hard going no place.

"Let me ask another way. What do you do to get clients coming to you instead of you running after them?"

Mark looked at me with a mixture of incredulity and cynicism.

Are Clients Calling You Up?

"What do you mean 'coming after me'? I can't even get them to buy my products when I find them. How can I expect that they're going to seek me out? You've got to be kidding!"

"No, I'm not kidding at all," I said with what I hoped would be a smile of encouragement. "How many people are there in your office, Mark?"

"About sixty-five or so. We're medium-size for this town."

"And how many other securities brokerages are there in this city?" I continued, probing.

"Probably five major houses with lots of smaller players. And then the banks, of course, are selling financial products. I guess there are lots of us," he concluded, still uncertain where I was leading him.

"And what makes you any different from any of those in your office?" I asked. Silence.

"What makes you different from any of those other brokers out there in other companies in town?" Silence again.

I continued, "For the most part, I don't think the difference is the products. A stock is a stock. Maybe a difference in commission, possibly service, but the product is pretty much the same. Right?"

"Uh-huh," he conceded.

"So, what's the difference between you and all the others offering the same product?"

"Nothing, I guess. At least right now," he again concluded, but this time I could tell he was thinking about what his words meant.

"That's my point. How can you expect anyone to tell you apart from all the masses of other brokers if you are exactly the same? You have to stand for something so that the *right* clients can find you. Then you not only have a real business but you eliminate your competition. Without bloodshed," I added with a smile.

"Does that make sense?" I pressed.

"Sure does. I guess that's what I'm here for!"

A niche distinguishes you from everyone else.

THE NICHE THAT "JUST SORT OF HAPPENED"

I met Ingrid several years ago after she'd returned from an extended trip around the world. The ostensible purpose of her trip was to figure out what her next business was going to be. Because her last venture had been enormously successful, she naively assumed figuring out the next one would be a piece of cake. She couldn't have been more wrong. A look at how that first business grew gives us a clue to why she was having problems getting on track with the second.

Ingrid's first business grew out of a series of articles she wrote for a nationwide magazine targeting the "larger woman." Ingrid's articles had grown into a book, her book had produced speaking engagements, and before she knew it, Ingrid had become a celebrity. She had also become a mini-empire. Books, patterns, and a host of other products came out with her name on them. Ingrid enjoyed her celebrity status as much as her significant income. The problem was, it all happened by accident.

"It just sort of happened," she told me. "I didn't really plan for any of it." She continued, telling me what I've heard too many others say. You know, the I-just-fell-into-it explanation for success. As she was talking, I heard myself thinking, The problem with falling into something good is that you could also just fall into something bad. Worst of all, when a niche happens by accident you can't replicate it, because you don't know the process that you went through in the first place.

"I've had several projects, but none of them go anyplace," Ingrid went on.

I thought about her term, *projects*, and the many people I've met who confuse a series of unrelated projects with a business that has any glue, a business that's going in a single direction.

With a frustrated look on her face, Ingrid announced the obvious, "It makes me crazy. I'm just so unfocused! So what do I do? How do I find a niche that will be as successful as the last one?"

"First off," I reminded her, "you're finished *finding* any-thing. We need to retrospectively unpack what you did the first time. Let's look at what you did that worked. And then you'll be ready to systematically begin our nine-step process, crafting your own new niche. And this time you'll do it inten-tionally."

Ingrid ignored Step 9—the critical phase that keeps you always looking ahead, preventing your business from coming to an abrupt halt with no apparent place to go instead of transitioning logically to the next stage. If Ingrid's plight rings vaguely familiar in your own business life, take comfort. Our event-consequenc-ing (Chapter 2) and trending (Chapter 3) exercises will keep you from making the same mistakes she did.

THE NICHE THAT WORE OUT

One of the saddest niche cases I ever met came packaged as an over-the-hill photography store. I say saddest because this is definitely one situation that didn't have to happen. But like so many niches that wear out, its owners had double sets of blinders on.

I walked into the store because I needed some custom printing work done and had heard this place could do the job very well. And they did excellent work for me. As I could tell from looking around the shop, which was like entering a time warp, something was not right. Inventory that looked old and dusty, too many items on sale, so many signs on the window you could hardly see in, and an overall sense of "we're tired" told me that whatever niche this place had had at one time was near death. Perhaps it had already expired. In talking with the owners I came to understand how this once-proud store came to be almost no more.

"Our father started this business nearly fifty years ago," Stuart told me. "He established a reputation for excellence before the term was cliché. For many years most of our customers were really large companies that wanted us to photograph their equipment. We made a lot of money on those big prints. We'd do them upstairs and the quality was unsurpassed."

I could see Stuart was understandably proud of the quality his store had stood for.

"So you decided you wanted to be in the photography business, too, Stuart?"

With that simple question, the expression on his face changed from pride to disappointment.

"Not exactly," he said. "Our father thought we should take this over and it was making money and looked like it had a future, so we did."

"But your heart's never really been in this, has it?"

"I guess you'd say that's right," Stuart acknowledged. "Anyway, the business did fine until a few years ago when a lot of our biggest customers went out of business. All of a sudden the commercial photography business just sort of turned upside down."

"So, what did you do?" I asked.

"Well, we got a second location, thinking expansion would help generate more revenue."

Egads, I said to myself. Expansion may sometimes bring in more money, but it also creates expense, something Stuart's over-the-hill store soon discovered. The second location lasted a few months. Unfortunately, the lease payments lasted two years.

"You have such a wonderful reputation as a photographer, Stuart," I said. "Have you ever considered holding seminars for special clients, perhaps offering photographic tours with yourself as the guide?" I was thinking to myself that with Stuart's reputation, many people would gladly pay just to watch him in action.

"I actually have thought about that," he answered, "but right now we have to figure out how to compete against the big stores that are destroying us. They are undercutting our prices on everything. I can't take time for seminars."

What would it take for him to realize *he* was the niche, I asked myself. If he harnessed the niche he was walking around with, he could have a vibrant, absolutely unique business. Granted, it would be different from the one his father had built. He opted, however, to try to stay afloat by staying the same.

As you've doubtless guessed, Stuart's business disappeared.

OH, SO NICHELESS

Though their symptoms were very different, Mark, Ingrid, and Stuart were ultimately suffering from the same ailment. Mark loved what he was doing. He knew his technology, he was an expert in his product line, and he worked hard. By all conventional standards, he was excellent. Unfortunately, he was also getting poorer daily, the reason being that his business approach was perceived as ordinary, indistinguishable from that of masses of other stockbrokers, making him basically invisible in the marketplace. Ingrid, on the other hand, formerly had a highly visible, very profitable niche. It's just that it happened by accident and she didn't know what ingredients had made it work so that she could replicate the process. Stuart also had a formerly prosperous niche. His disappeared by default. It wasn't that he didn't have fair warning that things were changing. Nor was it that he didn't know how his father had once created a good niche for the company. Stuart simply didn't want to change and he didn't. Maybe he was tired and wanted the store to die, which it did. So, while they each got there by different roads, each of our friends wound up at the same destination: sheer and complete nichelessness.

What we learn from these stories is that without a healthy, intentional, and highly disciplined niche, our businesses come to screeching and expensive halts!

By its omission, you are beginning to understand something about this idea of niche. There are a host of other ways to recognize a niche when you see one: features and characteristics associated with a niche, "critical attributes" if you will. And of course, the next steps will be those helping you enhance or develop the niche(s) that are right for you.

In simplest terms, a niche is something small. The corner where two walls come together is a niche. That niche can be very small, but it can run very deep. This is a case where small doesn't mean minimal business or limited success. Just the opposite. Most of the highly successful companies in this country—the ones that have thrived even in the worst economies—are highly focused, tightly niched entities. They don't just know who their audience is, they are also equally aware of who it is not. They are not trying to be all things to all people.

The publishing industry is increasingly sensitive to the *small is bigger* concept. Consider magazines such as *Road & Track*, *Air Transport*, and *Sports Illustrated*. Their subject matter is very specific and limited. So is their target audience. One of the more provocative target markets promises to be an extremely lucrative one for publishers of *PrisonLife*, a magazine tapping into a $2 billion captive market. Since the mid-eighties, the rapid proliferation of business journals and equally rapid decline of daily newspapers underscores the increasing significance of identifying and capturing specific market segments.

This point was driven home to me in a conversation with a highly successful business journal publisher located in the Pacific Northwest. In discussing his paper's ad rates and relatively small circulation, he reminded me that advertisers are no longer interested in paying just to be in a big paper; they want to be in the right one—the one they know their customers read. Better to be in a paper with a readership of 12,000 than one with 350,000 if they are 12,000 of the *right* people.

More than segmented
More than vertical
More than specialized

Lest there be any misunderstanding, I am not just talking about vertical or segmented marketing. Nor am I talking about being specialized. We are on our way to the next and critical step. Being perceived as *Special*.

THE STARBUCKS PHENOMENON

One of the most extraordinary examples of successful niching in the nineties is the Starbucks phenomenon. After nearly a decade of careful development, the Seattle-based coffee retailer exploded on the market in the early nineties. Actually, it would be more accurate to say that Starbucks is doing what every nichecrafter seeks to do; they are virtually making a market. They are reinventing attitudes toward coffee as no other retailer to date has done. Starbucks watchers recognize key steps the company has taken to achieve its unprecedented niche status. Just a few of them include:

1. Instead of competing against anyone, they are basically *making* a market. And it's a market that doesn't wince at price—even in a down economy.
2. They are creating a whole new culture surrounding coffee consumption. This new culture has norms, artifacts, and even its own language. No longer can you simply order coffee—not at Starbucks anyway. Choose from Espresso, Latté, Cappuccino, Americano, and myriad other coffee menu items; menu choices, however, all based around the single and simple coffee bean. The perfect example of rolling out multiple products from a simple, tight niche.

3. The "new language" of coffee introduces us to baristas instead of servers and shots of espresso instead of a cup of strong java.

4. Consistency within the organization appears to be a fanatical value. Wherever you walk into one of its stores, be it Vancouver, Portland, Seattle, New York City, or elsewhere in the nation, you not only see Starbucks but you feel it as well. The niche is through and through.

5. Like other effective niche achievers, Starbucks hasn't wasted any time moving itself to market. Once committed to rollout, it virtually blanketed its key target cities, making a presence almost overnight. No best-kept secrets with this product.

6. Most interestingly, Starbucks understands what so many otherwise excellent businesses fail to grasp. That is, when you're well niched, price isn't the issue. In years characterized by protracted recession and massive unemployment, no end is in sight to lines forming to pay $1.25 for a shot of Espresso or $1.75 for a cup of Latté aka coffee and steamed milk. Moral of the story? It's all in a niche.

So What Does This Mean for You?

Whatever kind of niche you are striving to create or make more profitable, the Starbucks story reminds us that even in the worst of times economically, success is possible if you create a niche that distinguishes you from everyone or everything else. Most of all, it reminds us that success in the nineties demands that we go beyond the ordinary to that which is perceived as truly *Special*. The challenge for Starbucks, of course, will be to sustain its niche in the market. Will knockoff artists niche away at its success? As you will be challenged to do in Chapter 6, Starbucks is undoubtedly assessing its niche's potential life span and planning for its re-niche.

Narrow but deep is one part of the good niche story. Another characteristic of a niche is that it is quickly identifiable with a particular feature, person, or product. The following exercise illustrates this point:

EXERCISE 1.1

NICHE RECOGNITION

Following are a number of names. Next to each one, write the thought or image that immediately comes to your mind when you see or think of it.

Motel 6	CHEAP
Avis	NAT
Coco Chanel	GLAMOR
BMW	LUX
Kleenex	HOUSEHOLD
Xerox	COP
Rush Limbaugh	CONSERVATIVE
Frigidaire	
Banana Republic	
Nordstrom	
The Gap	
Donald Trump	
The Grateful Dead	
McDonald's	
H. Norman Schwarzkopf	
Gypsy Rose Lee	
Rolex	
Archie Bunker	
Walter Cronkite	

Arnold Schwarzenegger	_____
John F. Kennedy	_____
Bart Simpson	_____
Michael Jackson	_____
Polaroid	_____
Madonna	_____
Burger King	_____
Eddie Van Halen	_____
Nike	_____
Orville Redenbacher	_____
H & R Block	_____
Eastern Airlines	_____
Hollywood	_____
Orlando	_____
Geraldo Rivera	_____
Roseanne	_____

Now that you've completed the exercise, let's give some thought to what happened as you were filling in the blanks. In most cases, it probably didn't take you more than a second to write down a response for each item. Ninety percent of my seminar attendees take less than a quick breath to say "Cheap" in response to Motel 6. No prompting or other clues on my part needed. Sometimes they embellish the description with "Cheap sleep." Instant recognition. No confusing Motel 6 with the Ritz! That's a real niche.

An almost equally fast, though different response occurs when audiences hear "Nordstrom." Customer service invariably is mentioned, though less now than in earlier days when I tossed the company name out for audience reaction. Perhaps this is a sign that Nordstrom has gotten lax about protecting its niche; perhaps it's a sign others have gotten into the customer service act, diluting its niche's impact today. At the very least it should be a signal to Nordstrom that the price of a strong niche is unrelenting vigilance.

Sometimes I ask my audiences about the difference between the BMW and the Mercedes. Some clever person always suggests "Forty-thousand dollars." Then someone else says, "Yuppies get one and the older, more established folks get the other." Again, instant response and solid niching. Central to the recognition test here is that not only are you identifying the product but, *more importantly, who is going to get it.*

Geraldo made my list for one reason, but he has stayed for another. The reason he remains is significant to each of us. Initially I put him on as an example of what I anticipated would be seen as a "bad niche." I anticipated (correctly so) that most people would quickly say something like "Sleaze" or "Sensationalism." Then, of course, I would be able to remind my audiences that not all niches are good ones. But whoa! I soon had to confront my own definition of a *good* niche and realized that Geraldo Rivera, regardless of what I thought of his journalism, met every last criterion.

A good niche:

1. Is intentional
2. Has a receptive audience
3. Takes you where you want to go (smiling all the way to the bank!)
4. Evolves
5. Distinguishes you from everyone else

For Geraldo, question marks must be put after this last criterion because what was once his unique, if dubious, approach appears to have set the pace for other major TV talk-show hosts, such as Donahue, Oprah, and Sally Jessy Raphael.

Mention another company on our list, the former Eastern Airlines, and you'll most likely hear customer service referenced once again, but a little differently. Unfortunately, Eastern had become synonymous with disastrous customer service. Not just poor, but awful. Lost bags, rude employees, equipment that was questionably maintained, late arrivals, late departures—if anything could be blamed on Eastern, it was! Whether its reputation was deserved is almost irrelevant. Had the company survived, it would have had a monumental job just turning around this negative public perception. The moral of the story is obvious: There are some niches you definitely don't want!

As you look at each of the items on this list ask yourself what the difference is between items in similar categories. Between Banana Republic and The Gap? Between McDonald's and Burger King? The difference is called niche. If there is no difference you know someone's in trouble!

AND WHEN PEOPLE HEAR *YOUR* NAME?

You've probably guessed that the real reason for the niche recognition exercise is so you can begin thinking about how others respond when they hear *your* name. What is the first thing that comes to their mind? Hopefully it will be exactly what you want them to perceive. And hopefully they'll respond in a heartbeat. No wondering what to say here. Since the best and fastest way to find out what people think is to ask them, get ready to pick up the phone! Your job is simple. Identify several people who know you at different levels of relationship (e.g., close friend, family member, business associate, client, prospective client). Ask them the following questions:

1. What is the first thing that comes to mind when you think of me personally?
2. What is the first thing that comes to mind when you think of my business?

These questions are simple, but the responses you collect will be very revealing. It is especially important for you to query people not yet your clients or customers but who you would like to do business with. If they haven't heard of you or have no reaction at all, that information is important in itself. Most of all, you want to ensure that whatever others perceive is what you intend.

A KIND OF ADDRESS

Thus we see that one important way of understanding niche is as *an address* by which you or your product is known to others. It's a reputation, distinguishable from that of the masses of otherwise excellent products and/or services. This is an address belonging to you and you alone. A curious, though fully accurate example of the ultimate in niche addresses is at your local mausoleum. That's right! Just as real estate salespeople sell houses, mausoleum salespeole will gladly sell you a niche of your own. We are coming to one of the most important aspects of effective niching—*uniqueness, singularity*, something you don't share with anyone or anything else.

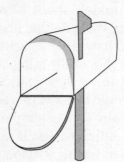

What's your specialness? Your niche address? The sheer practical necessity of having a clear and unmistakable address is driven home when you think about a trip to your local bookstore. Imagine going in looking for your favorite book. Unfortunately, someone has misshelved it, placing it somewhere other than where you are looking. Perhaps the book got misplaced because the person doing the shelving thought it belonged somewhere else, because the message wasn't clearly conveyed, or maybe it was a simple accident. Whatever the reason, the result was the same. The bookstore lost a sale because you, the customer, couldn't find what you wanted. The product wasn't in the right place. You went to its address, but it was at someone else's. If you are really serious about your business, *you can't afford to have anyone miss your shelf.*

What is your shelf?

More Niche Characteristics

Sometimes I think about niche as a kind of glue that binds (or should bind) an entire entity together. It's like our DNA—imperceptible but nonetheless present in every aspect of our being. It's that feature which, once again, is uniquely us—that distinguishes us from all the otherwise excellent businesses, services, and widgets on today's market. Other times I think of good niches being like bearing walls. They are the things that hold the rest of the building upright. Take them away and the whole thing falls in around itself.

As you begin the nichecrafting process—whether for yourself personally, your own business, or the company where you work—it's important to know how close you already are to your goal. The following self-test will give you a clue.

EXERCISE 1.2

YOUR BUSINESS NICHE SELF-TEST

Answer yes or no.

1. Am I (my firm) the only game in town?

   NO
   _____

2. Do people consider my service first and price later?

   YES
   _____

3. Am I perceived as sufficiently *Special* that prospective clients/customers can tell me apart from the masses of otherwise excellent professionals in similar fields?

   ?
   _____

4. Do I know clearly who my target clients are?

   ?
   _____

5. Do I know who my target clients are not? *?*

   _____

6. Am I prepared to turn down certain kinds of business if it detracts from my niche?

_____

7. Can clients tell what I stand for?

_____

8. Is my niche refining/evolving all the time?

_____

9. Is my niche one that a prospective audience wants?

_____

10. Do I have a plan and delivery system that can effectively convey to the right audience the need for my niche?

_____

11. Do I know the life cycle of my niche?

_____

12. Can my niche be rolled out into a variety of products or services (profit centers)?

_____

13. Do I have a sense of passion and focused energy with respect to my niche?

_____

14. Does my niche feel comfortable, natural—almost hand-in-glove?

_____

15. Will my niche take me where I want to go; that is, will the niche actively contribute to achieving the goals I have set out?

_____

16. Do I know what my clients' most important goals really are?

_____

17. Do my clients truly believe I am committed to *what they perceive to be their best interests?*

How to Score: Count total yeses.

17 = Excellent, but keep reading because niching never ends. It's time now to think about your re-niche.

16–15 = Above average but there is no such thing as almost niched. Step up the pace.

14–13 = Niche slippage evident. Caution.

12 = Don't let this book out of your sight!

More Than a Mission Statement

A commonly made error you want to avoid is confusing mission statement and niche. Your mission statement should reflect a niche, but the two are definitely not synonymous. Ask around to see other business mission statements. You'll rapidly find out that reams of paper, often taking hours and months of labor, frequently add up to sheer ordinary.

Beyond Specialization to *Specialness-ation*

Mention "niche" to most people and they'll gleefully start talking about specialization. They'll offer examples such as lawyers specializing in particular kinds of law (e.g., environmental, hazardous waste), restaurant owners specializing in "healthy heart" meals, retailers specializing in upscale clothes for larger women, banks specializing in loans to small businesses. These examples might have cut it a few years ago, but today they are nearly meaningless for anyone seriously wanting to niche a business for success and profits. Today's niche must go *beyond* specialized. It must be *Special*. It must have that something extra—that unique flavor or particular spin distinguishing it from everyone else.

When you simply specialize you cut an existing pie thinner

and thinner. Pretty soon the slices get so thin there's almost nothing left. This approach can work if you latch onto a slice that no one else can ever get to. The problem is that today no one owns any body of information. The same information and technology are available to almost everyone sooner or later. Increasingly it's not information or the product itself that makes the niche. Instead it's *what you do with that information or product*. That's where real *Specialness* comes in. You put your own stamp on something. Your DNA. Your fingerprint. The best part of *Specialness-ation* is that instead of sharing your pie with anyone, you wind up making a whole new pie. You create your own market. This pie is yours, and you don't share it with anyone else!

Is It a Field or a Niche?

It is extremely important for you to be able to distinguish your niche from the much larger field that may serve as its context. Some examples here will help clarify the difference. At one time people offering services in areas related to fitness were themselves unique. They had a corner on their market. By the mid-eighties, however, what was once a small niche had ballooned into an immense industry. Similarly, not long ago being an attorney was a niche in itself. By the 1990s this was yet another niche diluted into a formless mass. Those people who survived—indeed, those who prospered in the midst of the explosive growth in both industries—had carefully defined their niches and decided how to deliver them to their publics. Consider, for example, F. Lee Bailey and Johnnie Cochran. No need to put *Esquire* after their names. If you've been alive on this planet for the last few years, you know their names almost like members of your family. They did what you will learn how to do in this book, become bigger than a professional license or specific technology. They figured out how to be perceived as Special amidst the masses of other lawyers.

And from the pioneering efforts of names like Jack LaLane, Charles Atlas, and Joe Loprinzi emerged the now-massive health and fitness industry. By the early eighties athletic clubs had sprung up in every corner of the country. Fitness was no longer the domain of a few body-building types; it was going mainstream and fast. As the industry ballooned, scores of clubs went out of business. But some such as California-based Gold's Gyms not only stayed in; they prospered, franchised, and deepened their niche. And then, of course, there was Richard Simmons, who parlayed his approach to taking off fat into a huge and profitable niche for himself. Simmons, like our earlier lawyer examples, figured out that it's less *what* you do than *how* you do it that determines your business success or failure.

As you think more about your own business niche, you will want to also distinguish between the *process* you use to deliver the niche and the niche itself. For example, many times clients come into my office announcing that their niche is speaking, doing seminars, or writing. I have the unfortunate responsibility of informing them that *none* of those are niches. They are simply systems for delivering their product or niche. You may well have a whole menu of products or services to deliver your niche.

As we've noted, Starbucks has its Espresso, its Latté, and dozens of other coffee beverages. Whatever item is sold, however, you can be assured it will be keenly linked to coffee, lest Starbucks follow Sears to nichelessness. The following exercise will help you clarify the steps in the niche process and the differences between fields, niches, and process.

EXERCISE 1.3

THE NICHE PROCESS

Think about your own niche for a few moments. Then fill in the blanks.

Niche Field (the broad, encompassing area, e.g., food service)

PET GROOMING

Your Niche (the specific place, thing, or person, e.g., The
Bleachers Restaurant—see below)

_____ GROOMERS _____

Your Niche's Process (e.g., restaurant food/service)

_____ PET SERVICE _____

Remember, your niche-answer must clearly indicate (1) who
your target audience is; (2) who your target audience isn't;
(3) your specific style/approach; (4) what is *Special* about your
approach.

For example: The Bleachers Restaurant, Chicago—across the
street from Wrigley Field. Here *Special* is more than its hamburgers. It's *the* place to eat before a Cubs game. Cubbie fans
make loyal pilgrimages to The Bleachers before crossing the
street for their date with another niche, Chicago's losing-est
but most-loved baseball team.

Harry Caray's Restaurant is another well-known Chicago
niche—one also related to the Cubs but known as much for its
colorful owner and Cubs announcer. A case where the *persona* is
the niche. Not being an authority on sports niches, I tested Harry
Caray's niche-power out on my then-10-year-old nephew.
"Andy," I asked, "do you know who Harry Caray is?" Trying
hard to remain respectful, Andy couldn't hide the look of disbelief on his face, which nonverbally shouted, "Of course! Doesn't
everyone know Harry Caray?" He then launched into "Take Me
out to the Ball Game." Yes, Harry, *you* are definitely niched!

Not Just Any Niche

So far we've been talking about niches in general. It's important to emphasize that you're interested in far more than just
any niche. You want *good* ones. Good ones have very specific
criteria, including:

1. *They are intentional.* In other words, they don't happen
   by accident. You make them happen. They are part of

an overall plan. This rules out the lottery mentality—the niche-by-luck syndrome.

2. *They take you where you or your business wants to go.* This means that you must know where you want to wind up if you are to choose the right niche as the vehicle to get you there. That right vehicle must meet all your personal and business criteria of a good niche. All too often short-sighted people lock onto niches that divert their businesses from maximum success—niches that may produce immediate cash but have little to do with profit or business growth, much less wealth. Another way of looking at this is to think of your niche as a bus or train. Imagine getting on one you thought was going to San Francisco when it was really scheduled for Denver. No matter how nice Denver may be, it's not where you wanted to go.

3. *Someone wants them.* A good niche has a receptive audience at the other end. As a business owner, you are not making something just to go through the creative process. You are inventing a widget to make a profit, which means that a buyer must be at the other end of the niche. A good niche is always created with that ultimate consumer in mind.

4. *They have grow power!* A good niche is so rich that it can be developed with multiple profit centers if you choose to exploit them. It is the hub of a range of business activities all producing profit and benefit to your business. It is capable of growth while not becoming diluted.

5. *They evolve.* Like a healthy person, a good niche changes in response to its environment. In this case you are going to shape that evolution, maintaining control over its direction and outcome.

The Fear(s) of Niching

No matter how much you intellectually know and are committed to achieving a very tight and Special business focus, your emotions may get in the way. Doubts and fears often cloud even the most dedicated nichecrafter's vision.

One of the greatest fears many people have is of relying on something small to eventually produce something significant. It is understandable that an apparent contradiction exists, and I can easily empathize when my clients look bewildered as I tell them "Think small to get big." Alan, one of my favorite clients of all times, demonstrates this point very well.

THE CASE OF ALAN

I first met Alan at one of my earliest seminars many years ago. Tall, lanky, looking sort of like a modern-day Abe Lincoln, posture that could be better, hair that could be better cut, and clothes that definitely could be better fitted. Despite his rumpled appearance, Alan conveyed the kind of genuineness that created an instant rapport. You had to smile when he came in the room.

His initial introduction during that early seminar told me much about him. He informed the group he'd been a college professor in one of the Carolinas. It was physics that he taught. He'd been a full professor, in fact, but his job vanished when a statewide reorganization eliminated faculty positions in a host of "nonessential" areas. No matter that he was tenured and had been there nine years. No matter that he loved what he did and was good at it. Exigency, as it was called, meant he was dispensable. So it was that he moved to the West Coast, taking a job with a regional manufacturing company as Director of Human Resources. That position lasted approximately six months. The job was fine; the company folded. Another case where his life was in others' hands, and it wasn't being handled the way he liked it.

"I've got to have more control over my life. It can't go on like this," he told me later, during a private consulting session. "I've got to be able to set my direction and predict with some certainty where I'm going. I don't mind hard work—in fact, I thrive on it; but I can't stand this being tossed around by impersonal organizations."

"I understand," I said. And I did, having seen many cases of Alan and having heard the words many times before.

I had studied his interview form before his arrival and also remembered him from the earlier seminar—so I knew this next set of questions was going to be interesting, to say the least.

"I see here that you have a lot of interests. Have you begun to focus on any in particular?"

"Actually I plan to incorporate all of them into my business. I want to be a general consultant and business advisor," he informed me definitively.

Help! I'm a Wandering Generality . . .

"Uh-hum." I remained as noncommittal as possible. I ran down the list of high-priority interests: musician, athlete, communications, grant writing, speech writer, business-development advisor, stained-glass maker, banquet speaker. The list continued through even more items, all unrelated.

Kiddingly I asked him, "Do you do laundry, too?"

"My place or yours?"

Though the air was jovial as we talked, I thought of something that had gone through my mind many times with other clients. The hardest thing for Alan will not be deciding what he is going to do but instead *what he is not going to do*.

Just when I was about to emphasize his need for focus, Alan pulled out a newsletter featuring his incipient business. Entitled *Alan R's Enterprises*, it had one of everything on it, including a dog, a podium, and topics linked only by their lack of relation.

"To use your time efficiently, Alan," I said, "I can tell you right now what one major issue is that you have to deal with."

"What is it?" he asked, with expectation in his voice.

"Well, frankly, you have so many interests that none of them will be well served in a single business. The only things that seem missing here are a snowmobile and radon detector. As good as you doubtless are in all these areas you've listed, you can only do one of them and be successful. You can't be all things to all people and have it work. You've got to choose."

He looked glum. "I simply can't do it," he said.

"Well, for heaven's sake, why not?" I asked.

"The fact is, I need the money. I can't afford to limit myself right now. It's a luxury I can't afford. I've got to do whatever will bring in the dollars."

Short-term Gain and Long-term Loss

"And are you pleased with the dollars coming in now, Alan?"

"Well, no, not at all. But I'm still scared to say no or to limit the options."

I've heard variations on this story from scores of other excellent individuals—people who were too frightened to focus so they held on to a confusing array of services and products that led their business nowhere.

What does this mean for you and your own business? Alan suffers from the most common affliction affecting entrepreneurs and small-business owners. He is trying to be all things to all people. Lest there be any mistake, Alan is not in career crisis. He has already decided to be in business for himself. The problem is he isn't willing to clear his plate so the right people—his prospective customers—can tell what's on it. In fact, he can't even tell you who his customers are, other than anyone with a negotiable check. Alan's prescription for success must certainly include serious time with Step 1 (Identifying his wish list), Step 2 (Zeroing in on a preliminary focus), and extra time with Step 8, which requires him to commit and get on with a single direction. Probably he should just hole up and not come out until he's got each of the 9 steps nailed down.

AND WHAT BUSINESS CARD WILL I USE TODAY?

All-over-the-mappers are easy to spot by their business cards. They have lots of them. Actually they have lots of different ones. One for every enterprise they are involved with. Spencer is a consummate all-over-the mapper. I initially met him at a large meeting where he had done a magnificent presentation on behalf of his employer. I should say, *one* of his employers. Spencer wants to be a speaker, so he does programs for other professionals. When he's not speaking, he's selling his multi-level product. When he's not selling his multilevel product or speaking, he's selling his marketing services to someone. When I learned how many different business cards Spencer had to choose from, I realized the real trouble he was in. As gifted and ambitious as he may be, Spencer is sabotaging his own business success by refusing to commit to one business card, one direction.

"Spencer," I said, "there is only so much of you to go around. How do you expect to make each one of these successful?"

"Well," he said, "I can work on each one at a different time, and besides, they're good backups in case one of them fails."

I restrained my impulse to scream. But I could not pretend either. "Spencer, you've just used a phrase that can do you and your business in. Completely finish you off if you really believe what you said."

His eyes got big as he looked at me and asked, "Gosh, what did I say that was that bad?"

"You used the *B* word," I said.

"The what?" Spencer asked with a funny look on his face.

"The *B* word," I repeated for emphasis. "*Backup.* I won't say it again aloud because it is so dangerous. If you are really serious about niche success, you can't think in terms of the *B* word. You plan to succeed and that's it. You work with your widget until you have taken it as far as you can."

Watching Spencer's expression I could tell he was horrified with what I was telling him. I also realized that he and Alan were walking down the same path. Like Sony and Sears, they were undermining their own business success by going in so many directions at once they would never get anyplace of significance, except in debt. In essence they were busy creating a short-term gain and ensuring a long-term loss. Later chapters in this book will offer exercises to help you "think small to get big."

It is important to emphasize that although Spencer and Alan are small-business owners, they are a company in every business sense. This may seem pretty obvious, but frequently people (including the business owner) assume that *company* applies only to larger businesses. What this means is that regardless of its size, your business must adhere to sound niche-development and protection practices.

WHEN A NICHE BECOMES A TRENCH

Now that I have told you how important it is to begin thinking small, we have to prevent your niche from ever becoming a trench! A trench can easily happen if you don't use all the steps in the nichecraft process—especially the one matching what you have to offer with what someone else wants to possess. Or, if you grow a business that becomes a monster. That winds up building on your weaknesses instead of your strengths.

Your niche can also become a trench if you don't create a system allowing it to evolve, grow, and change. Alas, even the best niche can suffer the dinosaur's fate if it is not sufficiently elastic to adapt to its environment.

The 9 Myths of Niching

Successful niching is often derailed by the existence of several myths. Because a major goal of this book is to help you become self-sufficient in making your own business niche, it is important to dispel these myths immediately.

Niche-Myth #1: Niches Are Found

Nonsense! Scratch this myth right now. Niche creation is not like the childhood game of hide-and-seek, where the prize has already been placed out there and it's up to you to find it if you can. The fact is, successful niches or those taking you where you want to go in your personal and professional life don't just happen. They are *made*. Furthermore, that process of nichecrafting is a rational one, which can be described and replicated in an unlimited number and variety of settings. Most of all, nichecrafting is far too important ever to be left to accident, someone else's whim, or wishful thinking, an advertising firm, or public relations agency. Decisions about which niche is the right one go to the heart of your business or career. When you realize this last fact, it's easier to understand why the niche buck stops with you.

No wishful thinking or accidents here.

Niche-Myth #2: Once a Niche—Always a Niche

Toss this myth right now also! One of the few things we know for sure anymore is that things will surely change. Hence you must learn not only how to niche, but how to refine a niche, and finally, how to re-niche altogether. You will find that intentionally moving from one niche to another is not a sign of failure. It can be just smart, wise, or the right time for change.

You must build into your system a niche-review process to ensure that your business or career does not become obsolete. The danger of niche complacency can be seen all around us. Think about that wonderful retail store you enjoyed when you were a kid. It was so successful the owners succumbed to the "if it isn't broke, don't fix it" mentality. And they didn't. Not surprisingly, a few years ago that delightful store had a huge ugly liquidation sign on the outside and for a few days you could get real bargains. The world around the store had changed dramatically, but the owners seemed to wear blinders until they were forced to take them off. Even then, the concept of an evolving, intentionally directed niche seemed to escape them.

Good niches don't become dinosaurs.

Niche-Myth #3: Any Niche Will Work

Niches run the entire spectrum from brilliant and wonderful to negative and destructive. Sometimes a niche gets worn out or was wrong from the beginning. As you select your final niche(s), you will use a rational strategy for choosing among all possible ones. And there are many out there. Because there are so many possible niches for you to choose from, it's extremely important to approach your selection with as much dispassion as possible. Avoid falling in love with your niche. If you get emotionally entangled with your niche, it is going to be extremely difficult to assess its utility for achieving future goals. And that's what niches are all about. Appreciate them for what they are: means to an end. Paramount in distinguishing *good* niches from bad ones is that *good* niches are wanted by someone else *now*. When you are in business or developing a serious career, you can't afford to create niches that become unsold inventory. If the niche fails to meet all your tests of a *good* niche, it gets scrubbed and replaced.

Avoid falling in love with your niche.

Niche-Myth #4: Being Practical Detracts from the Joy of Niching

Of all the myths I hear about our subject, this certainly has to be one of the most foolish. Yes, making niches is an exciting, intrinsically rewarding process. But for those who don't arrive at them in due course (forever isn't due course), whatever joy exists at the process's initial stages is fast replaced by frustration, sometimes despair, and even anger. That's understandable. Shouldn't they be able to have it all? Yes, they should. So too should you and I. A central issue and key theme of this book, however, is that we are going to make that "it" happen, not just wish for it!!

Alas, the starving artist syndrome . . .

Niche-Myth #5: If I Just Work Hard at What I'm Doing, That Niche Will Surface

This is complete silliness. If you doubt what I'm saying, look about and count the scores of people and/or organizations you know where plain hard work goes on every day. Some of the best people you know are putting in long hours, doing excellent jobs, but going no place. In fact, they are working hard at digging a bigger and bigger hole. One of the first clues that you are mastering nichecrafting is when you can honestly say to yourself "I'm not working harder—just smarter!" In other words, it's not just how hard you work but *what you work at* that often makes the difference between your success or failure.

Working smarter, not just harder!

Niche-Myth #6: A Niche by Itself Ensures Success

This is one of the most insidious myths afflicting tens of thousands of people. The fact is, a niche in isolation is no good to anybody. Indeed, it can be a source of huge frustration to its owner. If you've been wondering why doing strictly what you love or offering a service that you think is great hasn't been getting you anyplace, this myth might be your core problem. A quality niche does not exist in a vacuum. It has a receptive, appreciative audience. Of course, the challenge is making that fit. Thus, we come to understand niche creation as an observable, dynamic process you can personally direct. It is a process that will call upon the best of your pragmatic and intuitive skills. It is in every sense of the word a true craft. Nichecraft, then, is the marriage of niches to the process giving them value. This union offers you nothing less than a blueprint for identifying, developing, implementing, and maintaining niches that will enhance your own life and the lives of those you touch.

Good niches aren't best-kept secrets.

Niche-Myth #7: Advertising Is the Same Thing as a Niche

Ridiculous as this sounds, I've heard the two terms used interchangeably and altogether confused on numerous occasions.

The problem in even remotely confusing the two lies in the assumption that you can find someone else to get a niche for your company. Just advertise and a niche will arrive. Right? *Noooooo!!!* Very wrong. For starters, advertising is simply a delivery system. It is only one way of getting your message out to market. Your niche is the message, which means it must be decided well before any marketing strategies are introduced. Niche drives the rest of the plan, not the other way around.

The biggest danger inherent in this semantic misunderstanding, however, is the assumption mentioned previously that niche responsibility can be turned over to someone else. The truth is, making the right niche is one of the most important steps an individual or business will ever take. It is a strategic decision and must come from those able and willing to take responsibility for the future it presents.

Niche first, market later.

Niche-Myth #8: If You Have a Mission Statement, You Have a Niche

Once again, total complete absolute nonsense. Granted, a mission statement is important. After all, it announces what you are up to and hopefully offers some sense of who your audience is and how you deliver whatever your service or widget may be. What we know, however, is that all too many mission statements are boring, ordinary, and absolutely nicheless—anything but *Special*. A mission statement not built around a *good* niche is destined for nowhere.

Your mission statement must be special.

Niche-Myth #9: I'm Too Small to Niche

Of all the niche myths out there, this one is among the most painful for me to hear. "Nordstrom is big. They can afford to be particular." If I've heard that mentality once, I've heard it a thousand times. What the person doesn't realize is that Nordstrom would not have gotten big had it not been particular, had it tried to be all things to all people. As soon as it loses its focus, its profits will go down. If you are not yet a believer in the narrow, deep, and profitable philosophy for small to mid-size businesses, Chapter 3 is filled with examples of how small businesses became very successful *after* they bit the niche bullet. You can do the same thing.

Nine Steps to Business Success

Until now we have concentrated on clarifying what a niche is and how you can tell it when it's staring you in the face. *Now* it's time to lay out the process for achieving this all-important ingredient. It's important to emphasize that the system you are learning is relevant to whatever kind of business you are establishing, whether it's a professional service, a retail operation, a manufacturing company, a for-profit or not-for-profit enterprise. The requirements for making good niches are all the same. They are also relevant if you are wanting to improve your own niche within an organization or enhance others' niches and improve their profits. In most cases, you will enter the system at Step 1. In some, however, you will enter with another step. The point is, good niches have considered all 9 steps.

By now you might be throwing up your hands saying, "Hey! I just want to have a decent business I enjoy that can provide me a fair income. And I want to keep it *simple*!!" If this is sounding unnecessarily detailed, relax. It won't take very long before the 9 steps become so much a part of you that you can throw all your checklists away. (And in case you decide you want more than a small, decent business, the basic rules outlined here will help you leverage small into as large as you want to make it! For now, though, you might want to make copies of *Nichecrafting in Steps* so you can keep them near you at all times, especially when you are doing your quiet-time thinking. Although each of the 9 steps is explored in detail in subsequent chapters, a brief discussion of them now will set a context for your use of them along the way.

Nichecrafting in Steps

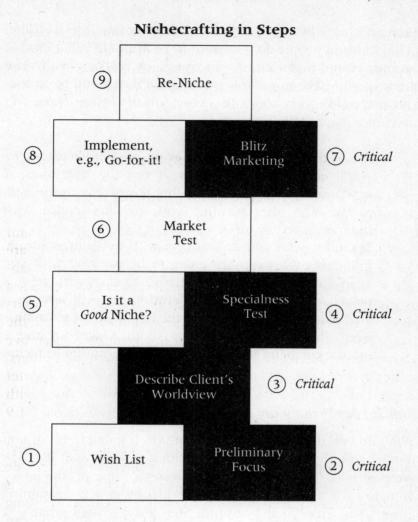

(9) Re-Niche

(8) Implement, e.g., Go-for-it!   Blitz Marketing   (7) *Critical*

(6) Market Test

(5) Is it a *Good* Niche?   Specialness Test   (4) *Critical*

Describe Client's Worldview   (3) *Critical*

(1) Wish List   Preliminary Focus   (2) *Critical*

Step 1: Identifying Your Wish List

Here you identify as specifically as possible who you want to do business with. Who do you see as customers or clients? Perhaps you have only a broad field in mind. If that's the case, still get names of businesses down on paper. Then get the names of decision-makers at the companies. Who will be deciding if your product/service is one they would want? If you truly don't have any idea who you want to work with, then another way to get to this task is to simply free associate. What kinds of people do you want to be around? What kind of businesses and organizations do you enjoy working with? The point is, you have to get this information down and be as specific as possible very soon. Two very critical reasons leave you no choice about defining your wish list:

1. If you don't know who you want as clients/customers, you'll *never* get them, especially not the *right* ones. A key to your success will be doing business with the *right* people—the ones wanting your product/service with the money to pay for it.
2. Secondly, who you do business with today dramatically influences who you are going to be working with five years from now. You should plan to start with serious players as customers/clients because they will serve as a vital marketing network over the long haul for your business. This issue is relevant to both a start-up and a mature company seeking to protect or recapture its niche.

Step 2: Your Preliminary Focus

What do you think your area of emphasis is going to be? If you don't know right now, then take a look at your wish list. Ask yourself what kinds of needs and interests these people have? Sometimes you can develop a focus just by closely examining groups you enjoy being around. Step 2 deals with what you ultimately are going to offer for sale. Many people have tremendous problems with this step, finding themselves unable to narrow from all their interests and activities. For that reason, an entire chapter (Chapter 2) is devoted to helping you focus and refine.

Step 3: Getting Inside Your Clients' World

This is the flip side of Step 2, which essentially looks at what you want to sell. Here you are making a fit between what you are selling and what the customer wants to buy. This step is vital because it helps ensure that you will not create a monster for yourself—a business that you love but that is an economic nightmare. If you can successfully execute this step, you will be able to merchandise and sell just about whatever product or service you offer. Should you want outside financial support from banks or venture capitalists, this step will be vital because you will have to show your financiers that it is in their interest to support your effort.

Step 4: Your Niche's Specialness Quotient

This is the most critical step in the entire ladder. Here you essentially add Steps 2 and 3 with an entirely new product emerging. Sometimes you may find that what you want to sell isn't interesting to your wish list. Your choices then are to go with another wish list or manipulate what you want to sell sufficiently so that it is desirable to them. Most of all, this is where you ask the vital question "Is my widget perceived as Special?"

Step 5: Is It a Good Niche?

You've just created a niche for yourself. But is it a *good* one? Does it meet all the criteria we've set out for good niches? If not, then you either scrub it altogether or rework some of the variables affecting it. The critical aspect of this step is that it gives you *choice*. It reminds you that not all niches are good ones.

Step 6: Test with Real People/Organizations

Here you take your service/product to market, giving buyers an opportunity to say yes or no. This step is very different from traditional market research, which is associated with Step 3. Here you find out what people will *really* pay for. This is the step happening when you go into your local supermarket and are greeted by a smiling person offering you the latest tasty potato chip, cake mix, or soda pop. Instead of saying "Do you think you'll like this product," they actually give it to you and then give you a chance to buy it at the cash register. They know that what we say and actually do are frequently two different things.

Step 7: Blitz Marketing

Sometimes this becomes your niche, depending upon your marketing strategy. Most of all, this step prevents your niche from becoming a well-kept secret. Specific strategies for getting the message out to the right people are detailed in later chapters.

Step 8: Go for It!

At first glance, this step may seem the easiest. but that's only at first glance. This is where you put your money where your mouth is. Commitment. Belief in your niche. If you're currently working for someone else, this is where you make the official transition to being your own employer. Everything that has gone before is fairly easy until now because all the previous activity has been purely theoretical. Unless you act now, nothing will happen. This is the step where everything is in your court!

Step 9: Re-Niche

You've got the niche rolling and it looks good. You know, though, that the world changes and so must your niche. No dinosaurs for you. To avoid ossification, you build in change ingredients. You have your sensors out at all times, predict trends and directions. You think about where your niche may go on its own unless you nourish and direct it.

The 9 Steps in Action

It's important to emphasize that although you need to understand and address each step individually, they aren't totally sequential. You must keep them all in mind all the time. Walk and talk and chew gum simultaneously is the key. The following example will help you see how applying these 9 steps helped two business owners get up and running fast(er)!

CASE ONE: SUZANNE'S STORY—FROM ALL-OVER-THE-MAP TO MEGA SENSATION

I initially met Suzanne when she attended one of my Niching for Success seminars. From the beginning it was obvious that she was not only one of the most talented, hardworking people I'd ever met, but that she was also a dyed-in-the-wool all-over-the-mapper. By her own admission. Suzanne acknowledged, "I don't have trouble focusing, but most of the things I focus on just never work for me." So she went from one thing to another. From having her own frozen yogurt restaurant to managing resort properties to meeting planning to marketing products for others, she sought the direction that would work. Hearing that at the time I was franchising my seminar program, Suzanne thought this could be something she'd like to do.

It could have worked. She was a good presenter. She knew her subject matter. People loved her. The only problem was, every time she was supposed to be getting ready for a program, Suzanne was back in the kitchen cooking. She simply loved to cook. And then one day I got a call. It went like this:

"Lynda, I reread *Nichecraft* last night and I figured it out! I know what I'm going to do!" She sounded excited, relieved, and filled with anticipation.

"Well, don't keep me in suspense," I said. "Just what are you going to do?" I realized that I was probably about to lose a great seminar leader.

"I'm going to cooking school!" she announced.

"Why cooking school?" I asked. "You could probably teach at one yourself."

It was clear she'd thought this one through. "I don't just want to learn to cook. I want to learn how to make money at it. I'm going to manufacture food products."

Within one year after Suzanne called announcing her decision, her food manufacturing company was selling millions of pounds of Ritzy Rollups throughout the United States and Canada, and today there is talk of her organization going public in a few years. Following is a more detailed description of how Suzanne used *Nichecraft*'s 9-step process to make the American Dream her reality.

Step 1: Wish List?

The ultimate consumer would be an upscale person wanting an already prepared but Special light food for entertaining. The way Suzanne would get to those people first would be through Club Stores (e.g., PriceCostco and other similar networks).

Step 2: Focus?

"Indulgence food." Delicious and sinfully rich. Food that is perceived as more a treat than common-sense good for you. Ritzy Rollups would be her first product, soon to be followed by a full line of other items.

Step 3: Clients' Worldview?

Ultimate customer: upscale, valuing efficiency and convenience, time at a premium, and wanting to entertain easily; caterers looking for the same; buyers in club stores wanting a product that will sell high volume and fast. Must meet all FDA requirements, be packaged to appeal to the specific customer.

Here Suzanne addressed multiple levels of customer. First the store buyer whose worldview she had to satisfy to get the product on the shelves. And then there were the caterers looking for convenient appetizers for their own customers. And finally, there was the end user whom she also had to satisfy to get the product off the shelves.

Step 4: Test of Specialness?

In a society moving toward fat-free everything, "indulgence food" is increasingly *Special.* Much like Ben and Jerry's rich and richer ice cream, Suzanne's Ritzy Rollups go against the trend. Most importantly, by entering the market through club stores, Suzanne was able to penetrate her market fast, another way to be perceived as *Special.*

Step 5: Evaluate Against Good Niche Criteria?

On all counts, it fit. This time Suzanne had a niche that produced money. Most of all, she had created something that built on who she really was. Now she doesn't have to feel guilty when she thinks about food and cooking. It's her niche.

Step 6: Test with Real People?

Suzanne tested her product at scores of delis, restaurants, and within the club stores themselves. Professional demonstrators offered customers tastes. The cash registers told the rest of the story.

Step 7: Blitz the Market?

This was Suzanne's strong suit. From the beginning she had a dynamic system to get her product to market. She knew she could sell to all the stores by herself, but she educated herself about and enlisted the help of others such as key buyers, distributors, and suppliers. Her product packaging carried a huge photograph of her own smiling face right on the front, guaranteeing that consumers identified with a real person, not just a product.

Step 8: Go for It?

And she did. Going from a cottage industry at home to big-time manufacturing almost overnight required Suzanne to acquire outside capital. For this she had to offer almost everything she owned for collateral. With confidence in her product and her plan, Suzanne went for it. No plan B.

Step 9: Re-Niche?

Although Ritzy Rollups will most likely sell in increasing numbers over the years, I'm sure that Suzanne is exploring additional products to add to her line. The challenge will be in ensuring that whatever she adds hugs and reflects her company's core as do her Ritzy Rollups.

CASE TWO: STEVE'S CONSULTING PRACTICE

Steve retired from the Navy two years ago after 25 years of active duty service. Before his retirement, he experienced considerable nervousness about the future, wondering if he would be able to survive in an unpredictable business climate. Although he didn't talk a lot about it, he wasn't totally convinced he had anything anybody would pay for. Even with his officer's retirement pay, Steven felt sure he would have to continue generating income so his family could continue to live well. He decided to start a consulting business. Using the 9-step *Nichecraft* system, Steven created a business that provided him with both pleasure and money!!

Step 1: Wish List?

Large organizations such as General Motors, General Dynamics, Nordstrom, and Pepsi.

Step 2: Focus?

Conflict resolution and negotiation. He wanted to consult to organizations needing assistance with these issues and perhaps provide training programs to employees, increasing their skills in these areas.

Step 3: Clients' Worldview?

Steven arranged informational interviews with dozens of people on his wish list. He asked them about their priorities, their hopes and dreams, their pains, and the ambitions and goals they held for their businesses. He listened hard, identifying what their pains were and what they perceived as blockers to their successes.

Step 4: Test of Specialness?

Fortunately Steven learned early on that no one perceived his service as particularly Special. He literally went back to his drawing board and decided to figure out what he stood for. He decided to write a book describing his approach to negotiation and personnel management. He knew that once the book was written, his Special way would be increasingly clear to prospective clients. They would be more likely to take him seriously because he had taken himself seriously. Ultimately Steven was his niche, but the book was a vehicle for putting him out front.

Step 5: Good Niche Test?

On nearly all counts, his book and new approach promised to produce a good niche. His one concern, however, loomed larger all the time. He realized that to make full use of the book, he would have to travel, being away from home a great deal. This was something he definitely didn't want to do. He would have to monitor this carefully.

Step 6: Test with Real People?

Steven called several key people on his wish list and found them very receptive to hearing about the approach being described in his new book. He invited them to previews and focus groups to ensure that he was on track.

Step 7: Blitz the Market?

Seminars, speeches, TV, writing articles, and a host of other strategies to make him highly visible were approaches Steven would use to get his niche to the right people.

Step 8: Go for It?

He did go for it and was very successful.

Step 9: Re-Niche?

Steven's niche is good for the next few years, but he is already thinking about the next book and next niche. Niche #2 will be an extension of #1, but as yet remains undefined.

CASE THREE: MARIE'S AUTO BODY SHOP

Marie is a talented artist. She paints and sculpts. For many years she had a highly successful business, selling her products to well-to-do individuals and businesses. Because of a host of family-related concerns, Marie had to move to another area of the country where she was virtually unknown within the art community. She needed to establish herself quickly and wanted to continue doing what she loved, which was working with metal and paint. By coincidence, as she was worrying about satisfying her material and artistic needs at the same time, she ran across an ad in the paper: Auto Body Shop for Sale. "Wow, it's a long shot," she thought, "but I'll check it out." And she did. Next thing she knew, Marie was the proud owner of an auto body repair shop. Lots of metal and paint around. Her challenge now was to make it pay for itself.

Step 1: Wish List?

People who wanted highly personal attention paid to their cars—especially collectors of vintage and expensive autos.

Step 2: Focus?

Auto body repair.

Step 3: Clients' Worldview?

Feel they want the best, can pay for it, and expect it. Want flawless attention to detail. These clients *love* their cars. They expect personal attention almost to the extent of pampering.

Step 4: Test of Specialness?

Since there were other auto body shops in the area, Marie needed to distinguish herself clearly and quickly. She realized that being female gave her a potential edge. Marie would be her own niche. Her strategy would be to elevate her persona, emphasize the artistic and personal care her shop provided, and extend her market area through articles in newspapers and other media. Her new goal was to have people sending their antique cars to her regardless of where the owners lived.

Step 5: Good Niche Test?

On all counts this approach passed the "good niche test." Marie found herself loving life around metal, paint, and people who wanted a real artist to handle their cars.

Step 6: Test with Real People?

This step passed with flying colors because even before Marie saw the ad in the paper, people were asking her advice about how to repair their special cars. The market was already coming to her. What remained was for Marie to ensure that people took her business seriously regardless of where they lived.

Step 7: Blitz the Market?

Antique car shows, articles in papers, TV interviews, speaking regularly at local civic groups, and a range of other strategies keep Marie's name out front, reminding her wish list clients she's there when they are.

Step 8: Go for It?

She did. Go for it meant that Marie not only would expand her shop but undertake a massive "Marie-is-the niche" campaign.

Step 9: Re-Niche?

Re-niche is sometime in the future for Marie. When that time comes she will probably sell the shop and find another way to have fun and profit from her metal and paint!

Your Own 9 Steps

Now it's time to complete your own 9 steps. Your first attempts at these several steps may result in some empty blanks. That's fine! Each of the 9 steps is explored in subsequent chapters. As you continue reading, you will find yourself redoing the exercise, each time with more depth and refinement. Plan to keep all your copies. You will enjoy comparing your early attempts with ones you complete later on.

Most of all, you will want to keep your eyes on the 4 critical steps essential to successfully starting your new business. Without them, good niches simply don't exist and neither will your new business, or at least not for long!

EXERCISE 1.4

APPLYING *NICHECRAFT*'S 9 STEPS TO YOUR OWN BUSINESS

Step 1: *Identify your wish list.* Who do you want as clients or customers? Be very specific with names, locations, etc.

Step 2—*Critical: Identify your preliminary focus.* Even if you are not certain, describe your tentative focus or niche.

Step 3—*Critical: List your potential clients' major interests or concerns, ambitions and goals.* Begin thinking about what is going on in your client's head, *not* your own.

Step 4—*Critical: Does it meet the test of Specialness?* Add Steps 2 and 3. Describe this new product. Is it perceived as Special?

Step 5: *Does it meet the tests of a good niche?* Does it meet all the tests of Specialness?

Step 6: *Test with real people and/or organizations.* Forget market research; test market instead.

Step 7—*Critical: Blitz the market.* Like Sherman through Georgia!

Step 8: *Implement; that is, go for it.* Nothing to fill in here. Just do it!

Step 9: *Re-niche.* Go back to Step 1 and repeat the process.

Why the Fuss?

The payoff can be very big, which explains why more and more people in every conceivable business type, size, and location are willing to invest serious time and effort in making the right niche. Some of the outcomes you can reasonably expect once you become adept at the nichecrafting process include:

1. You won't have to worry about competing with anyone or anything because you'll be unique and there won't be anyone else! In essence, you will have eliminated your competition nonviolently!

2. Your potential customers and clients will be able to find you rather than your having to run out looking for them. They will be able to tell you apart from the masses of otherwise excellent and competent people by virtue of your niche—the "address" that belongs to you alone.

3. If you have a product or service to sell, customers will ask "How fast?" not "How much?" They will be concerned primarily with your product, not its price.

4. You will reduce the likelihood of inventing a widget destined for your eyes alone because you will have thoughtfully matched it with a potential audience beforehand.

5. You will be able to niche and re-niche regardless of where you live, which means you will never be a prisoner of geography.

6. You should enjoy the highest level of intrinsic satisfactions—the kind that come from knowing that you are not just doing what you want to do but that you are building a profitable, healthy business at the same time.

7. Most of all, your meticulously crafted niche will put you—to the extent possible—in control of your own life and business. You will find that for all these outcomes, but especially this last one, nichemaking is well worth any "fuss" it takes to get you there!

Where Are You Now?

So that you will have a gauge for measuring your nichemaking progress, you should take a moment now and consider just where you fall on the diagram below. This simple self-test will show up many times throughout coming chapters, making it easy for you to track your new skills of niche development.

EXERCISE 1.5

MY NICHE PROGRESS SCALE

Place your initials on the portion of the scale that most accurately describes your niche progress up to now.

1   2   3   4   5   6   7   8   9   10

I'm a niche wreck/   Hallelujah! I did it

totally unfocused.   in one chapter.

Your Essential Nichecraft Vocabulary

Every discipline has its own vocabulary. Although it doesn't pretend to be a discipline per se, nichecraft also has its own language—words and terms essential to understanding the intent and process of this approach. Since all language is subject to many meanings, it is important that we start out with some common understandings of the key terminology you will encounter later in the book. The following list will provide you with an edge in your understanding and application of the nichecraft process. Read each of the following terms carefully. Consider how each of them may apply to your individual situation. Mark this page with a bookmark or dog-ear it so you can access it readily as need dictates.

B word: Backup. A dangerous attitude if you are serious about getting focused. Keeps you from committing fully to your niche.

Competition: What you don't have when you are well niched.

Consequence of consequences: Systematically thinking ahead about what happens beyond the immediate result of a particular action. Something most people don't do.

Craft: Skill, art, knowledge; what you do to a niche to make it worth anything.

Critical attributes: Absolutely vital and essential elements of a thing; the features giving an entity definition. Those features without which something does not exist.

Divestiture: The term describing what happens to companies that lose sight of their niche and actually think bigger is better. Sometimes greedy. Always foolish.

Evolving niche: Has the same features as a flexible niche. This is what happens to all healthy niches over time.

Flexible niche: A niche that grows and responds to reality.

Focus: The single vision required for success; doing what most people don't want to do—staying on track, avoiding doing all the things you love to do just because you love them even when they don't take you anyplace except all over the map.

***Good* niches:** Niches that meet the minimum criteria of (1) taking you where you want to go, (2) being wanted by others, (3) being purposeful, and (4) having the capability to evolve and grow.

Intentionality/purposefulness: Taking control over the shape and direction of your niche; not allowing important directions to take place by accident.

Market saturation: Something else you don't have when you are well niched.

Niche: Something perceived as *Special*, unique, one of a kind, singular, exemplary. *Not ordinary*.

Niche advantage: Your goal. You know it is no longer possible to be successful by competing; your true advantage comes when *you create the niche you own*.

Niche case: A person or organization in shambles because they went nicheless too long.

***Nichecraft* Group:** The group so valuable in helping niche-crafters check each other out to ensure they are headed in the right direction. Some groups call themselves study groups and others, support groups. The issue is, don't go it alone. Let others help you create the niche that works best for your business, career, or organization.

Nicheless: A state of floundering, zero focus, all-over-the map; not a place to be.

NicheThink: The mindset, perspective, way of looking at the world that always seeks *Specialness*.

Niche wreck: Same as niche case. See above.

Ordinary: The opposite of niched.

Plan B: Not an option if you are planning to succeed. Get on with A. That's it.

Platinum Rule marketing: The ultimate in client-centeredness; looking at the world from the customer's perspective instead of your own. A major key to success in the nineties.

Re-niche: What you do as soon as you think you have finally made the niche; structured evolution of the niche, not radical change.

Sabotage crew: Those people who prefer that you remain satisfied with your station in life, thus not rocking their boats and never threatening others with what appear to them to be foolish ambitions and dreams.

Segmentation: Sometimes confused with niche. Anything can be segmented. Only niche is *Special.* Many steps are required between merely segmenting something and creating that which is perceived as one of a kind.

Self-discipline: Knowing what you're willing to give up to get where you or your organization wants to go; not just knowing what you want.

Special/**unique:** One of a kind, niched.

Specialness: Never settling for the ordinary.

Specialness-ation: Beyond specialized. Having that something extra that distinguishes you, your service, or product from everyone else. Your signature. That spin or flavor uniquely yours.

Synthesis niche: The new entity arising from melding what you want to sell or offer with what someone else wants to possess.

Trending: Thinking ahead, understanding what needs will arise from events and directions in motion today. Getting out of the mental boxes and conventional frames of reference preventing *good* niche development. A must strategy for successful nichecrafting.

Wandering generality: A person or organization that is nicheless. All-over-the-map. Flits from one thing to another. Uncommitted. Usually unhappy and unfulfilled. If a business, nearly always unprofitable.

Summary

During this warm-up, you have been introduced to a process that will influence every aspect of your business. You have learned that it is essential for you to do more than make just any niche. You want *good* ones. The kind that will take you and your business where you want to go, that distinguish you from everyone else, that are truly Special, singular, unique, one of a kind, and that are wanted by others. You have learned that arriving at a good niche is an active process. It's something you can't hand off to an outside agency. Niche doesn't just go to the heart of your business. It *is* the heart. And you have also learned that a good niche is a fragile entity. If you want to keep it, *guard it well* and nourish its growth. Unfortunately, we've seen that a niche that doesn't grow may be here today but not on the scene tomorrow.

While this chapter has emphasized the fate of the nicheless, it has also reminded us that businesses that focus can and do win and they do it in *any* economy. The rest of this book guides you through *Nichecraft*'s 9-step process so that you too can achieve and win with your own great niche.

2

ELIMINATING THE COMPETITION

It's time to put all your eggs in one basket, then watch them like a hawk.

—ANONYMOUS

Now that you know what a niche is and how to recognize one, it's time to get on with the actual process of making them—of deciding what your business is going to be about. What its *Special* focus will be. Our first step is going to be to look at the possibilities for good niches already within you or your organization. At first blush this may seem frivolously simple. After all, who knows you better than you?

The issue is, of course, that often we are too close to ourselves to see the picture accurately. Whoever said "The fish are the last to discover water" was probably looking at someone trying to make a niche!

Narrowing the Focus

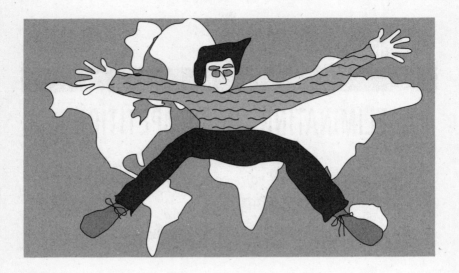

"Dr. Falkenstein, I can do so many things—and I love all of them—and I'm good at them. People tell me I can do anything I want!" When I hear this series of self-descriptors from a client, I can't help thinking to myself that the only thing worse than being able to do everything in the world is thinking you can't do anything at all. All-over-the mappers, whether sole proprietors like Alan, whom we met in Chapter 1, or huge conglomerates like the former Gulf and Western Industries, are in clear self-destruct modes.

When confronted with this situation, I immediately assign the following exercise. As you will see, it forces us to focus in spite of ourselves. You don't have to be an all-over-the-mapper to benefit from Exercise 2.1, so before going one step more you, too, should answer the following questions and fill in the blanks.

EXERCISE 2.1

BASIC FOCUSING

---

1. List the things you personally do best. Don't limit your thinking to what you do on the job or in your

current business. "Best" may be in any aspect of your life.

2. Identify the skills implicit in each category; for example, analysis, interpretation, synthesis, listening, problem-solving. Be specific.

3. Now prioritize the things you do best according to those you like to do the most. Cross off any that are very unpleasant for you. Remember, you are creating something you will implement in your business or professional life. It makes sense to create something you will like.

THE THINGS I DO BEST   WHAT SKILLS ARE REQUIRED

_____   _____

_____   _____

_____   _____

Now take a few minutes and think carefully about the implications of the items on your two lists. What professional or business applications might there be? Write them down.

Potential Business Niche Applications

_____

_____

_____

_____

In case you're thinking the above exercise really only applies to someone trying to figure out their career and not their business niche, stay close by. The central thing we are going after in creating a niche that works is a focus distinguishing your business or organization from everyone else's. To do that we need to "unpack" all your resources—everything you bring to the business table, especially your skills, achievements, your style, and those features that may ultimately set your business apart from other excellent companies in a similar field. Once you have a clear handle on what your own personal resources are, you can rationally decide which, if any, should be intentionally applied to your business. If this particular exercise still eludes you, consider the following metaphor. Assume you are looking to paint your store a color that will really set it apart from all the others on the block. Paint is a resource. Your own skills, achievements, and other personal features that we are distilling are resources. Unlike the paint, however, you don't have to write a check to get them.

Building on Your Strengths

Strange as it may sound, many people build on their weaknesses—not their strengths. Scores of businesses do the same thing. Some, in fact, lose sight of what those strengths actually are—the features that made the company successful in the first place. Do you know what your own personal strengths are? What your company's greatest strengths are? Make a list of each from your own point of view. Then ask some friends and business associates to answer from their perspective. In a sense you are creating a mirror for yourself by inviting others to provide information you may not be aware of.

Some time ago a client asked me if it wouldn't also be useful to make a good list of his weaknesses. Without hesitation I said *no*. I still say no. You can't build a solid house on a weak foundation. If GE had done this simple exercise, it probably would never have bought Kidder Peabody, a transaction that got the company far afield of its core and finally blew up in its face with the 1994 Jett scandal. GE ultimately sold Kidder to PaineWeber, hoping to stem a massive tide of red ink and enormous public embarrassment.

YOUR ACHIEVEMENTS AND ACCOMPLISHMENTS

Powerful niches are frequently buried beneath years of achievements and accomplishments that have become second nature to us. We are rarely reinforced for the good things we do. Few people get praised for going through green lights or making an accurate prediction, but go through a red light or guess wrong sometime and see what happens!

The following exercise will help you see how some of those achievements and accomplishments can be turned into niches that work for you. As with the previous exercise, it may be hard at first to even think of the things you have accomplished over the years. Don't limit yourself to achievements within a formal setting. You may find out that your strongest suits have played themselves out in avocational or volunteer situations. Don't limit your thinking exclusively to your adult years either. Think back to your earliest childhood and the things that you were recognized for—the achievements that made you happiest and most proud.

EXERCISE 2.2

ACHIEVEMENTS AND ACCOMPLISHMENTS INVENTORY

PART ONE

In the spaces below, list the achievements and accomplishments *you* consider most significant.

_____

_____

_____

PART TWO

Now that you have listed what you perceive to be your most important achievements, it's time to find out how others would answer the question for you. Many times outsiders see strengths and skills in us we just took for granted. Things we didn't even consider as *Special*. This part of the exercise is simple. Identify a range of people who know you in various degrees—from family to business associates. Before you ask your question, it's important to set the correct tone. Do this by saying, "I have a favor to ask of you. I'm doing a little work on my business niche and I have two questions I'd like you to help me with. I'd appreciate it if you would tell me what you think my most significant accomplishments and achievements have been." Ask them to respond from a *personal perspective and then from a business perspective*.

After you ask the question, *shut your mouth*! Don't load the deck or bias your respondee. Whatever answers you get will be right. It is *their* perceptions, not yours, that you are looking for. List their answers in the spaces below:

PERSONAL ACHIEVEMENTS   BUSINESS ACHIEVEMENTS

_____   _____

_____   _____

_____   _____

THE SIAMESE TWIN CONDITION

You might wonder why we are spending time asking so much about you personally when this book is about growing a business, something that has a life and form of its own. The fact is, regardless of the size of your business, you can't separate yourself from it. You take yourself to work every day. If you take a package that doesn't match with the job needs, you've got a mismatch, regardless of the employer. I suggest you think of yourself as a Siamese twin, only in your case there will be no surgical separation. The niche that runs through you will also nourish the business you grow. Since you are in charge, it is your responsibility to keep both twins healthy.

YOUR COMPANY'S ACHIEVEMENTS AND ACCOMPLISHMENTS

Now it is time to ask exactly the same questions about your organization. What do you and others perceive to be its most important achievements and accomplishments? Its greatest strengths? Ask this question of enough people, including past and present customers and those with whom you've never done business, and you'll find patterns that may delight you. It's entirely possible that others will identify strengths in your company you'd never see yourself. Once again, those strengths may suggest a niche waiting to be exploited.

What are the implications of the information you're collecting for your business or organization? If you've found out something especially interesting, you'll want to highlight it and make sure it gets written into Step 2, Preliminary Focus, on your 9-step chart.

The Patterns in Your Life and Business

As you were completing Exercises 2.1 and 2.2, you may have begun to notice certain themes repeating themselves over and over again. The following exercise helps you describe those patterns.

EXERCISE 2.3

PATTERNS IN MY LIFE AND BUSINESS

Describe patterns you've begun to notice in your life. Use language that is specific rather than vague.

_____

_____

_____

Describe patterns you've begun to notice in your business. Once again, be as specific as possible.

_____

_____

_____

It would be a good idea to dog-ear this exercise, since you will most likely be coming back to it throughout the nichecraft process. It may turn out that inside one of these statements lies the germ (more aptly put, gem) of a niche. Continue to study these accomplishments and achievements for yet one more feature: *consequence*. Too often people look only at what they did, and not at what happened as a result of their action or presence. Their view is much too short-term. By looking at the consequences or impact of your own actions or those of your company or organization, you may come to see niche potential you never thought about before. Once you become adept at consequencing, you sharply reduce the likelihood of becoming obsolete or a victim of circumstances. Move now to the following exercise.

EXERCISE 2.4
CONSEQUENCE NICHES
---

1. Look at each of the accomplishments and achievements you listed above. Now identify the consequences of those achievements. Play out the consequences of the consequences of the consequences.
2. Now can you identify any interesting patterns?
3. Can you spot any business niches for the making?

CONSEQUENCES OF CONSEQUENCES	CONSEQUENCES FOR THE MAKING	NICHES FOR THE THE MAKING
_____	_____	_____
_____	_____	_____
_____	_____	_____
_____		

To identify your business niche, ask yourself what needs are being produced by the consequences of what you did. From the *difference* you have made.

Event Consequencing

Now it's time to systematically begin "event consequencing," a skill you'll find invaluable in creating just the right niche for

yourself and your business. This is similar to the basic consequencing exercise you just experienced but concerns itself with
a specific happening instead of a longer-term sequence of
events. Operation Desert Storm produced many consequences,
but one of the most interesting was something the medical
community reported as Operation Desert Stork. According to
an October, 1991, *USA Today* report:

> Operation Desert Storm is over, but Operation Baby Boom is
> about to begin. At bases across the country, medics are gearing
> up for a phenomenon not seen since the troops came home
> after World War II and Korea: babies, lots of them, . . . filling up
> hospital clinics and generally straining the resources of the . . .
> U.S. military. . . . The baby boom is the entirely expected fallout
> of the war in the Persian Gulf when 500,000 soldiers flew off for
> up to a year.

Babies would not be the only thing produced by Desert
Stork. Business opportunities opened up overnight. Think for a
minute about some of the more obvious consequences of our
baby boom:

More medical supplies required—particularly in obstetrics
More medical services—baby doctors, nursing services
More baby care services and supplies needed—day care,
    infant clothing, baby foods
More maternity and parental leaves granted
Businesses having to fill existing positions with temporary
    workers or existing help
More home-based business developing

One of the best recent examples of an event producing huge
and profitable consequences—especially for those who were
awake to the possibilities ahead—was the introduction of
Microsoft's Windows 95. The interminable ballyhooing about
the product's introduction put millions of people on notice that
an opportunity was in the offing. Not just the opportunity to
buy Windows 95. I'm talking about the thousands of support

services and products generated by this single product. Training classes in how to use it, software experts to install it and ensure other programs were compatible, and new hardware opportunities taking advantage of the 95 technology are just a few of the endless consequences arising from this one product. The best thing about this, of course, is it was all predictable.

The Desert Storm and Windows consequence lists can be played out for pages. At every consequence you have a possible business niche waiting to be exploited. The moral of their stories: If the niche fits—take it! In the space below try your own event consequencing. This time, think very hard about business-related consequences. As you complete this exercise, I am confident you will agree that with every consequence comes a special present. It's called opportunity.

EXERCISE 2.5
EVENT CONSEQUENCING

Identify a significant event, either one that recently happened or one you predict will happen. (It's preferable to work with a forthcoming event since you have more opportunity to capitalize on its implications.)

The event

_____

One major consequence of the event

_____

Consequence of the consequence

_____

This consequence's consequence

_____

This consequence's consequence

_____

Continue consequencing your event

---

1. What, if any, impact will the above consequences
   have on your business regardless of whether you
   decide to turn one of them into a niche? (This is a critical question to ask yourself, since consequencing can
   also alert you to possible minefields and problems well
   before you get to them.)
2. Is a potential niche for your business suggested by any
   of these consequences?

If you have trouble figuring out the niche, ask yourself what
problems—what needs—will be produced by the consequences
you identified. Remember, a synonym for need is opportunity!

The Microchip Mentality

These last few exercises are useful for all of us engaged in
nichemaking. They are especially valuable, however, for a group
of people I've come to describe as having the "microchip mentality." These people are especially vulnerable to seeing themselves
and their businesses with dangerously limited perspectives. If
they have been building a particular kind of microchip, their
identity is governed by that chip. Unfortunately, it can also be
limited by that same chip. If the chip becomes obsolete (as many
are prone to do), these people also see themselves and their
enterprises as obsolete. Jack Lombard's story demonstrates this
point all too well.

Jack had recently been let go from one of the world's largest
aerospace companies. Though his story was one I'd heard

many times before, it was no less poignant the nth time around.

"I was with CRM for nearly 30 years," he said matter-of-factly. "I was with the company when it started. We only had seventeen employees at the beginning. I remember . . ."

His voice trailed off.

Picking up again, he continued, "I helped develop the SuperTech for the XCT–9000. But then I volunteered to work on the control panels for the MRN–50. That was my big mistake, Lynda. Research won out and the MRN–50 flies without people."

I inquired, "Then what happened to you, Jack?"

"Well, I got shifted to *quality control*. Do you know what quality control is, Lynda?"

I felt obliged to confess I was not an expert on the subject, though I'd met other people from companies similar to his and in situations similar to the one he faced. I went on to say, "Jack, it seems to me that you are viewing yourself very narrowly—defining your value in relation to the specific product you were last associated with."

What I meant was this: People from two extremes come to see me. At one extreme is the person I call the all-over-the-mapper, and at the other is the one I have come to know as the microchip mentality. Where all-over-the-mappers can't focus at all and think they can do everything, those with the microchip mentality are as narrow as a pinhead in defining what skills and abilities they bring to a situation. The microchips almost always underestimate their true capabilities.

"Look, do you think there is any market out there for me in quality control?" he persisted.

"I don't think you're going to like my response, Jack, at least in the short run. What I think is that you are going to have to create a whole new niche for yourself—one that is not dependent upon the whims of a huge corporation or an external circumstance.

"Furthermore," I said, "you are going to niche yourself in a way that enables you to stay flexible and foresee trends so that you don't ever again become obsolete."

"So how do I do this thing you're talking about?"

"Well, the first thing you're going to do is start thinking about yourself in very broad terms. We're going to look first at your many skills and achievements. Then we'll identify something Special that you can offer to just the right market or audience."

"What does this have to do with quality control?" Jack asked.

Whew, I said to myself. This is definitely one person who shouldn't be in business for himself! His excessively narrow vision of what he has to offer limits his services to what *was* instead of what *can be*, much less what his clients will want. Since Jack's quality control buzz phrase has been replaced with a newer model, total quality management (TQM), our friend probably finds himself very depressed. Once again he is obsolete.

Unfortunately, Jack Lombard has a lot of company with his inflexible view of the world. And the price of that rigid, unimaginative outlook is very high. Applied to your business, it can easily produce bankruptcy, liquidation, red ink, and debt.

What Business Are You Really In?

Though Jack Lombard was employed by someone else, his story is nonetheless relevant for all of us in private business. Jack's extreme tunnel vision prevented him from asking a very basic question; that is, "What business are you really in?" He did not allow himself to see the bigger picture into which his widget fit. And when the picture changed, he had no place to go, or so he thought.

Once again, lest any of us think Jack and the "Mom and Pops" of the world have a lock on denial or refusal to acknowledge change going on around us, we have but to look at some of the once-huge industries that found themselves out of a niche before they woke up to the real world around them. Smith-Corona's 1995 announcement that it was closing its doors for good because people weren't buying typewriters any more was a pathetic reminder that microchip mentalities come in all sizes. Instead of asking what its real business was, Smith-Corona just churned out typewriters, never adapting to the larger environment around them called office systems and communications. Their story is not a lot different from that of the asleep-at-the-switch daily newspaper industry. With hundreds of dailies having bitten the tunnel-vision dust, the industry as a whole is finally accepting as reality that communication and information, *not* newsprint, are its real business. This long-overdue recognition allows those "papers" that have survived to implement technology that achieves the organization's basic purpose. That fundamental purpose must yet house a good and flexible niche.

No less a giant than IBM appears to have asked the same question—"What's our real business?" Following major reorganization in the mid-nineties, the company found itself almost re-niching, trying to recast itself as mainly a supplier of solutions instead of just a seller of hardware. Commercial printing is still another example of an industry that must rapidly redefine what its real business is or face extinction. Printing has been compared to the steel industry, where you traditionally talk about the products you make and are defined by them. Printers have traditionally defined themselves by the process of printing. In today's world that is tantamount to suicide.

What is your real business?

What Are You Willing to Give Up?

Your success in business will be affected by many variables. One of the most important is your skill in self-discipline. The kind of self-discipline I'm talking about extends beyond simply knowing what you want, setting goals to get there, and following a tight plan; it includes *knowing what you're willing to give up* to get what you want. This component is crucial because, as you already know, successful niching requires a tight laser-beam-like focus. You can't be all things to all people. Regardless of how good you are at any of the things you want to do, be, or sell, if you expect the ultimate consumer to be able to find you among the masses, you are going to have to decide not just what you're going to do but what you're *not going to do.*

Alan, whom we met earlier, is an example of someone not willing to give up anything on his business's grab-bag menu of services. On the other hand, Carole Meyer, a Portland-based photographer, understands the importance of self-discipline—of giving up to get what you want. A brilliant portrait photographer, she made a strategic business decision that to achieve her goals she should change clientele from professionals to graduating high school students. I was personally chagrined to learn she was taking no more professional shots. Only graduating seniors, please. Alas, no amount of begging or pleading would work. Her office graciously refers out to other photographers, unless, of course, you're a graduating high school senior.

Closely related to this concept is understanding and knowing what kinds of trade-offs you are making. We make trade-offs every day. The difference now is that the ones you make are going to be conscious and intentional. Most of all, you will have thought through the consequences of those trade-offs. Some of the most common trade-offs my clients mention concern time with family and financial security.

I personally have also dealt with trade-offs. In building my own business, I spent several years traveling from major market to major market performing seminars. I'd made a conscious decision that for a certain period of time I would trade off time with my family and friends. At a certain point I realized that the trade-off was neither necessary nor something I wanted. While I still travel, it is on much different terms than earlier in my business development.

The point is, we all make trade-offs. If you and your business are going to be successful over the long term, however, you need to think carefully about those trade-offs, ensuring that you are willing to accept and anticipate them. The next exercise will help you clarify the idea of trade-offs in relation to your own business or organization's goals.

WHAT I AM WILLING TO GIVE UP

1. Identify your major goals.
2. List the trade-offs associated with each goal. For example, if you wish to create a successful business operating out of your home, one of the trade-offs you would be making is a more limited interaction with the public than if you worked in a traditional office or business environment.
3. Identify what you are honestly willing to give up to achieve your goals.
4. What are you *not* willing to give up?

My Major Goal	Tasks to Achieve Goal	What I'm Willing to Give Up	What I'm Not Willing to Give Up
(e.g., become world-famous fine art photographer)	(e.g., develop portfolio of fine-art-quality photographs)	(e.g., $ from weddings)	(e.g., time with family)
_____	_____	_____	_____
_____	_____	_____	_____
_____	_____	_____	_____

As a final part of this exercise, look carefully at all your goals. Prioritize ones you consider absolutely essential. Then do the trade-offs exercise again. The more you do this exercise, the more you recognize that having it all rarely means all at the same time. It is up to you to decide on the order of the pieces.

With your trade-offs list made, you have a rational way of deciding what kinds of goals make sense within the larger context of your business dealings and even your personal life. Trade-offs are not inherently good or bad; they become destructive only when they come as surprises. You should also be able to see how easy it is to have so many things going on at once that you confuse your potential audience about what you stand for. When that happens your business is in trouble!

Going Back to Spam

Instead of waiting for disaster, many companies have been proactive, seeing handwriting on the wall saying "You're inviting big trouble." There was General Motors jettisoning EDS, a mid-eighties acquisition from Ross Perot. From the beginning, this had to be among the stranger marriages. Probably not as bad as Sony going into the movie-making business but a mishmosh nonetheless. And then Federated Department Stores not surprisingly dumped its dowager I. Magnin chain, saying the store was "inconsistent with the aim of the company to expand its core department store business." And we can't overlook what may well be the biggest corporate divorce in history; that is, AT&T's decision to quit the computer business before it was too late. Cut its losses before they really gushed blood. By ridding itself of NCR, the corporate giant allows itself to focus on its most basic core, telecommunications.

But my favorite refocus in recent times has to be Hormel's move in selling off its slaughtering operation. Well before any hint of "too-late" being around the corner, Hormel decided to return to its core. Back to hogs. Back to Spam. Realizing they were really in the business of selling commodities, the company basically said they were not in the butchering business. They asked the question we all must ask ourselves if we are going to achieve the kind of niche that is profitable and enduring. That is, "Who are we?"

What's your Spam?

THAT'S ALL WE DO

In case you're hearing yourself saying, "Yes, but they're so big, they can afford to pare back," let me remind you that it's not a matter of being able to afford to cut back. They can't afford *not* to cut back to the essential core. No business is too big or too small not to have to do this. A recent announcement from a client of mine caused me to smile, thinking to myself, Yes, they've got it; they understand niche.

Brooke and his new partner have both been in commercial real estate for many years. Thoroughly professional, they gained their stripes working for one of the nation's major real estate brokerages. Having committed to going into their own business, they knew they could not compete against another established company. They would have to do something very special. And the right clients would have to know about it. Unlike so many young companies, Brooke and his partner bit the niche bullet. From the beginning, they made no pretense of trying to be all things to all people. They knew who their clients were and who they were not. The announcement I received told it all. Very simply it said, "Tenant Representation: THAT'S ALL WE DO." Yes, they do "get it." They are *narrow* and *deep* and *prosperous*.

LETTING GO AND COMMITTING (AKA JUST SAY NO!)

As I work with clients at early start-up or well into their business development, I find that a significant number of them feel guilty about letting go of their treasure chest of unfocused activities and mutually exclusive priorities—things that get in the way of, dilute, or simply detract from their primary business focus. I hear statements such as "I can't bear to give this part up—I've worked too hard to develop it"—"I enjoy this one so much"—"This other is so interesting"—"The fact is, I can't toss any of them out the window." You may even defend your right to stay unfocused as Alan did when I kiddingly said to him, "Alan, my goal in life is to get you niched!" He shot back with, "Rotsa ruck!" So much for my goal.

Granted, it may be hard for you to turn your back on some of these old and familiar activities, products, or services. But from now on, a hard-and-fast rule will apply: If something is detracting from or diluting the strength of your consciously selected niche, it must be removed from the shelf. Maybe you can keep some of the items around for after-hours time or hobbies. But if it's a detractor, it's gone! It is entirely possible that from time to time you will have some internal resistance to cope with as you firmly say no to the temptation of adding just one more "fun" thing to your already full cup. The following exercise will give you clues about how much resistance you can expect from your irrational side.

EXERCISE 2.7

YOUR QUIT LIST

1. Identify your niche. To the extent possible, be very specific.
2. List the activities or other focus points you are putting away—quitting—in favor of your niche. If you are engaged in any activity detracting from achieving your niche goal, that activity should be on this list. Another reason for putting aside a particular activity or product is if it is not profitable now or shows no sign of ever being profitable. (In a later chapter you will learn to track where your real profit comes from.)
3. Write a word or phrase to describe how you feel about putting this activity or focus point aside.
4. Complete the feeling scale, indicating how you feel about giving up each of the items you identified.

My business niche is _____

_____

_____

_____

WHAT I'M GIVING UP TO ACHIEVE MY NICHE	A WORD OR PHRASE TO DESCRIBE HOW I FEEL ABOUT QUITTING THIS THING	VERY BAD		NEUTRAL		VERY GOOD
_____	_____	1	2	3	4	5
_____	_____	1	2	3	4	5
_____	_____	1	2	3	4	5
_____	_____	1	2	3	4	5
_____	_____	1	2	3	4	5

After the above exercises you know more clearly which things will get in the way of your niche success. Even so, you may still find yourself fighting off internal messages to keep doing the same things. A part of you is going to be resistant to change. If this is the case, be prepared for some direct confrontations with yourself!

Moral of this story: Just say no!

The Lessons I Have Learned

Another way to identify potential niches residing inside yourself is to think about the most important lessons you have learned over the years—whether those lessons have come from your experience in business, working for someone else, volunteer work, or even your leisure time. These lessons go way beyond textbook data. They are more than the experiences you've had. Instead, they are *what you have made* of the experiences. They are how you look at the world *after* the experience. The reason they are so valuable is that each of us processes an experience differently.

Consequently, what we make of it becomes something unique, reflecting our own way of looking at the world. That uniqueness may be the niche or core of your business. Some of my own clients' experiences may help you understand your own lessons better.

Perry was a principal in a large family-owned equipment manufacturing company. The business produced huge machines used in agriculture and was one of the world's largest companies of its kind. Despite its size and market, the company nearly failed because of serious internal family issues. In assessing the experiences of his own company, Perry realized that a significant number of similar firms throughout the world were also family-owned and vulnerable to the same issues that nearly killed his company. He also realized he understood many of those issues and could help similar organizations avoid the disaster his family and company had experienced. Shortly after his family's business was on its feet, he sold his portion to his brothers and opened another company. This one is devoted exclusively to advising companies manufacturing agriculture-related machinery. But he isn't advising them on the nuts and bolts of the equipment. He shares the lessons gained from his own experiences in a similar business. Without those experiences he'd have no lessons.

EXERCISE 2.8

THE LESSONS I HAVE LEARNED

List your lessons below.

The Lessons

_____

_____

_____

_____

The Patterns I See

_____

_____

_____

_____

Now take a look at your entire list. Ask yourself what these lessons tell you about the person they belong to. What are you learning about that individual's perspective or style? Where might these lessons be put to use?

What These Lessons/Patterns Tell Me About My Business

_____

_____

_____

_____

If you had trouble listing your lessons, complete the following sentences:

Based on my experience, I would advise you to _____

_____

Here is how I would do it differently this time: _____

_____

Do this exercise enough and you are likely to isolate a specific observation or lesson that is uniquely yours—one that you can build on and exploit in your own business.

Your Opinions May Be Your Niche

"Polite people don't express opinions in polite company!"
"Don't be controversial!" "Don't upset apple carts!" Regardless
of how you have treated your opinions in the past, it is time to
get them out front—at least to add them up and see if collectively they might reflect an important niche for you and your
business.

Earlier you learned that a key attribute of a niche is singularity, uniqueness, being one of a kind. As you review your
lessons and opinions lists, you will see that they certainly meet
that criterion. The reason is that while you might have shared
similar experiences with someone else, or a whole group of
people for that matter, what you made out of the experience—
the synthesis of the experiences—is uniquely yours. It may
well be that your way of looking at things can help others lead
their lives more efficiently or enjoyably. Ben and Jerry's Ice
Cream became famous not just because its founders figured
out that indulgence food would never go away. In addition to
billing their product as lush and rich, they also let it be known
that a percent of all the company's profits would be directed to
specific nonprofit efforts. Ben and Jerry's was among the earliest and most successful of the organizations promoting themselves not just on the basis of their products but on what they
do with the money derived from them! The term *socially conscious organization* emerged to describe the trend Ben and Jerry's
helped set.

Oftentimes, then, what you personally bring to your service
or product can be the key feature setting your business apart
from everyone else in your field. Most importantly, once you
know what you stand for, a system can be put in motion to
convey that message to others. No chance that you will be like
pasteurized milk—bland, homogeneous, indistinguishable from
the masses. You understand full well the words of songwriters
Aaron Tippen and Buddy Brock who remind us, "You've got to
stand for something."

EXERCISE 2.9

MY OPINIONS

Think for a few minutes, and in the space provided list key opinions you have on subjects of priority concern to you. Identify the kinds of opinions you would go to the wall for—the ones that come from the essence of your person— the ones that add up to you.

I believe _____

_____

I believe _____

_____

I believe _____

_____

   Summarize any patterns you see in your opinion statements. How can your opinions be translated into a business niche?

What does your *company stand for?*

Niche Your Style

Your style—your way of doing something—is one more aspect we should consider as a viable niche source. By style I mean your approach to resolving issues—your way of doing things—the unique touch that is yours alone. Regardless of what kind of product or service you are delivering, capitalizing on your style can lend the kind of singularity that is definitely a characteristic of good niches. For example, the late blues singer Billie Holiday was said to have a sound of her own. It was a sound no one could replicate no matter how they tried. Similarly, a *New Yorker* article

described Barbra Streisand as having "a voice as immediately recognizable in its way as Louis Armstrong's." The article went on to
say that "What she does so ingeniously is *Streisand* each song." It
was a sound no one could replicate no matter how they tried. Yet
another way to think about style is to ask yourself what it looks
like when you put your own signature on something.

And What Is Your Streisand?

To clarify the concept of style even more, think about some of your
own favorite artists, athletes, and even politicians. Then identify
the style that comes to mind when you think of their names.

EXERCISE 2.10

NICHE YOUR STYLE

1. List your favorite people in each of the following cate-
    gories.
2. Describe as clearly as you can the style you associate
    with each person.

PEOPLE   STYLE

Sports _____ _____

Music _____ _____

Art   _____ _____

Now list several words or phrases that would describe
your personal style or the style you bring to your product
or service:

_____

_____

If you can't figure out *your* way, ask yourself how the outcome of several very important activities in which you are involved would be different if someone else were in your particular role instead of you. Or assume five of you are each assigned the same task. A panel has to identify who executed each task. How would they know which one you did? Or say your business and four others are each working on identical projects. How would we know which one was yours? Once you can answer that, you'll also know your style!

What Is Your Signature Statement?

Lest there be any misunderstanding that style may be important only to artists, sports figures, and politicians, we have but to look at winners from other major industries. In discussing his company's expansion move to New York City, Gordon Segal, President of Chicago-based housewares and furnishings chain Crate and Barrel, emphasized Crate's sense of its own style. Quoted in the *New York Times*, he said, "We never take a manufacturer's product straight off the floor. . . . No matter what the style, we'll have our version of it." With knockoff companies sprouting up all over, Crate's challenge, as with Starbucks and other niche leaders, is to stay ahead of the very pack they started.

Crabbe Huson, a mutual-fund management company based in Portland (Oregon), provides another example of an organization not only understanding its own style but refusing to compromise that style at any cost. Company President Jim Crabbe explained why his firm refused to go ahead with a marriage to Prudential Insurance, one of the nation's deepest pockets. In an interview with the *Oregonian*, Crabbe said he felt like the renegade penguin in a "Far Side" cartoon: the one standing on an iceberg in a crowd of identical penguins, crooning "I Gotta Be Me." For Crabbe Huson, that "me" is its contrariness, its relatively small size, its way of doing business. If you will, its style.

Going Against the Grain

One of my all-time favorite examples of someone who not only understands his style, but has been enormously successful capitalizing on it, is Brad Fletcher, one of the nation's leading commercial real estate professionals. His story sheds valuable light on how "your way" can also be the most profitable way.

Since Brad entered his profession of commercial real estate in the late 1970s, his income has grown steadily and is now in the strong six figures. I asked him why he thought he'd been so consistently successful. He thought for just a second and answered, "I've always gone against the grain." With that admission, it's not surprising he started his career in commercial real estate when he did—a time when interest rates were running in the 20 percents. A crazy time to go into commercial real estate, you might say, a time when the deck was so loaded against you. Crazy like a fox, if you are Brad.

It seems his career started one day when he was driving down the freeway and saw several dilapidated houses lining the highway. The houses were boarded up ready for demolition. In a flash Brad said to himself he could do something with those houses. So it was that he bought them up for $50 each. After borrowing some start-up money from his father to redevelop them, he was off and running. Instead of demolishing the houses, he had each of them moved to attractive sites, rebuilt, and of course resold at considerable profit.

His niche? Creating opportunity out of someone else's discards.

Today he still works against the grain.

He works with government officials putting teams together, helping young companies get started. Although many of them ultimately go out of business, some of the fledgling start-ups that Brad nurtures prosper, and some become world-class in their field. Today, one of those former start-ups is the world's largest electronic company. Not surprising that Brad still works closely with them. And you can be certain his commission is a tidy sum more than what he collected when his now world-class client was just venturing into the light of day. They, like so many of his other clients, appreciated his help when they were young and poor. They are loyal to him now that they have money and power. He says it's right to help those young companies. He also says it's smart.

The last few years in his city have seen large numbers of old warehouses converted to chic, upscale loft space. Because of Brad, buildings that would otherwise have been razed and torn down have been converted to highly desirable properties. Once again, he created opportunity out of someone else's discards.

In so many ways Brad is interesting, which of course is one of the major characteristics of people who have created niches for themselves. For one thing he doesn't even use a computer, though he is sort of thinking about getting one. He understands that technology alone won't create success for him. Most of all, he understands the essence of making the best niche of all—doing it *your* way.

Now that you know what Brad's way is, *what's yours?*

YOUR STYLE CHECKUP

Should you decide that your style is going to be a key dimension of your niche, you will cultivate it deliberately and aggressively. Most importantly, you will create a marketing system methodically carrying the message of your style to the ultimate consumer. As I've already confessed, I am especially partial to this approach to creating the good niche—it crosses so many fields and products. I particularly like it for individuals wanting to strengthen their personal images. A carefully grown style— protected from distractions as any niche should be—can set you apart from the faceless crowds. And as Brad Fletcher has shown, it can also recession-proof you. The following short checklist will give you an idea how the style component of your own niche is faring.

MEASURING YOUR STYLE

Mark the number most closely matching your style quotient.
My style is:

Clear

1	2	3	4	5	6	7	8	9	10
Zero, invisible!				Evident			Strong, vigorous		

Intentional

1	2	3	4	5	6	7	8	9	10
Zero, invisible!				Evident			Strong, vigorous		

Consistent

1	2	3	4	5	6	7	8	9	10
Zero, invisible!				Evident			Strong, vigorous		

Invent Your Own Language

"Invent my own language?!? Come on, enough's enough! Are you serious?" you ask, aghast. Couldn't be more so. And here's why. You may already have found out that when you try to add up your opinions, experiences, and lessons into a single phrase describing you or your perspective, existing language is sometimes not adequate. This makes sense, though, because in summarizing those lessons, you created something new for which there may be no language yet available. Look around and you will see that often our world moves faster than available vocabulary, which has to run fast to keep up with all the changes around us. Many words or terms become archaic and are used only because no one has come up with better ones to date.

Take the word *retirement*. Taken literally the word is a

dinosaur. The vast majority of people retiring today aren't looking at rocking chairs and a life of do-nothingness. Increasing numbers are planning next careers and most of all anticipating highly productive years ahead. Hence, if taken literally this simple word can cause considerable problems for people about to experience it because it's discrepant with a desired reality. Hence, a new word or phrase is desperately needed to describe society today. I tell my clients not to retire—but to reformat.

Some examples of terms that have made their way into our lives courtesy of authors and inventors include *megatrends* (Naisbitt) and *futureshock* (Toffler). On the sports front consider *in-line skates,* one of the fastest growing athletics-related industries in the world today. As you work toward defining your niche more precisely, think about the metaphors you already use to describe what you do or your product does. By looking closely at themes emerging from your own lessons and opinions, you may find yourself inventing terms to summarize the essence of you. Best of all, once you invent your new words, they will always be associated with you and your niche!

Creating Your Own Culture

One of the most important reasons for creating your own language is that in so doing, you are also creating a *culture* associated exclusively with your business. Once again, Starbucks demonstrates the power of creating your own language. Terminology such as Caffé Americano, Espresso, Caffé Mocha, and Caffé Latté certainly sounds far more upscale than just plain coffee or extra strong coffee or coffee with cream. And if you plan to get between $1.50 and $2 for a cup of coffee, you better have something special associated with it. In this case it is the *language* of coffee. Excuse me. I mean *caffé!*

And of course, our new caffé culture includes its own norms and artifacts, aka products. One of the best things about creating your own language is that you are in a powerful position to define products new members of your culture will need to appropriately carry out their roles and obligations. In other words, you have multiple profit centers. And no niche is ever happier than when multiple profit centers nourish its cash register.

And finally, it's worth noting that the new language of coffee is being learned not just by customers but by potential competitors. As we know, it's one thing to invent or market a language in a unique way; it's another to ensure that the rest of the world continues associating it with your company. Vigilance will be the price of Starbucks keeping and deepening its niche.

Take a few minutes now to try your hand at new-language development. On a separate sheet of paper, list your own terms or personally crafted words describing what you, alone, stand for.

The Test of Discrepancy: What Your Firm Doesn't Stand For

One of the fastest ways to figure out what you or your company stands for is to identify what you absolutely don't represent. While the discrepancy test is nothing more than square-peg/round-hole analysis, it is also tricky for many people new to NicheThink. The reason is that what you *don't* stand for also means what business you *won't* take. This is a reminder that you can't work for just anybody; in some cases you will turn away business because it's the wrong kind and may take you down the wrong road. A road that will produce a niche from hell.

EXERCISE 2.12
THE TEST OF DISCREPANCY

In the following spaces, list situations which if they actually occurred would be so completely out of character for your business that you would know something had gone wrong. The thing going wrong, of course, would be niche confusion.

I (we) don't stand for this: _____

_____

_____

_____

_____

Critical Attributes and Your Business Success

If you are having trouble attaching language to this "thing" that you sense you or your business are about, the critical attributes exercise might be just the answer. Critical attributes are simply those features that must be present for an idea or product to exist.

Think for a moment about the difference between a table and a chair. If you were going to explain the two items to someone totally naive, what would you say? Is the fundamental difference that one has legs and the other doesn't? Or is it the number of legs? Is it that you put something on one and not the other? (That one doesn't work for long either: dishes on the table and your body on the chair!) If you continued the exercise, you'd soon recognize that the primary difference between chairs and tables is not one of form but, indeed, *function*. A table's primary purpose is not seating! The critical attribute distinguishing these two otherwise similar-sounding structures from one another is function.

Understanding or being able to recognize the critical attributes of your business is far more than an academic exercise. It is essential for your long-term success. If you are unsure what distinguishes your company from others in your field, you certainly can't do much with your niche. Chances are you don't even have one. The following exercise will help ensure that you consciously define what distinguishes your organization from others in your industry.

CRITICAL ATTRIBUTES TEST

In the following spaces, list the critical attributes associated with your business; that is, the characteristics without which your business or organization's identity really doesn't exist.

_____

_____

_____

Now that you have these attributes listed, review them carefully, determining if they reflect any patterns or perhaps an altogether new idea. Better yet, come up with a phrase summarizing the essence of these attributes. This phrase might be the new term describing your company's niche!

_____

As you are listing your company's critical attributes, subject them to the test of Specialness. In other words, so what's new?

DESCRIBE THE OTHERS TEST

Objectively describing other businesses in similar fields can help you refine and develop the niche singularly belonging to you. Complete the following:

Your field (e.g., retail): _____

_____

_____

Others in your field (e.g., Banana Republic): _____

_____

_____

_____

Their key characteristics (e.g., stylish, sporty, upscale):

_____

_____

_____

Now compare the lists you just made. Set your own critical attributes list alongside that of the others. Write a big *S* over similar characteristics. Circle those that are singularly yours. Perhaps you want to capitalize on those features. Be very careful that any unique feature you define is truly that. You needn't write off the *S*'s as having no potential, but if you are going to count on them to do anything for you, plan to define your company's own approach, style, audience, or critical attribute!

Turning Free Advice into a Profitable Niche

When was the last time you gave out some free advice? The kind that someone came to you and asked for, that is. How many times in the last year have people come to you asking the same question? If you find yourself being called upon regularly by uninvited, nonpaying "customers" wanting your help with a particular issue, it may be that others see you as able to deliver something they need. Apparently they see something in you that you may not even see in yourself. This something might be your niche.

This question is especially important to think about in the

context of your business. Sometimes people wind up asking advice about things you may think have nothing to do with the main purpose of your business. If enough people ask the same question, however, you'd better take it seriously. For some reason, they perceive you and/or your business as able to help them with that specific issue. In fact, it may supersede in their minds what you perceive your business to be about.

Suzanne, whose Ritzy Rollup empire we talked about earlier, was in part a product of the free-advice syndrome. Recalling her process of achieving focus, Suzanne realized that whenever her friends were having a special event, they would call her to help prepare the food. Or they'd ask for advice on how to organize the  event themselves. Thinking about the category of free advice she dished out (quite literally), Suzanne, as she put it, decided she was done being a "closet cook." Why not come out and make money at it? And so she did. And so she is.

What free advice are you serving up?

Following my hunch about the free advice syndrome proved the impetus for solidifying my own business niche and professional practice. After leaving my position as a university professor, I opened a private consulting practice. Shortly after my doors opened, an interesting phenomenon began. The phone started ringing with people saying such things as "So and so at the university said you could help me start a consulting practice. Can I come and take you to lunch and pick your brains?" (To this day I still cringe when I hear this expression, since it invariably produces a Hitchcock-like image in my mind of birds feasting on my gray matter.)

The calls continued. "Lynda, a friend of a friend five times removed said you could answer some questions I have about

consulting. Could I take you to lunch and p . . . y . . . b . . . ?"
The phone rang from up and down the coast and from the
widest spectrum of people. A common denominator existed,
however. They were all serious in their calls and, more importantly, they perceived I could help them. And what's more, I
hadn't invited a single one to call me! I wondered how many
more potential callers existed out in that wide universe of con-
sultants and what would happen if I did invite them?

To my delight I discovered an enormous industry with few
available mentors. A strong preliminary focus was in the offing. My real niche had to wait a while until I realized that the
single biggest difference between winners and all the rest
(regardless of industry) was the individual or company's ability
to distinguish itself from everyone else—to describe its own
perceived Specialness. You know. To define its own niche.

Now, when I go to lunch, it's to enjoy someone's company,
not to have my b . . . p . . . .

And What Do You Do?

Have you ever asked someone what they do and had them
respond with "Well, it's sort of complex"? Five minutes later
you weasel out of the conversation with a polite "Do you have
a brochure?" hoping that ploy will end the confusing monologue. A reminder once again that if you aren't perfectly clear
about what you offer *and* how you are Special among all other
providers in the field, don't expect your customers to be clear. If
they aren't clear, don't expect them to buy. The following two
exercises will help you refine your business focus even more.

EXERCISE 2.15

THE FRIENDLY STRANGER

As you have already learned, good niches have receptive,
appreciative audiences. That is, someone wants what you
have to offer. It is important for you early on, then, to
begin understanding how your audience perceives your

niche. The following exercise will provide important, per-haps even provocative information that you can use later in refining and managing your niche(s):

1. Identify someone who doesn't know you very well to assist with this short exercise; for example, a neighbor down the street, someone in your office building, a colleague down the hall.
2. Taking not more than 2 minutes, describe what you perceive your niche to be.
3. Then ask your "friendly stranger" in his/her own words to relay back to you the niche you just described. That playback should not take more than 2 minutes.
4. Are you hearing something that shouts Specialness, singularity, one of a kind, all with high focus? Are you hearing what you thought you said?
5. If possible, have a third party listen to your description and your "stranger's" interpretation and ask the third party to compare the two statements against your cri-teria of a good niche.
6. Discipline yourself to the suggested 2 minutes. Remember, a good niche carries with it nearly instant recognition. If it takes more than 2 minutes for your customer to figure out what you are about, your niche needs work.

You will find this exercise useful regardless of what kind or size of business you are building. The paramount issue here is that a niche is only as good as it is perceived to be by someone else. It is important to take constant readings on that perception.

Outside-In Views

You just received important information concerning how oth-ers may interpret your explanation of your niche. Now it is time to invite assistance again. This time, however, you are going to ask for help in clarifying what may be an existing *unintentional* niche. Where you told the "friendly stranger" what you perceived your niche to be, this time around you are going to be told by others what they think it already is!

EXERCISE 2.16

FROM THE OUTSIDE IN

---

1. Identify several different individuals who have known you well over the last several years and in a variety of situations, including your business, leisure, and personal life.
2. Give each of these people a set of 5 x 7 blank cards. Ask them to note on each of the cards a word or phrase that they believe aptly describes your most interesting and/or important qualities.
3. After you have collected all the cards, go through and put those seeming to go together into stacks of their own. Take cards out of each stack and see if they go in other groups.
4. When you are satisfied that the cards belonging together are in fact in the right stacks, give each group a name. This should be a descriptive term suggesting a common denominator linking all the terms to each group. You put the cards in specific groups because they share some things in common. Now it is time to say what those things are. Write down the name(s) you have given to describe each group.
5. After you have found the right phrase or term for each grouping, study those terms carefully. The language you selected may in fact describe a potential niche that others see in you and your business. You may want to consider elevating it from its status of unintentional to that of purposeful and cultivated.

It's very important to invite people's reactions to you on both personal and business levels. In today's world, it is often difficult to impossible to separate the two. Take a particularly hard look, however, at people's first response to your existing business operation. They may well see something in it that you have taken totally for granted. Perhaps another niche for the intentional crafting!

Missing a Niche

From time to time I meet someone appearing to fiercely resist acknowledging a potential niche when it is almost beating them over the head. Max's story will illustrate that point.

Max came to me on a personal referral. When he called, Max suggested he just wanted to ask a few nitty-gritty questions about setting consulting fees and organizing some business matters. Early in our discussion, however, it became evident to me that virtually all of Max's life was built around something he did in his off hours. Max pumps iron. He is a body builder. He is a gym freak. He lives, breathes, and loves working out. His first love is not a new one. Since he was a teenager, Max has always made sure that wherever he goes, he has the names, numbers, and addresses of health clubs with facilities consistent with his high standards.

Were it not for one other fact, Max's obsession with working out and physical fitness might be construed as just that. The other fact in Max's story is that people have always sought him out, wanting his assistance, guidance, and support in their own physical fitness routines. As a young adult, Max found himself besieged by others wanting information about how they too could improve their physiques through workout routines similar to his.

"A niche! A niche!" you're saying. "He has something someone—in fact a lot of people—want! He's got a niche!"

Right—and wrong. Max could turn his personal interest into

a powerful and intentional business niche, if he wanted to. Sensing that so many of the right ingredients were in place for him to do this, I asked Max, "Why do you ignore what the world has been trying to tell you for over twenty-five years? That you have something people want."

"Well, I guess I'm comfortable where I am now. I don't have to worry. I can pretty much count on what I'm doing. You know," he went on to say, "it's just too risky making changes . . . and besides, I don't know if I'm good enough."

As he spoke, I thought to myself about two other ingredients effective niching requires—both of which appeared to be absent from Max's repertoire. First is a willingness to publicly say to the world, "I believe in this product enough to take it to you." As long as Max operated in a casual, noncompetitive situation, he was fine. But he could not tolerate the thought of taking himself to market with intentionality, meaning he would open his product to scrutiny and—as he implied—the risk of failure. Successful business people must have unwavering confidence in their product and sufficient tolerance for risk, which in turn allow them focus and commitment. Max had neither. Hence, his decision was logical: take the safe road. The trade-off, of course, was a missed niche.

Whereas Max missed a niche out of fear, IBM missed what could have been an absolute blockbuster niche. And it missed it for an even simpler reason. It just "didn't get it." Having perfected electromechanical calculation (the Harvard Mark I, 1944), IBM initially dismissed the potential of computers. Only after Remington Rand's UNIVAC (1951) began replacing IBM machines did it offer a serious response and for a time captured an 80 percent market share. But then it missed the niche of all niches. By staying heavily wed to the waning mainframe computer market, IBM all but missed niche opportunities related to personal computers, networking, and software. It appears that IBM took its original niche vow too seriously. Till death do us part does not mean till your niche causes the death of your business. A good niche grows and evolves. In our next chapter you will improve your trending skills, ensuring that you will never have to play niche catch-up.

YOUR NICHE CHECKUP

Place your initials on the portion of the scale that most accurately describes your niche progress up to now.

| 1 | 2 | 3 | 4 | 5 | 6 | 7 | 8 | 9 | 10 |

I'm more confused   Making progress   Wow! It's great!
      than ever

Summary

This chapter has been about getting to your most basic core, whatever it may be. It has also been about getting rid of whatever may detract from that core. Though there are many ways to make good niches for your business, one of the best places to start the process is by distilling the essence of you—your skills, perspectives, style—the lessons you've learned throughout life. This process can be used by companies of all sizes and types seeking to establish a strong niche presence. In all instances, the issue is defining a central organizer—an ethos if you will. Once articulated, this ethos must be rigorously adhered to, avoiding scattered all-over-the-mappism. We have learned that size of company is no indicator of its niche intelligence. Huge organizations demonstrate niche incompetence with the same ease and frequency as the little guy. The difference is that it costs a lot more when Sears screws up than when you and I do.

And finally, this chapter introduced an ingredient so vital that even the best niche will most likely fail without it: an unwavering confidence by the niche's owner or manager—the kind of confidence that is willing to take a public stand saying "This is what I stand for and I'm proud of it."

3

MAKING YOUR NICHE WORK
IN ANY ECONOMY

One of the major reasons for crafting a strong niche is that a really good one protects you in any economy. As we have seen with our earlier Starbucks example, when you are well niched price isn't the issue. People want your product or service and will stand in long lines to get it. Brad Fletcher, whom we met in Chapter 2, achieved his early success in commercial real estate at a time when interest rates were going through the roof. People said he was crazy. Instead of crazy, he was just niched and on his way to considerable prosperity. This chapter provides more strategies for creating a niche that will be successful in any economy.

Intentional Themes

We start with one of the most powerful niching strategies you will encounter; that is, *intentional* theming.

You may wonder why I emphasize *intentional* theming. After all, who cares how you get a theme as long as you've got one. Right? Wrong. Sorry, that just isn't the case. The issue of intentionality—of purposefulness—is central to the idea of good niching. Too many businesses have themes that are merely accidental and don't meet the tests of a good niche. Most of all,

intentionality reminds us that choosing a niche is a strategic
decision and everything else in your operation must be prepared
to support it.

WHAT DOES YOUR BUSINESS STAND FOR?

One of the most well-known intentional themes associated
with a specific American business has been Nordstrom's customer service. Especially in its more youthful years, this
upscale specialty chain did everything short of deifying the
customer in its relations with the media, advertising, and the
ultimate consumer. Though they have tried, few other businesses of any size have been able to match the Nordstrom
niche for customer service. In many sectors Nordstrom and
customer service became virtually synonymous: "customer service the Nordstrom Way." Much like Starbucks, Nordstrom
didn't wait around to jump on a major trend. It set one. Or at
least it set the pace, the standard for customer service.

Now a mature company, Nordstrom is challenged to keep up
with the very reputation it established. As you may know from
personal experience, it is much easier to maintain a consistent
culture when your organization is very small. As Nordstrom
has expanded well beyond its flagship Seattle store, preserving
that service ethic has doubtless been challenging. The real
trick, though, for a company like Nordstrom comes in figuring
out how to keep *and* deepen the niche they've got while looking to the future and figuring out what curve they want to be
ahead of next.

The fact is that however excellent it may be, "customer service" is quite ordinary. If, by chance, you have been thinking
about growing your niche around something to do with customer service, you don't need to groan and throw in the towel,
however. What you need to do is niche the concept even more
by deciding *what your specific approach to customer service will be.*
For example, Marilyn Sangmeister, a Northwest business advisor, designed the *Customer Service from the Heart* system reflect-

ing her own values and approach to life. What is your own style? Your own way? Answer these questions and you'll be on your way to a great niche!

WHAT'S YOUR THEME SONG?

Whatever theme you select for your own business, it will act as a kind of warp and woof, weaving its way through the entire company. It will be nothing less than a glue or ethos binding departments and employees to one another. As you prepare to select a theme that can be applied to your business, keep the following criteria in mind. A good theme will:

1. Be understood and implemented throughout the company
2. Be consistent with the overall goals of your business
3. Convey authenticity and an appropriate relationship to the products with which it is associated
4. Have the principals' long-term commitment rather than being a faddish, short-term response to long-term profit and productivity issues.

Intentional theming works well for virtually all organizations, including the thousands of small to mid-size towns throughout America. Increasingly, these formerly bustling entities find themselves withering and dying, victims of nichelessness. Some, though, have realized their imminent demise and have taken steps not just to survive but to thrive in the shadows of the new malls and shopping centers filled with retail giants. They have committed themselves to clear, understandable themes. Just a few of the most successful include:

TOWN	NICHE/THEME
Leavenworth, WA	Bavarian village
New Orleans, LA	Dixieland jazz
Williamsburg, VA	Colonial village
Freeport, ME	Factory outlet

Poulsbo, WA	Scandinavian village
Ashland, OR	Shakespearean productions
Nashville, TN	Country music
Santa Fe, NM	Native-American art
Gilroy, CA	Garlic

DON'T LOOK TOO FAR

The good news is that many of the best niches are very close to us. The bad news is that sometimes we have myopia and can't see what is right in front of us. Forest-for-the trees syndrome. I'm reminded here of the story of the two children on their first trip downtown by themselves to see the parks and other lovely sites in their city. Their mother had told them not to miss a particularly beautiful building designed by a famous architect. The problem was that the children kept losing the building. They'd walk toward it and it would disappear. When they finally asked a police officer to help them, they learned the real problem. They were simply too close to see the whole thing. They had to stand farther back to get the full picture. Once we learn to do this on a regular basis, good niching becomes infinitely easier, much more fun, and certainly more profitable. In a sense, achieving a good niche requires you to be a bit schizophrenic, temporarily, that is. You have to get far enough outside yourself and your business to have a clear perspective on the changing times.

WATSONVILLE: DISCOVERING THE NICHE WITHIN

Watsonville, a small town in northern California, was like many towns of its size across America. Originally with an agricultural base, it had been for many years bustling and prosperous. And like many of its counterparts, Watsonville was also quickly relegated to off-the-beaten-path status when freeways and air shuttle service became commonplace. As if freeways were not enough of an insult, add the slick nearby shopping centers and more recent arrival of superstores and you could have a pretty pathetic picture. You *could have*. But Watsonville is niche savvy.

The downtown association's leadership realized they certainly could not compete against the cookie-cutter mall stores—stores targeting a mass audience. Similarly, they would be no match in a bout against the superstores going in just down the road. So what was left? What was left turned out to be the town's richest asset. An asset no one could clone, knock off, or steal. That asset was none other than its people.

Watsonville's population is now dominantly Latino. The Latino culture has for many years permeated the region, but as in so many similar situations, it was, if not intentionally buried, at least overlooked. Under the leadership of its MainStreet Project Director, Jerry Hernandez, Watsonville launched a full-scale effort to highlight and capitalize upon a niche that was already there—its Latino culture and tradition. As a major regional Latino center, Watsonville would be on its way to becoming a destination—a place people would travel long distances to visit, enjoy, and spend money in. It would become its own version of Chinatown.

Perhaps the most powerful aspect of Watsonville's decision to build on its people's roots is that it builds on something completely natural, exquisitely authentic. It is the town's natural core. In most cases, that which is most authentic is also the piece that is strongest. So it is that Watsonville has identified its core and is building on its most Special and unique strengths.

To Thine Own Self *and* Business Be True

Remembering that many of the best niches may be right under your nose with no new widget needed, it's time to think about potential themes that can define your own niche. It may be that a feature you take for granted can be capitalized upon and developed as a serious theme associated with your enterprise.

MY INTENTIONAL THEME POSSIBILITIES

In the spaces below, list possible themes that your business or organization could adopt and cultivate.

Example: Nike-Swoosh/"Just Do It!"

Example: Health/fitness for the mature market (Note: At one time, health and fitness constituted a theme on its own merit. Today, demographic trends lend themselves to further refinement of the field—indeed, a budding niche).

_____

_____

_____

Mom and Pop Get Niched

Once the backbone of American retail, successful traditional "Mom and Pop" shops are an increasing rarity throughout the country. With tens of thousands of smaller stores gobbled up by larger conglomerates, many of the rest appear on a fast track to becoming invisible. Mom and Pop are definitely on the endangered species list if they operate in traditional fashion, oblivious to the world about them. But so are all businesses, regardless of size. Using good niche sense, Mom and Pops can be profitable while providing their owners with a high quality of life—a feature usually at the top of any entrepreneur's wish list. If you dream of having your own Mom and Pop operation or simply want to make your existing business more profitable, keep the following guidelines nearby:

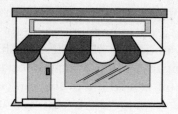

Mom and Pop Niche Rules

1. Quit talking about or buying for "what used to be." Most of all, get rid of any vestiges of mass marketing attitudes you may still hold. Don't plan to resurrect them in either of our lifetimes.

2. Expunge, eliminate, banish from your vocabulary any idea of competing with the "big boys." You can't. If you think in terms of competing you will fail because you will wind up thinking about being similar instead of capitalizing on establishing singularity and uniqueness. While this issue is relevant to all businesses, its impact is most obvious in retail. To remind yourself of this, write down the following reinforcement phrase, and keep it close to you at all times: Niche! Don't compete!

3. Play to your strengths. Of all the messages in this book, the importance of this one cannot be overstated. Think of Watsonville. It could not compete and win against the superstores and shiny malls. But it could win by building on its inherent strengths. Your smallness can be a strength. Since you aren't appealing to everyone, your merchandise can be upscale. However you decide to proceed, the first step should be in clearly identifying and then leveraging those strengths you *already* have.

4. Give serious consideration to capitalizing on yourself as the theme of your niche. If you establish yourself as a personality to be reckoned with, that image can be more powerful than a specific tangible product. And most of all, it is *Special*. It's all yours. Think about transcending a single product or technology.

5. Get your neighbors on board. Don't go it alone—it won't work. If customers are going to stop at your store, it will be essential for you to establish a critical mass or sufficient impact so that your potential customers know you exist. You can dramatically increase this impact by involving several other businesses under a common theme. There is no little irony in the fact that independent businesspeople who try to operate in isolation today are probably setting themselves up for failure. Telescope the time needed to get where you want by thinking and creating a niche group (see Chapter 6). This important support system may make the difference in whether your small business ever creates the large profits it is otherwise capable of producing.

6. Think of yourself as a *destination*. Don't limit your thinking to the several square blocks around your operation, whatever it may be. Create the kind of niche that draws people to you from all over.

Does Your Franchise Have a Niche?

Franchising is one of the fastest growing industries in the world. It is especially exciting to people wanting to own their own business but not wishing to start it from scratch, people who would prefer to buy something with a track record and a marketing support system. Today franchises come in every flavor, from hotels to hamburgers to motivational seminars to pizza to mobile dry cleaning to dentistry to mail boxes to executive office suites. It seems there is almost nothing that is not available in franchise format. The problem is that with even the best franchise, you still have to protect and grow its niche. Too many people think just buying a ready-made franchise will do the trick. Despite the consistency required among franchises, despite the tight regulations franchisees must adhere to, the key to most of their success boils down to creating the niche that distinguishes them from all the other franchise owners in their area. Bruce and Joyce are a "Mom and Pop" franchise couple who successfully did just that. Their story provides an important lesson for all of us.

A NICHE SUCCESS STORY

Shortly after Bruce "retired" from his executive-level position with a Fortune 500 company, he and his wife, Joyce, became franchisees. As owners of a high-tech print shop, this husband-and-wife team found themselves with a multiyear lease, no backlog of customers, and no cash flow to count on! One week after opening, they learned to their chagrin that a shop from the same franchise and located down the street had just folded. Bruce and Joyce's shop looked exactly like the one that had gone out of business. The products were essentially the same. They were competing for the same business. Not surprisingly, Bruce and Joyce wondered if they were going to make it.

When I visited with Bruce several months later, I realized that any concerns they may have had about their ability to succeed were not justified. Already Bruce and Joyce's shop had broken sales records across the entire franchise operation. A simple throw-away statement revealed to me why their business was light years ahead of so many others operating in the same overall environment. He said, "I had to tell them to go somewhere else. I simply couldn't shave my prices the way they wanted. You know if I did that, I wouldn't be able to pay my rent." And finally he said, "The truth is, it costs me just as much to get a small customer as it does to get a large one so why should I fool around with nickel-and-diming?"

Regardless of who *your* customer is, the lesson from Bruce and Joyce is clear: you can't do business with everybody. You have to know who your audience is *and who it isn't*. Most importantly, there may well be times when you have to turn away business because it's the wrong business. It's business you can't afford. Alan, our all-over-the-mapper, could take a lesson from Bruce and Joyce.

If you think franchising may be for you, the following additional rules for franchise success will help you ensure that your franchise comes niche equipped:

Rule 1: When you shop for a franchise, make sure the franchisors are very clear about the company's overall niche in the market. Do they even have a niche? What's its potential life span?

Rule 2: Does the franchisor have a marketing strategy that will help make your unit a household word?

Rule 3: Make sure you know how you are going to grow that niche at your local level. Especially with smaller franchises; corporate can sell you a set of products, but it will be up to you to develop the niche that makes you successful. Without that niche, you will most likely never pay off the franchise fee and you most certainly will be disgruntled that you ever got into the mess to begin with.

Rule 4: Know your own personality. Yes, I know you've heard this one before. But the issue is extremely important when investing time, self, and money in a franchise operation. Successful franchisees are definitely team players, which is something of a trick for dyed-in-the-wool entrepreneurs who desire independence and decision-making autonomy. It's a very fine balance you walk between the two, and if the scale tips on one side more than the other, it's definitely in favor of teamwork.

Rule 5: Don't plan to invent or implement a whole new product line along with your franchise system. You won't be able to do it. Franchisors neither want nor allow their products to be messed around with. The agreement you sign guarantees you will deliver them as promised. If you are a classic entrepreneur, start your own business and franchise it, but don't buy one for yourself.

When you buy a franchise, you are buying someone else's niche. Make sure it fits yours.

Niching Prices and Fees

In every economy, there will be people who buy something because it's the least expensive in the category and those who buy because it's the *most* expensive. Because of this, pricing is one of the most frequent niche strategies—especially at the extremes. Some examples:

Watches: Timex—Rolex
Lodging: Motel 6—Ritz-Carlton
Apparel: Ross Stores—Neiman-Marcus
Pens: Bic—Montblanc

You might argue that the above examples are really quite different. After all, the Ritz does a lot more than just leave a light on for you. The fact is, the basic category of service both companies fill is hospitality. That is, while one will give you more sheets in one night than most people use in a week, the *fundamental* difference is price. One is high. The other is budget.

So obvious it's hardly worth mentioning. Right? Wrong! As you are niching your own product or service, remember that price conveys a message every bit as strong as the service itself. If you decide to go after a price niche—especially a low one—also remember that sooner or later someone else will come into the market and undercut you. You should either be prepared for a price war or, better yet, have established yourself so firmly in the market with household-word name familiarity that newcomers don't have a chance against the incumbent. Most likely, though, you'll want to implement one of the best niche-protection strategies of all, adding perceived value to your product or service.

JOINING THE CLUB

Warehouse and membership shopping clubs are prime examples of how niching according to price requires constant vigilance. For example, PriceCostco (formerly Price Club and Costco) and Sam's Warehouses are two of the nation's earliest and largest discount shopping clubs. Initially they offered low prices in no-frills environments. As these companies grew, their product lines also grew to the point where today they take up acres of space and sell everything from cars to steaks, all at deeply discounted prices. But they are not the only games in town anymore, and price alone definitely cannot guarantee them the business they want.

Following PriceCostco and Sam's success, the market was flooded with other membership shopping clubs, many of them focused on specific kinds of products. Office Club, later to be Office Depot, is just one example of more recent entries into the burgeoning office products field. Challenging price even more, many newer companies don't require membership to purchase. The point is, if you are selling on price alone, you can't win for long, because someone will always figure out a way to undercut you. So when you can't win on price alone, what do you do? You do what a senior official from one of the dominant shopping membership clubs told me. He said, "We can't just be a club anymore. We've got to become a *clubhouse* instead." In other words, value-added for members.

MAY I BORROW YOUR PEN?

It used to be that borrowing someone's pen was just that. You used it for a minute and returned it to the pen's owner without a second thought. If you haven't already had it happen to you, don't be surprised if your next request for a writing loaner is received with disdain, a shake of the head, and "I'm sorry, I don't lend my pen out to anyone." Alas, even the rules surrounding pens have changed. And so have the price tags, especially at the upper end, which has stretched itself out of sight. How intriguing that in a $5 billion worldwide market for writing instruments, the fastest growing segment is the premium segment—the one where pens cost more than $50 each. Some more than $1,000. But then writing isn't just getting something down on paper anymore. A Montblanc ad invites us to consider "the art of writing."

So it is that niching on the basis of price extends to virtually every service and commodity. The issue is being excruciatingly clear who your audience is and who it's not. The happy camper Bic customers are probably not thinking about the "art of writing" and how it will enhance their lives!

When Your Business Is a Professional Service

If dramatic changes have occurred in business generally in the last decade, a virtual revolution has taken place in the professional services. Just yesterday, it seems, life as a professional was secure and predictable. You finished college, went to some kind of graduate school or professional training program—maybe law, medicine, engineering, architecture—got a big certificate that you immediately framed and hung on your new office wall, sent out engraved announcements, and waited for the clients to come in. And they did. At least for a while.

That "while" ended when services got saturated with tens of thousands of other excellent, bright, energetic souls in similar fields, and in the same breath laws changed allowing advertising! All of a sudden being a lawyer was no big deal in itself. Regular architects became a dime a dozen. Even declaring yourself a doctor no longer raised eyebrows out of respect and awe. What happened was that professions formerly qualifying as niches in themselves grew in numbers so dramatically that they ultimately represented huge fields, at best. If you were truly serious about your professional status and long-term success, you realized that it would take a lot more than a shingle, license, expertise, or even massive advertising to keep you in business. The key, of course, became niching.

As you would expect, the basic rules of effective nichemaking apply to the professions. A few nuances deserve some special attention, however. If you are involved in any professional service, keep the following tips close by for frequent reference:

Special Considerations

1. Remember, professional services are distinguished from conventional products largely because they are based upon someone's knowledge or expertise. Hence, your image and reputation become critical features of whatever niche you create. And therein lies the central reason professional services don't go on sale!

2. Don't plan to own any specific technology or body of knowledge. Information per se is available to virtually everybody. More than data by itself, the thing that will set you apart from other experts in your field is what you make out of the data—how you approach the information, how you apply it.

3. More than in any other aspect of business, you and your personality—your style, your presence—are central to successful nichemaking in the professions. Yours is a business where "people buy people." The bigger the issue you are asked to address, the more the client wants to respect you as a person whose judgment, whose approach, whose style will get the job done fast and well. As you define your niche within your professional services field, it should highlight you the person and what you stand for.

   People buy people.

4. Don't plan on potential clients automatically picking up on your personal niche. You must systematically cultivate the image and actively send the message out to the right people.

5. Niches in the professional services should create situations where potential clients are more concerned about what you offer than what you cost. "How fast?" not "How much?" should be their first question. One of the key differences between selling professional services and other products is that you don't go on sale or negotiate your fees. This underscores the need for a tight, clear, and powerful niche message. Your potential clients must perceive you to be indispensable in their world.

6. Since it is vital that clients perceive you as already successful, *you will not be doing cold calling* or other things
that set you up to look like a beggar. Your niche must
distinguish you sufficiently from everyone else in your
field to encourage the *right* clients to call you—and lots
of them!!

You Are It

Although many issues affect professionals growing a prosperous niche, the biggest single issue rings very loudly and very
clearly. It is that *you are it.* In a professional service, people buy
you. If you really want to be successful, you cannot hide
behind your technology or service or certification. This point
was driven home to me repeatedly during a study I conducted
identifying factors causing clients to choose one professional
over another. The landlord of a major downtown LA office
building summed it up best; in explaining what causes him to
select one real estate broker over another, he put it this way:
"Well, when it's all said and done, I gotta be able to work with
the guy."

The implications of this statement are especially important
for professionals working within a large organization. While
solo practitioners take more responsibility for cultivating relationships, people within large organizations tend to assume
that the company is the dominant reason clients come in the
door. In most cases, that simply isn't the case. They nearly
always come in because of a particular individual. And even if
they came in because of the company's larger reputation, it is
specific people who bring them back. The implications of this
are very powerful. Most of all, it means you can't rely on your
company to create customers for you. That doesn't necessarily
mean the company isn't doing its job. It's that *all things being
equal,* your customers are more interested in buying you as a
person than they are in the larger company.

The power of understanding who you are as a person and
exploiting that to the fullest as your niche is illustrated by the

dramatic success experienced by one of my clients. As you read her story, think about your own version of her niche.

No General Law Practice Here

When I met Kay Wakefield a few years ago she'd already built a decent law practice. Out of law school a few years, she had a general practice made up of a little bit of everything and a lot of domestic relations cases. Though her time was occupied, it was clear that at the rate she was going her firm would get by but not get great. Kay was not prepared to settle for "get by."

After exploring her options for creating the right niche, one especially intriguing feature of Kay's background emerged. She came from a long line of people with successful family-owned businesses. Her father and uncles had been in business together as had other members of her family. From the time she was a child, Kay had experienced first-hand the rewards and punishments family-owned businesses provide. As an adult she didn't give it a lot of thought, but she instinctively knew that growing a successful family business required more than just getting the right business plan or product. It required an intimate sensitivity to the complex human dimension of the business.

On that point Kay certainly scored Bingo.

But she scored bigger when she started trending, looking at the explosive growth of family-owned businesses in America. And the score got even bigger when she combined the essence of who she was with her law practice. The focus was natural. A law practice focused on the family-owned business.

That was step one. And it was a big one. But there was more to do. The first part of the "more" was getting rid of the law practice that had nothing to do with family-owned businesses. Kay knew she could not clutter up her practice, because it cluttered up the client's perception of who and what her firm was about. Away went domestic relations. In one swoop she gave away more than 30 percent of her practice. She did what so many professionals are deathly afraid of doing: turning down business because it's the wrong business. She knew that by narrowing the playing field she would wind up with a very deep and profitable niche.

It did not happen overnight. But approximately two years after sending paying clients to other lawyers, Kay's practice mushroomed. She added new partners and moved into attractive and much larger offices. Her business is about one thing: helping family-owned businesses be more successful.

Of course the moral of the story is that Kay was walking around with the niche that would ultimately serve as the core of her growing law firm. Her niche was neither her law degree nor the body of law affecting family-owned businesses. All lawyers have access to the same information. It was *what she as a person brought to the table*. Her experience. Her view of the world. Best of all, these are commodities no one can steal from her. They are hers, alone.

Following are case studies of two more of my clients for you to learn from.

CASE ONE: BILL AND HIS BOOKKEEPING SERVICE

Bill bought his bookkeeping service nine years ago from the firm's founder, Herman. Herman had named the company Keep You Secure because it seemed to say what he did for his customers. Herman had established himself as a respected businessperson in the community, and for years the business got along. Nothing great. Mid- to low-end customers and start-up businesspeople used his services. Basic bookkeeping with a lot of clerical. Some tax preparation.

For the first few years under Bill's ownership the business seemed to be going in the right direction, but more recently it's taken a nosedive. Bill says it's because there are so many others doing "the same thing he's doing." (The killer statement.) And most important to him, Bill is tired of what he calls "nickel-and-diming" clients. He wants to spend the same amount of time with less labor-intensive work. He has been taking sophisticated classes in tax preparation and special IRS auditing procedures so that he can consult to corporate clients with annual revenues of at least $200K. Although he isn't starting a completely new business, Bill must establish himself as a significant figure to his new clients. Let's see how he uses *Nichecraft*'s 9 steps to achieve his goals.

Step 1: Wish List?

Corporate clients with annual revenue of $200,000 and having IRS tax problems.

Step 2: Focus?

Tax support and consulting concerning their tax problems.

Step 3: Client's Worldview?

Keep IRS off their backs. Pay least amount of taxes. Reduce paperwork.

Step 4: Test of Specialness?

This is where Bill begins to get into trouble. He knows that to attract the kinds of clients he wants, he is going to have to elevate himself and be visible as an important problem-solver. The name of his company will have to change to include Bill's name—since people will be buying *him*. He reluctantly agrees to put his name out front, but he isn't ready to kill the Keep You Secure part, even though it isn't bringing in the customers he wants and is likely to confuse those he does hope to attract.

Step 5: Good Niche Test?

The niche passes all tests. It certainly would take him where he says he wants to go.

Step 6: Test with Real People?

Bill inquires of a few prospective clients if they would buy a service such as the one he is proposing. He gets some positive response and believes his service would be saleable. He is timid about implementing a more thorough market test strategy.

Step 7: Blitz the Market?

Bill freezes. He can't implement any marketing strategies that would make him personally visible. He won't undertake a newsletter or speaking or other strategies that would establish him as a major player in his field. He keeps talking about the niche. The same conversation every time.

Step 8: Go for It?

Bill flunks. He isn't ready to believe in himself, which is the major downfall of many other professionals trying to sell their services but reluctant to put themselves on the line to do it. Their confidence factor is zero. So is their business.

Step 9: Re-Niche?

He's trying to do it, sort of. But it won't work until he commits to himself. Bill is destined to wish and not do.

CASE TWO: WHEN A LAW DEGREE AND A MEDICAL DEGREE ARE NOT ENOUGH!

Burke holds both medical and law degrees. A member of the bar in one of the nation's largest states, he has achieved extraordinary success as a preeminent litigation attorney. If a large corporation has a significant matter to be tried in court, Burke is called. Especially if it involves a medical-related matter. But Burke isn't excited about being a trial lawyer forever. "It burns you out," he says. "You have to be young to handle this kind of life. It's not what I want to be doing when I'm 50."

"Well, what *do* you want to be doing?" I asked. Here's what his 9 steps to success look like.

Step 1: Wish List?

Hospitals, universities, and other institutions dealing with bioethical decisions, an area of deep personal interest and commitment to Burke.

Step 2: Focus?

Surrogacy. On the increase, surrogate births will generate a whole new body of law requiring experts to assist others in their interpretation and application.

Step 3: Customer's Worldview?

Apply existing law in an appropriate manner to avoid legal and ethical problems with clients/patients. Be recognized as a leader among organizations offering similar services, but most of all *stay out of trouble*.

Step 4: Test of Specialness?

Burke knows that he is the real niche—his persona is what his public buys. His vehicle for getting that persona out there will be his book on surrogacy. It will elevate him above all others in his field and establish him as a person to be reckoned with.

Step 5: Good Niche Test?

His approach meets all the criteria.

Step 6: Test with Real People?

Burke checks with some key professional associations about his subject and they immediately invite him to talk to their members at major meetings. Interest is hot.

Step 7: Blitz the Market?

Burke's plan includes the full range of print and nonprint media. His book will be the engine driving his entire business.

Step 8: Go for It?

Burke has to write the book and he does.

Step 9: Re-Niche?

Burke thinks ahead to his book's sequel.

Niching Your Multilevel Business

Network or multilevel marketing(MLM) is not new. The difference today is that not only has it gone mainstream, but network marketing is experiencing explosive growth. As with franchising, you can get virtually anything—from algae to purified water to cosmetics to tours of the Orient—through a multilevel source. That it's entered mainstream America is evidenced by the arrival of MLM courses on many college campuses across the country. By 1995, millions of people worldwide described themselves as being involved with one or more multilevel businesses. So, what's the issue? The issue is that although huge numbers of people get themselves involved in an MLM, estimates suggest that nearly as many people drop out as drop in! The sad thing is, they think they flunk MLM. The real culprit is niche. They don't have one.

If you are involved in an MLM and are serious about becoming successful, you must address the issue of creating a good niche for yourself every bit as much as people involved in traditional forms of business. The following tips will help you niche your MLM for success:

1. Shop. Make sure that whatever MLM you select fits your personality. You cannot sell something over time unless you really believe in it. There must be a niche fit.
2. Most of all, you must realize that the product or company by itself will do you no good unless you are prepared to develop your own niche as you would for any other business. The product is not a niche. *You* will be the niche. If your multilevel is like most others, there

are tens of thousands of people selling exactly the same product line you are, so obviously product is not the niche. Furthermore, hundreds of those salespeople may be in your backyard. In fact, you probably recruited more than a few of them yourself.

3. Accept the fact that once again, *you're it*. Decide early on what your own style, your own approach will be to growing your organization and to selling whatever your product or service may be.

4. Be prepared to focus and commit. Unfortunately the vast majority of MLM people are destined to fail from the beginning because of a seriously flawed belief that goes something like "I can do this part-time and make some extra money at it." The reality in most cases is, part-time anything is not worth much. Extra-money-mentality most often means a max of one or two sales, at least one of them being your own. If you are going to be truly successful, you've got to commit. How many people do you know who are in real estate today and out tomorrow? The reason isn't a lot different from the one explaining MLM's huge attrition rate. Part-time usually adds up to waste of time. So, if you are giving thought to MLM or network marketing as a business, I say great. But I also say you've got your niche-work cut out for you every bit as much as any other businessperson.

In an MLM the main issue is not your product, it's you.

The Consistency Criterion

Whatever focus you ultimately select, one attribute above all must exist if you are going to achieve maximum success. That attribute is consistency. Good niches are predictable. Your customers or clients must know what to expect. The message must be consistent regardless of where or how they hear it. And they are going to hear it in many different ways. More than anything else, you need to avoid mixed messages, confusion, or, worst-case scenario, no message at all. Invisible.

Colorless. Blah. Consistency is a crucial feature in successful nichemaking. It not only reinforces your obvious message but underscores its intentionality of purpose.

To understand the power of the consistency issue, look no further than the most successful businesses in the country— especially those with multiple locations such as franchises (e.g., Dominos, Pizza Hut, Sheraton, McDonald's, Alpha Graphics). Located throughout the country, in some cases the world, these businesses nonetheless share common and visible threads with their franchise associates. Customers know what to expect. That "thing" they expect is called niche. It's the tie that binds. It's what allows your customers to distinguish you from others in the same field. Without it, you're little better off than our all-over-the-mapper in Chapter 1.

Predicting Trends and Likely Niches

Whether you are already highly focused or still exploring the best direction to take in starting your business, your ability to take maximum advantage of trends will be critical for your overall success. By trending I mean anticipating consequences of events and current directions. Good niches respond to needs that grow as society changes. More specifically, one of the most effective ways of identifying powerful niches is by tuning in to the art of trend prediction and thinking about problems and needs (opportunities) likely to be generated by those trends.

The familiar adage of physics—for every action, there is an equal and opposite reaction—is one of the nichemaker's best friends. A recent conversation with the person seated next to me on a long-distance flight makes the point. By not giving the frequent flyer's easily recognized don't-bother-me signal (yawn, read paper, go to sleep, look the other way), Mr. X set himself up for my inquisition, which revealed that he was marketing director for one of the world's large disinfectant companies. In answer to my question, "How's business?" he responded, "Great, but we're always looking for those new markets." He went on to say that his product had recently found an interesting market niche—day care centers. Who would have imagined day care centers as a major market even ten years ago, I thought to myself. Of course the issue is thinking ahead. Mr. X was ensuring his company's continued success by addressing Step 9 (Reniche) and Step 1 (Wish List). His product remained the same, but it now had a huge new audience.

STAYING AHEAD

Thus, it's not enough just to keep up with your niche; you've got to be ahead of it. Ahead of the curve to ensure you're in the driver's seat. Or the pilot's seat, for that matter, because keeping your niche working is a little like flying a plane. Like the airplane pilot who constantly scans the instruments looking for all information possible about the flight, you must always be doing weather checks and looking ahead. One of the things I learned a long time ago when I took my first flying lessons was that if I was going to stay in the air, my head had to be well ahead of the plane. I had to be thinking about what was coming up not just a few miles ahead but well beyond my immediate line of sight. If I didn't think about what was ahead before I got there, I stood a good chance of running into big trouble. The faster my plane, the faster I had to think and consider the always-changing environment ahead of me. So it is with making a good niche. Don't ever expect yours to stay in one place.

Although trending a good niche may bear some resemblance

to flying that plane I spoke about, there is one huge difference and that difference is the moral of the story. Though you can get away with it in an airplane, there is *no such thing as niche auto-pilot*. You must be awake, directing your craft, whatever it may be, at all times.

Since we live in a virtual sea of trends of all kinds—including economic recession or recovery, draw down or right-sizing (depending on whether you are civilian or military), computerization, societal aging, and electronicization of information—your niche-trending opportunities are enormous. The following trend-consequence exercise will help you identify problems and niches to address them.

EXERCISE 3.2

TREND YOURSELF A NICHE

1. Identify a major trend affecting business, society, education, health, etc. (e.g., home-based businesses increasing rapidly).

   _____

   _____

2. Think about and list the problems likely to be generated as a result of the trend (e.g., home furniture inadequate to manage business needs, personal relationships strained because of role confusion created by family members working in the home environment, more people wanting to take work home instead of spending all day in the traditional corporate setting).

   _____

   _____

   _____

3. Now identify the consequences of those problems (e.g., new home office furniture designed to meet new

needs, psychologists find more domestic issues related
to new roles and closer interaction of family members,
and managers in traditional work situations looking
for ways to assess productivity of employees not always
under the same roof).

_____

_____

_____

4. Play out the consequences of the consequences for
    several generations.

_____

_____

_____

5. At each consequence, stop and ask, "What need is
    going to exist at this level?" This need may well be an
    exciting niche for you to seize and fill. List all the new
    niche needs here.

_____   _____   _____

_____   _____   _____

_____   _____   _____

_____

MORE EXAMPLES OF TRENDING IN ACTION

Following are some more examples of trending with possible
niches waiting to happen.

Trend: Peace ⇒ military draw down ⇒ tens of thousands of
career military involuntarily released from their jobs ⇒ more
people thrust out onto job market ⇒ longer period of time for
people to find conventional employment ⇒ potential frustration, anger, dysfunctional attitudes and behavior. Niches? Career

counseling specializing in transitioning military personnel and families, advisors to home-based businesses.

Trend: Down-sizing and right-sizing of various companies resulting in mass layoffs of civilian personnel throughout the country ⇒ glut on market of qualified personnel ⇒ permanent disappearance of former job slots ⇒ out of necessity people move toward home-based businesses ⇒ people with little experience developing and promoting own businesses seek advice. Niche? Advisor to home-based businesspeople.

Trend: Increased use of sugar substitutes in food ⇒ fewer cavities ⇒ less conventional business for dentists ⇒ dentists wanting increasing patient load ⇒ dentists engage marketing firms. Niche? A particular approach to practice management for dentists.

Trend yourself a niche.

Tracking trends and zeroing in on a possible niche is unusually effective when done with a friend or small group of people brainstorming together. This approach to nichecrafting is especially exciting because it allows you to be the first—No. 1! By being at the head of the line you can penetrate your market early and deeply. Being first can definitely help you make a niche. It can also be a problem if you are so far out front that no one—especially your potential client—understands what you are talking about or selling. If you create a niche destined to make you a leader, you are also likely to have to educate many others (buyers) to get there. This can take time, money, trial, and error. Most of all, it takes acute and sensitive attention to every step on your nichecraft ladder of success.

Making Yourself Indispensable

We said that a key feature of a good niche is being perceived as indispensable. As you are thinking about how to create the kind of Specialness that will do just that, you may want to consider the strategy Jim shared with me some months ago. A former corporate executive who "reformatted" himself into an entrepreneur, Jim confided his key to success (which was considerable). He said, "You just decide you're going to get very good at all the things the other guys don't like to do . . . and then you do them."

This strategy can be invaluable whether you are still wondering which direction to go or are in a more advanced stage of business development. The following exercise gives you an opportunity to see how your business might grow by leveraging other people's dislikes!

EXERCISE 3.3

MAKE YOURSELF INDISPENSABLE

---

1. Identify your preliminary focus area.
2. List the major things that must be done to achieve the goals of that focus.
3. Which of those things do people like to do least?
4. What things, if any, can you pick up on and do?
5. How will this influence your business focus?

Get niched, get noticed, get profitable.

Drawing Outside the Lines

One of the best things about NicheThink is that we get to think and draw outside the lines. Actually we *have* to get outside our conventional thinking if we are to be successful creating the kind of niche that achieves our goals in today's world. In a very real way you have to be willing to *play* with ideas. Instead of saying something can't be done, you say, "How can I do this?" "Why not?" Instead of assessing an idea on its face value, you want to turn the idea inside out and upside down. Ask yourself, "What would it look like if I did it this way?" What would happen if . . . ?

While NicheThink is a very rational process, you must think of yourself as an inventor. An inventor of new ideas. Don't allow yourself to say no just because you've never done it that way before. By the same token, just because something is new doesn't mean it gets a medal either. It means all ideas get subjected to the same merciless 9-step process for making a good niche.

Your Niche Within the Large Organization

So the company is on its way to getting focused, on target with a good niche, and more profitable. But what about *your* niche within the organization? Regardless of how long you plan to be with the firm, it's vital that you be clearly distinguished from all the other good people looking for many of the same things you are—professional advancement, more money, more job satisfaction, more freedom, more recognition, etc.

This was brought home to me clearly by a young CPA who during a private consult said, "I don't just want to be one of the masses in the firm. My plan is to definitely be a partner. But I know I must be noticed. How can I make myself seen, heard, appreciated—indispensable?" The answer was to deliberately niche him in an area that virtually all the other member CPAs needed. A strategy closely related to Jim's earlier admonition to find out what the other guys need and/or dislike doing the most and become expert at it. My client hasn't made partner yet, but he's well on his way.

A Niche That Goes with You

One of the most important reasons for creating a niche you own—one transcending any organization—is that organizations disappear. In the last decade law firms have provided us with one of the most frequent examples of this phenomenon. Instead of creating a niche that worked, many smaller law firms of the 1980s sought refuge in the bigger-is-better Sears mentality. Merging and merging with firms they shared no

interest (or niche) with other than more money, many formerly closely knit small firms found themselves with lots of
expensive real estate and hallways filled with cubbyholes where
no one knew anyone else, nor did they want to!

For a host of reasons, including the emergence of warring
internal factions, their bigness being perceived by clients as
impersonal and inaccessible, firm lawyers wanting more entrepreneurial opportunities, and blatant nichelessness, big firm
after big firm has dissolved, often leaving their former partners
facing the same frustration and fear experienced by others
whose jobs left while they were still there! But as always,
exceptions to the rule exist, and in this case the winners are
very clear. D.S. is an example of such a winner.

THE D.S. STORY

I met D.S. when I was franchising my own business. Although
he was referred to me through a mutual associate, I was finally
persuaded to see him after reading a book he had co-authored
on franchising. On my initial visit to D.S. I found my way to
one of the biggest law firms in this area. His corner office
looked over the city, and for all apparent purposes D.S. had a
pretty sweet deal. During one of our conversations about my
niche, D.S. described how he had decided years ago to focus
exclusively on franchise law because he saw that field holding
massive growth possibility. Since his entry into the field, D.S.
had systematically written articles, prepared his own book, and
above all never wavered from his focus.

The real test of his niche came not long after I met him. The
papers broke the news this way: "X Law Firm Collapses."
When he called me the day before the information appeared in
the press, D.S. sounded more confident than ever. "You know,"
he said. "I'm almost glad it happened this way. I would never
have made the move to be on my own if I'd not been nudged.
But I realize I don't need the big firm. In fact, it needed me."

D.S. couldn't have been more right. Just a month later the
same paper showed him standing on his deck overlooking a
beautiful meadow and reported his success in taking his niche

to his home office. D.S. had created a niche he could take any-place—home office, traditional office environment, wherever! He had established himself as someone to be reckoned with on his own terms, allowing him to be successful wherever he lived!

PS: When I last talked with D.S. he had just completed a new addition to his home because his business had grown so much and the rest of the family wanted to reclaim the family room. Another testimony to the value of a niche that can live anyplace.

It's all in a niche!

Summary

This chapter has described myriad ways to create the niche that works for your business in any economy. We learned that some of the best niches are right under our noses ready for exploitation. Furthermore, we have been reminded that some of the most important features of good niching are purposeful-ness in directing its course, being willing to shelve old ways of looking at the world, and most importantly, being ahead of the curve. One of the most significant strategies you were intro-duced to was trending and rationally anticipating where your business is headed. You learned to think about niche opportu-nities in time to make them happen. And finally, you were reminded that a niche that thrives in changing times is a proactive animal, never taking its success or future for granted.

4

MOVING IN WITH YOUR CUSTOMER

Anything that won't sell, I don't want to invent.

—Thomas A. Edison

Thomas Edison is probably best remembered as a genius inventor. But he was much more. As his statement above suggests, he was also a genius at nichemaking. Indeed, Edison's pragmatic approach to the creative process (which to some might be considered a contradiction in terms) may well account for the overwhelming success of his dozens of inventions, which collectively revolutionized society. He knew, apparently instinctively, that a niche is useful only if it has a receptive audience. As a business owner you know all too well that the life blood of any healthy business is the *right* customer base. You want an eager audience—and a good-sized one. The question, of course, is how to get it. How to ensure that you haven't invented a monster—something you *love* but that has no commercial value. What we know for sure is, *you aren't interested in becoming another statistic.*

A Niche with No Place to Go

The pervasiveness of niches and potential niches with no place to go is brought home to me almost daily as I listen to clients diligently trying to be successful in their organizations and businesses. Just a few examples will make the point.

Janet owns a small computer training company, which she opened two years ago. The firm's offices are in the back room of a computer retailer located in suburban Portland, Oregon. She came in to see if I could advise her how to better develop her business, which by any stretch of the imagination was mediocre at best. After an initial series of questions about her background, I asked, "And what seems to be the problem, Janet?"

"Well, I sell training in computer software X and Advanced XX. My target audience is the small-business owner—you know, the ones who don't have a lot of money to spend on expensive classes."

She went on, "Here's the problem. After I went and bought all the software—and you know, it's very expensive—I found out that a lot of these people use cheaper programs than I have in my training. The programs are simpler and not as good overall, but that's what they are buying."

To make sure I understood what she was saying, I summarized: "So you have invested in something and found out customers don't want it—they want something else?"

Her head nodded yes.

"Seems simple to me," I went on. "You have some clear choices. Either change your target audience, buy new software, or find a better way to get to the audience you're after."

"But I can't get rid of this software. It's so expensive. I have to have a set for each computer station. Don't you understand how much that will cost me? And I don't want to work with anyone else! I like the small-business owner." Janet continued outlining all the reasons why the product she had already bought—customer unseen and virtually unknown—was the product she was going to stick with. She hadn't learned yet how much it would cost her to hang on to something that no one wanted.

It turns out Janet went out of business not too long ago. I heard she is planning to open a restaurant of some kind.

Can't help wondering how she's going to select her menu offerings.

In one form or another I hear Janet's story time and again.

Officials from a large federal agency came to my office not long ago to talk about ways of getting more people to participate in the services the agency offers.

"Our client base is declining all the time," the agency representative told me, "yet we know the need is still out there. We just can't figure out how to get those people in to see us. How can we persuade them they need us?"

The agency's problem was starting from a faulty set of assumptions altogether: you don't persuade someone of their need.

And then there are people like Sandra who arrived in my office a while ago, carrying two huge boxes.

"Looks like you could use a little push cart?" I smiled. "That's a good idea. I've been thinking about it and I think I'll do it now that I've placed my big order for products," she said. "I'm going to be *very* busy," she exclaimed with excitement in her voice and eyes. And thus began the saga of Sandra's jewelry business. It was a short saga.

"I make jewelry from all these different junk pieces you see here," she said. As she spoke, Sandra hauled out dozens of funky-looking bracelets, necklaces, and earrings. I guessed that she was planning to sell her wares to teenage girls—probably through Saturday-flea-market–type vehicles. Then she said, "And I'm going to sell these to other women about my age."

"And where do you plan to do that?" I asked.

"All over," she said, "but mainly through retail stores."

"Have you checked how those stores feel about your products?"

"Not really," she answered. "But I know they'll want the pieces. They're really popular where I live."

"OK," I said quietly, trying not to let my eyebrow rise too much as I questioned how an urban market would respond to her concept.

At my suggestion, Sandra took her wares around to some retail stores similar to those in which she wanted to sell her products. She not only asked the managers and buyers about their level of interest in her products, but she asked for feedback from distributors as well. After all this homework, Sandra found out that few were interested in her products as they were put together, but they did express interest in a modified version. This was great! Unfortunately, Sandra was about to receive a huge shipment of materials to create more of exactly the same items. She had ordered the nonreturnable items before checking out who, if anyone, wanted to buy her new widgets!

The ultimate tip-off to me of a niche headed no place, however, comes packaged in the following statement from otherwise bright, hardworking, excellent people: "My clients don't know what their problems are!"

Examples exist everywhere of individuals and organizations promoting products and services without considering the ultimate consumer: "I love what I do, therefore others will too." If that alone is the criterion for taking a product of any kind to market, disaster looms on the horizon. For as all successful business owners know, that philosophy fails to take into account the customer. The rest of this chapter addresses that issue: how you can make the vital fit—take something to market that you do enjoy and that is consistent with your business or professional goals but ensure that it is ultimately accepted by a strong customer base. The concept applies to virtually every kind of business. More than any other subject in this book, this issue can determine your success or failure in your new business.

Remember, characteristics of a good niche include the following:

1. It is always intentional.
2. It helps us achieve our goals.
3. It is wanted by someone else.
4. It has the capacity to evolve and grow.

By coming back to these four criteria you avoid the likelihood of creating niches destined to exist in a vacuum, encouraging your frustration and disappointment. "OK," you say.
"I'm being intentional about this process. I have a tentative
niche, which I think will achieve my goals. But this idea of
being wanted by someone else? This sounds tricky. Where do I
start?"

The answer is, "We will start right here by undoing the
Golden Rule!"

A niche by itself is not enough.

Applying the Platinum Rule*

"Undo the Golden Rule? That's crazy!" Before tossing the idea,
consider that I am not urging you to dismiss the spirit of the
Golden Rule. Instead I want you to look at the exact language
and the assumptions the language carries. Then you will better
understand why I suggest that successful nichemaking is best
served by applying what I have heard described as the Platinum
Rule.

Think for a moment about the Golden Rule: Do unto others
as you would have others do unto you. Consider the assumptions implicit in the statement. You're right, of course, if you're
saying that the major assumption is one of similarity. Taken literally, the statement presumes that everyone has the same
starting place; what pleases you, pleases others, or at least
should. If you invite friends for dinner, please them by serving
your favorite foods regardless of how divergent they might be
from your friends' tastes. Examples of far greater consequence
abound, but the issue remains the same. By itself the Golden
Rule assumes we all think and feel alike. Of course, nothing
could be further from the truth.

Let's see what happens, however, when the Golden Rule is

---

*Bennett, Milton. "Overcoming the Golden Rule: Sympathy and Empathy,"
Communication Yearbook, 1979.

replaced by our Platinum Rule, which in essence says: Do unto others as they would do unto themselves. Now this may sound very simple, but its meaning is truly profound for anyone seriously concerned about creating a successful business, which of course requires just the right niche. What it means is this: Instead of looking at the world exclusively from our own point of view—from the point of view of what we want to sell—we are going to get outside our shoes and look at the world from our customer's frame of reference. The issue is not whether you wind up agreeing with or even liking your customer's views, values, and ideas. It is not a contest of whose point of view is right or wrong. The issue is simply accepting that diversity as reality and addressing it effectively.

You know full well that you and someone else can be listening to the same music and hear something different. You and a friend scrutinize a painting; you each see things a little differently. Certain images stand out more to you than to your friend. Your mood is affected one way by the painting; your friend responds with other feelings. You go to a speech attended by a thousand other people. You listen to the same words as everyone else, but the nuances are different for each of you; the way you interpret it—apply the meaning to your own life—is uniquely yours. Again, we are reminded that the issue is not to quibble about whose reality is the accurate one; rather it is to acknowledge that our *perceptions* of reality vary, and if you are to be successful in *good* nichemaking you must understand, accept, and address your customer's perceptions.

YOUR NICHE ACHIEVES YOUR CUSTOMER'S GOALS

Understanding your customer's perceptions of the world is an absolute must for one major reason; that is, no one buys something just because you want to sell it. That "it" must help your customers achieve their goals. It must put them in a better place than they were before, or at least they must perceive that it can help them or fulfill some perceived need. It is rarely the widget, per se, that is significant. It is *what your customer perceives the widget or service will do for them.* A fine point, perhaps, but absolutely *critical.* Too many people put the widgets first when they should be understanding their customers' goals. Your widget is the vehicle for achieving those goals. If you don't know what those goals are, you can't sell to them. And you may have found out already that it's hard to even give a product away if a customer doesn't see a need for it in his or her life.

Blatant examples abound of hardworking people virtually undoing themselves by refusing to understand that their widget is the solution to a problem or a means to an end. It is not the end in itself. For example, in commercial real estate, too often I see brokers trying to sell or lease properties as if they were the client's ultimate goal. The actual goal, of course, is what the properties will achieve for the client. And not all properties will achieve the same thing. In a sense this approach requires that you reposition your thinking from selling a particular product or service to problem-solving for your client.

Although I have singled out real estate, be assured that the Platinum Rule applies to anyone and everyone serious about creating a niche that eliminates the competition and guarantees success in any economy.

It's time now to stop talking about the Platinum Rule and actually see what it can do for your business. The following exercise will get you started thinking from your potential niche consumer's perspective.

EXERCISE 4.1

YOUR WISH LIST'S WORLDVIEW

Complete the following:

1. Your niche focus (e.g., international trade: Mexican-American, disability and compliance consulting)

YOUR WISH LIST

Identify your wish list of clients or niche audience. If you're targeting a specific person or group, that's OK (e.g., large corporate clients, developers, nonprofit organizations).

_____

_____

_____

_____

YOUR WISH LIST'S PRIORITIES/CONCERNS

Use terms/phrases that your clients would use to describe their priorities (e.g., increase profits, avoid lawsuits, stay tax-exempt).

_____

_____

_____

_____

2. Describe ways your widget can help improve your niche consumer's world. Remember, you are thinking about their worldview—not yours. Ask yourself what your prospective customers' goals are. Sometimes those goals are not formally stated. Sometimes they are related to their own audience's goals.

_____

_____

3. Your niche/wish-list match. Now that you have objectively identified your potential clients' views of the world, evaluate how closely your niche will be perceived by them as addressing their needs.

1   2   3   4   5   6   7   8   9   10
Not strong at all   Iffy   A connection
                                               will be made

BECOMING AN AUTHORITY ON YOUR CUSTOMER'S BUSINESS

You've probably already figured out that getting inside your customer's shoes is just the beginning. You're actually on your way to becoming an authority on your client's business. If you are going to help your clients achieve their goals, you have no choice but to understand what is going on in their industry, including the pressures, trends, and other factors influencing their potential success or failure. And now it becomes even more clear why you must focus, focus, focus. You simply cannot be an authority on a broad range of industries. It's a contradiction in terms. There is not enough of you to go around. Your clients' worlds are becoming increasingly complex. Knowing what it takes to make those worlds succeed is a job in itself. It's your job.

Become an indispensable part of your client's world.

If your score on the exercise above was less exciting than you'd hoped, it's clear you've got to do a better job of looking at the world from your client's point of view. Following are two very simple exercises that will help you do just that.

EXERCISE 4.2

BASIC NICHE INTERVIEW

You have doubtless done many versions of the following exercise in the past. This time, however, you are going to concentrate exclusively on its implications for clarifying your niche direction. Do the following:

1. Identify several wish-list clients or key people associated with this list. You are looking for people bearing a strong resemblance to your potential niche recipients.
2. Call them up and request a short amount of time on the telephone or a personal interview. Be very straightforward about your purpose in calling. Tell them you are seeking to understand their industry better and they have insights you believe may be helpful. Additionally, you'd like their opinion about your potential niche. *Don't* ask for advice, since people customarily pay for

that commodity. What may seem like a small semantic difference between the words: *opinion* will get you an interview; *advice* will get you a bill.

3. Ask questions such as the following: What are their priority concerns? What kinds of behaviors/widgets would help resolve those concerns?

4. How do they respond to the concept you propose or are proposing?

5. To what extent will your widget address their concerns? Are you describing what you are up to in terms that make sense to your potential audience? In terms that will be heard appreciatively from their point of view?

6. Do they know anyone else selling a widget such as yours? If so, what does it look like? Who is getting it? Etc.

7. Listen carefully to the language used and concerns expressed by your interviewee.

At the conclusion of this interview you may decide that in fact you are right on track; your developing niche is going to be received with open arms! On the other hand, you may find you are trying to sell something no one wants. Janet's software, if you will. If you listen hard enough, though, you should be able to hear what kind of software is wanted. Instead of saying, "My clients don't know what their problems are," you will realize that their perception of the issue is your starting point for a relationship with them.

You must know where your clients "live."

EXERCISE 4.3

THE FELT-TIP PEN

A simple felt-tip pen can help you identify how closely on target your niche is with your audience's perception of reality and need. Do the following:

1. Get yourself a big red felt-tip pen.
2. Locate copies of various trade and professional publications that your wish-list clients read regularly.
3. Go through the various articles, circling issues and problems that surface over and over again.
4. Once you have completed Steps 1–3, again evaluate your tentative niche in relation to its effectiveness for addressing the perceived issues you just identified.

1	2	3	4	5	6	7	8	9	10

Zero relationship   A connection   Wish list will
                                             clamor for my niche

If you find that your niche and your client's perception of need still appear divergent, think how what you are selling can be "massaged" or restated to reflect the consumer's point of view.

Although there are infinite examples demonstrating the importance of understanding and niching to your consumer's worldview, few are as powerful as those we see in the retailing world—especially the world of fashion buyers. Think for a moment about the most successful apparel stores you know. Then ask what criteria the buyers use in making their merchandise selections. If the store is successful, you can be sure they are buying according to one criterion—what their customers' tastes are, not their own. In fact, the kiss of death for any retailer is buying according to the manager's or owner's personal tastes. Though this example is a simple one, it requires commitment to accepting the client's worldview as the critical starting point of any niche transaction.

But what happens if after you give all possible consideration to your customer's perception of reality, you determine that the niche you are growing is not viable—that it cannot possibly meet the goals you have set out to achieve? If, after all the exercises and evaluations you complete, this is your decision, you will

want to carefully, deliberately, and swiftly cut this niche's cord. Depending on exactly what the widget is, you may not want to discard it altogether; you may save it for a hobby or recreation or keep it in mind for sometime in the future. Remember, if it doesn't meet *all* our criteria of a *good* niche, it goes!

Deep-six it!

Your Clients' Hot Buttons

Now that you have methodically considered your niche-consumer's worldview, you are ready to take the next step, of teasing up the "hot buttons" that will be the focus of your later marketing effort. For now, though, we will simply pinpoint those buttons.

"Stop!" you once again are saying. "Define your terms. What is a *hot button*?"

A hot button is a pressure point belonging to your niche consumer. It elicits a visceral response. It is their "pain." The thing they want fixed or goal they want to achieve. Everyone has pressure points. Hot buttons typically produce emotional instead of strictly intellectual responses. Strong niches connect with the consumer's hot buttons. In other words, your niche will help your client or employer achieve that person or organization's existing goals. A good starting place for thinking about hot buttons is with yourself and your own pressure points.

EXERCISE 4.4

YOUR PERSONAL HOT BUTTON LIST

In the space below, make a list of the things or people causing you to feel before you think—that create an emo-

tional response well before your intellect intervenes (e.g.,
your child or loved one; the IRS).

_____

_____

_____

_____

   Now that you have had some practice thinking about hot buttons, it's time to consider those owned by your potential niche
customer. Remember, as you make your list, think about your
customer's perception of the problem—*not the solution*, which is
most likely your niche. Two examples from my own experience
working with clients may help clarify this important distinction.
   Several years ago I worked with a client who, at the time she
came in, was offering a virtual grab bag of staff training programs to business and industry. One of her favorites dealt with
customer relations. She wanted to introduce that training program to hospitals and the healthcare industry. After previewing
her entire program, I concluded it was one of the best I'd seen
and from a substantive standpoint should succeed in a heartbeat. Unfortunately, she wasn't getting in the door of any of
her prospective clients. Together we realized her training program would never see the light of any healthcare center's
training room if it didn't connect to her consumer's worldview.
   All it took was a simple change of title and the doors opened
wide. The program title went from "Improved Customer
Relations" to "Reducing the Incidence of Medical Malpractice
Suits through Improved Customer Relations." Instead of selling
her solution, my client connected to her client's own sense of
the problem. We had isolated a hot button that caused the
right clients to call her up and move her business from sluggish
at best to the fast and profitable lane.
   Another of my favorite examples comes from Helen, a CPA
client of mine who had spent much of her life moving from
one place to another as her husband was transferred while he

moved up the corporate ladder. Now it was her turn to build a serious practice. But once again she was in a new city where she knew virtually no one. When we met, dilemma was written all over her face. How could she quickly build a practice in a city where she had no network, much less a referral base? Why would anyone want to come to her when they could work with people who'd lived in this area for a long time? Not long into our conversation, however, I knew she was only a hot button away from success.

It seems our CPA had spent much of her volunteer time doing work for nonprofit organizations. In the process of giving something important to them, she also came to understand many of the increasingly complex issues nonprofits come up against on a regular basis. Issues which, if not confronted effectively, can result in the same death knell as for their counterpart organizations in the for-profit sector. In one of our early sessions I asked her to think about the biggest issue she thought nonprofits face today. What if any issue keeps their leaders awake at night worrying? Without a second passing, she looked at me and said, "Probably it's just staying tax-exempt." And there it was, a hot button that provided instant and intentional focus. It has also provided her with an enormously successful practice working with nonprofits from all over the country that have a concern about maintaining their treasured, though vulnerable, nonprofit status. Whoever said the market for CPAs is saturated hasn't met Helen. And I guarantee you, they haven't figured out their own clients' hot buttons!

You need to understand the world from your customer's viewpoint. The following exercise will help you get even more inside their shoes.

EXERCISE 4.5

GETTING CLOSER TO YOUR CUSTOMER'S WORLD

Look over the list below. Are your wish list clients linked by any of the following variables or categories? If so, write the commonality next to each category.

Age _____

Economics _____

Industry _____

Goals/Accomplishments _____

Attitude/Outlook _____

Frustrations/Concerns/Pains _____

Condition/Needs _____

Beliefs/Shared Cause _____

Dreams _____

Other _____

One of the most efficient ways of pinpointing a viable niche is figuring out very specifically how what you want to offer can help your prospective customer or client. The following exercise will help you do just that!

EXERCISE 4.6

ADDRESSING MY CLIENT'S HOT BUTTONS

CLIENT CONCERNS/PRIORITIES   WAYS MY BUSINESS COULD
                                     ADDRESS OR SOLVE THEM

_____   _____

_____   _____

_____   _____

HOW DO I FIND OUT WHAT THESE HOT BUTTONS ARE?

If you're like many people, you are saying "Hey this is a great idea, but I don't know my wish list clients personally. How do I find out what they're really thinking about?" Exercises 4.2 and

4.3 introduced some of these techniques. Following are things you can do very quickly that will shed important light on what's going on in the heads of your best prospects:

1. Read what they read. Get copies of the trade and professional publications your clients use. Go through and circle the issues that come up over and over again.
2. Call up key people in your industry or general field. Ask them what they perceive the major issues to be. What trends do they foresee? What problems will emerge as a result of these trends? Who's currently addressing these issues? In what manner? (Sometimes people are embarrassed to make calls like this. If you are among that group, relax. Almost everyone is flattered if you ask for their *opinion*. Don't ask for advice, since that suggests payment for services.)
3. Conduct a survey. Again, identify key people in your prospective industry. Call or write to them, inviting their participation in your study. Indicate that the study will be published in a forthcoming newsletter. Their names will be confidential unless they give permission to share their identity. You will send them the results of the study for their own company's use at no charge.

A CASE STUDY OF SUCCESS

Architectural Banners That Weren't for Architects

The story of how the Platinum Rule turned one business around in a hurry will give you a hint of how helpful it can be in the start-up and growth of your own enterprise.

Sheryl and Keith had been in business for nearly five years. Former school teachers, the couple had left education to pursue their real love, the design and manufacture of beautiful banners for use in commercial and business environments. Both Sheryl and Keith had strong artistic backgrounds and for years had longed to use that background in a serious business endeavor. So it was not surprising that when they set up their business, their niche, as they perceived it, was architectural banners. Their products were truly beautiful, eliciting compliments from almost everyone who saw them. The only problem was that no one was buying them. Sheryl and Keith accumulated an inventory of banners they loved. But they were in business to make money, not just love what they were doing! When they came to see me, I asked why they called their products "architectural banners"?

"Because these are the people we want to sell the banners to," they said.

"Why do you think these people want your banners?" I asked.

"Because they will make the buildings and offices these people design more attractive to others," I was told.

"Let me ask another way," I said. "Why should these people pay you for the banners? What's in it for them?"

"Hmmmm . . . well . . . hmmm. . . ." Both heads shook from side to side as their owners searched for a satisfactory reply. But there was none. The reason? Because there was *nothing* in it for their prospective architect clients. There was no "win" reason for architects to invest in my clients' banners. It was clear Keith and Sheryl weren't interested in changing their product. What, though, about selling it to another audience? What audience would have a vested interest in their product? It didn't take long before our rapidly brain-stormed list produced just the right audience and we all knew it! Instead of architects, the logical buyers were building managers, shopping center managers, and marketing directors. For these people the banners would perform a distinct function by being attractive to potential customers.

This simple exercise of asking who would win from having my clients' products around produced another win. Sheryl and Keith now knew who their *real* clients were and from that point on directed their marketing efforts to those people. A quick, low-cost solution to what could have been a very expensive problem. The Platinum Rule provided the answer. Manipulating Steps 1 and 3 ensured their business a prosperous future.

DREAMS AND AMBITIONS—NOT JUST PROBLEMS!

Listening to your potential customers' perceived problems is certainly important. Equally important, however, is identifying what their most important dreams and ambitions are. These may be dreams and ambitions for themselves, personally. They may be dreams for their company. Remember, whatever you're selling, ultimately you are selling to another human being. It must help that person achieve his/her goals. Most importantly, you achieve your own goals by helping others achieve theirs.

Listening to Your Customers' Wants

As you are niche-customer matching, it is important to begin distinguishing between what people say they need and what you hear or see that they want. The difference can be huge. It can also mean the difference between a successful niche and one falling flat on its proverbial face.

Coca-Cola's marketing fiasco of the mid-1980s demonstrates this point. Thinking it time to bring out a new product, Coca-Cola mobilized its massive forces for worldwide market research. At thousands of sites people were asked if they liked the new soft drink. When a sufficient number answered yes, company executives concluded that a winner was ready to enter the market. Unfortunately, those same company executives soon found out that researchers had omitted one critical question from their market study. They never asked, "Would you buy this Coke instead of our classic or traditional cola?"

If they had asked this question, it's likely they would have heard what they were soon to learn, that liking the new product was not enough to make customers change habits. The researchers' fatal error was in conducting a study focusing on their own point of view— not the potential consumer's.

How does your niche sound?

Hit 'Em Where They Ain't!

In an interview with the press, one of baseball's earliest Hall of Fame members, Wee Willie Keeler, described his strategy for success. He said simply: *"You just hit 'em where they ain't!"*

And that short one-liner offers one of the most powerful strategies for our own niche success; that is, figuring out who doesn't yet have our widget. It's the case of the unserved or underserved audience.

Remember, we said *Specialness is in the eye of the receiver.* As you are finding out, there are many ways to achieve that perspective. It may be you don't have to invent a new widget à la Edison. Assess where your potential niche is right now.

EXERCISE 4.7

WHO DOESN'T HAVE YOUR WIDGET YET?

Who already has your widget?

_____

_____

_____

What groups don't have access to the kind of product or service you may offer?

_____

_____

_____

You've identified some groups that don't have your potential niche available to them at the moment. But you are not done! Remember, you need to check their reality to better assess whether your product is even perceived as a want—not a need from your vantage point.

Reaching unserved or underserved markets has been the basis for huge success stories within business and industry. The copy machine story is one of the best illustrations of this point. If you are over 40 you doubtless remember that early copy machines were large in scale and equally large in price. (If you're under 40, file this story under history!) And virtually all of them had the same name: Xerox.

Though Xerox didn't invent the photocopy process, the company was the first to market the product in a serious way to the large corporations and big organizations that could afford the equipment. Tactically, Xerox officials made a decision early on that their machine would be marketed almost exclusively to high-end customers. The machine would not be available to everyone. Even companies with a Xerox machine on the premises did not have it all. For many years consumers could rent only Xerox machines. And of course regular paper would never do. Xerox's "special" paper had to be used.

Xerox's tightly controlled marketing strategy limited the number of people with access to this product. The product was so tightly controlled that the company's name became synonymous with copy machines, regardless of brand! The niche was narrow, but it was rich and deep.

Of course, all that changed. You are doubtless ahead of me, thinking about the Japanese entry into the personal copy machine market. In almost one fell swoop, personal copiers became available to small and mid-size businesspeople, just as personal computers have become a way of life for increasing numbers of them today.

The point of all this is that by identifying who doesn't have your widget—the unserved or underserved audience approach—you may find the single feature needed to transform something ordinary into a special entity. Hence, the real niche product in the copy machine story was not the technology but in fact who had access to it. Of course, if you decide to take this direction, you will want also to put a game plan in place to penetrate your market—regardless what it is—very rapidly. The knockoff artists will never be far behind. (Knockoff artistry is a niche in itself, these days. Ask Gucci or Louis Vuitton if you don't believe me!)

JIM'S CHERRIES: AN UNSERVED AUDIENCE GOLD MINE

Simply manipulating the audience variable can produce such powerful results, the strategy is well worth your consideration. Jim's story illustrates how simply changing audiences can make the difference between marginal survival and tremendous success.

Jim is one of the largest, most respected, and well-established fruit growers in the Pacific Northwest. Having grown up in the fruit business, he was a natural in developing his family's business, taking it from a modestly profitable operation to a virtual empire, which included fruit products of all kinds. And especially cherries. Cherries and more cherries of every conceivable variety. For several years the cherries produced the highest profit margins of all the company's fruit.

But all of a sudden, cherries seemed to be glutting the market, year after year after year. The glut wasn't just in the Pacific Northwest. The entire country seemed overflowing with cherries. Of course, that sent prices through the floor to the dismay of orchard farmers. If something didn't happen soon, growers would have to sell off property just to sustain themselves.

Jim didn't plan to be among those converting beautiful orchards to housing developments. His answer? Let's see, who doesn't have our cherries? The answer? The Japanese.

So it was that Jim began exporting to Japan the same cherries whose prices had plummeted in the United States. Of course the prices there would have to be higher. And they were. But not just a little. Starting at $6 per pound, Jim's cherries became high-end delicacies, sought out by the well-to-do Japanese consumer. By simply looking for an audience that didn't have his cherries, Jim turned a liability into an asset. What could have been the end of a business turned out to be a tremendously valuable re-niche. This also underscores a point made earlier. That is, when you're well niched, price isn't the issue. People are interested in your product first and foremost.

Once again we see the power of methodically shifting our audience variable. This approach is particularly important in today's world of emerging global markets. Too many people get stuck thinking too small. Thinking the only audience for their product is the one that has been getting it for years. If this is you, get out of the box. The issue is no longer the widget itself, but who has access to it.

Just Say No! (Again)

Our discussion of targeting a specific audience is closely related to one of the major themes of this book. It is also one of the keys to the success of your new business. That key is knowing who your audience is *and who it isn't*. It's being willing to turn away business if it's not the *right* business. It's not trying to be all things to all people. *You can't do it.* Not if you want to win, that is.

Same Widget + Different Use = New Niche!

If you've shifted your audience variable around and still aren't satisfied your widget has a future as a good niche, it may be time to give fresh thought to what it's being used for. Or perhaps it's more accurate to ask, "What *could it be* used for?"

One of the best examples of a widget with two completely different lives arrived in my office not long ago. Reviewing his business background and all the I-should-have-could-have-but-didn'ts, a client pulled out a small rectangular box. My first thought was that it contained a pen. And I wasn't far off. Actually, it was a laser pointer. The kind seminar presenters use to highlight key points during their programs. Its virtues were so self-evident, I personally wanted to place an immediate order. But my client didn't bring it in to sell. And he was less interested in what its original use was than in what he had just found it being sold for.

"I knew it a few years ago when I first saw this thing," he announced.

"You knew what?" I asked.

"The first time I saw this I said it would make a great cat toy. It drives cats crazy. It's better than catnip." As he talked, he flashed the laser light on the wall, making the little red dot dance and jump.

He went on with a note of chagrin in his voice, saying, "And wouldn't you know where I found this thing? At one of the big pet store chains! They were blowing out of there."

I smiled, once again realizing that many good, profitable niches are staring us in the face. Already invented, already tested, all ready to go. Many times you don't have to start from square one. If your own widget seems to have run its course, ask yourself what other uses it may have. It's entirely possible it may have a whole new life ahead. And you may have created a new and profitable niche for yourself.

The Juggling Act

By now, you've figured out that the process of making good niches involves keeping many things in mind at the same time. Keeping an eye on your end goals, tending to a focused but evolving and dynamic niche, and always thinking about the ultimate receiver of your product are but a few of the mental gymnastics each of us has to perform to ensure a niche that is worth anything. The following Nichecraft Matrix will be helpful as a "watchdog" for you—a reference check on your niche. Take a few moments now to do your own nichecraft checkup.

Important! Set a date now to redo your Nichecraft Matrix.

EXERCISE 4.8

YOUR NICHECRAFT MATRIX

1. Study the following matrix. Consider the points you can get in each category.

2. Place a number from 1 to 10 to 20 as specified in each category in the matrix boxes. Assume 20 or 10 is very high and 1 is very low.

Check one:
This niche is ____ personal ____ business ____ organization ____ career ____ other.

Possible Points	Categories						
	Niche	Field	Products	Target Audience	Focus	Hot Buttons	What You Stand For
Clear 10 pts							
Consistent 10 pts							
Intentional 10 pts							
Client-Centered 20 pts							
Achieve Short-Term Goals 10 pts							
Achieve Long-Term Goals 10 pts							

How to Score: Count up to 490 possible points.
    490–475 = Excellent
    474–450 = Above average
    449–400 = Average
    400–350 = Tricky but survivable
Less than 350 = Trouble ahead, close to being ordinary

Making the Big Fit: Shifting the Variables Around

By this point you've also learned that niches can be a function of many things, *least of all* magic. The kind of Specialness central to any niche can be achieved by manipulating one or a constellation of variables. We have already considered several of those variables. Now it's time to look at them in relation to your own developing niche and determine what aspect of the product is Special by itself or what variable needs to be manipulated to achieve that critical feature.

EXERCISE 4.9

MANIPULATING VARIABLES

Using the tests of Specialness, mark yes or no in each of the blanks to the left below, indicating what variable(s) contribute to the singularity you are seeking. In the column to the right, describe the variable in concrete terms (e.g., target audience = high-end retired/retiring executives).

Your niche _____

VARIABLES		SPECIFY
_____	Target audience	_____
_____	Your style	_____
_____	Your widget	_____
_____	Cost	_____
_____	Location	_____
_____	Marketing strategy	_____
_____	Your service	_____
_____	Theme	_____

_____ Your personality _____

_____ Type of advertising _____

_____ Use or function _____

_____ Other _____

As you continue to think about ways to create the kind of Specialness that will set your business apart from all the others out there, allowing the *right* people to find you, think about your preliminary focus and your clients' needs. Play with the following formula, applying it directly to your own business situation:

Your Preliminary Focus **+** Your Audience's Perceived Needs
= Your Niche

Ask yourself: Is the sum of my focus and client need Special in itself? If not, add a twist to it from the list of variables, or sources of Specialness.

Earlier you assessed how closely your product was meeting the perceived needs of a target audience. Once again, grade yourself on this important question. This time take into consideration any variables you may have recently adjusted to make the ultimate fit between your niche and its consumer even better.

EXERCISE 4.10

MEETING YOUR AUDIENCE'S NEEDS

Give yourself a grade:

1   2   3   4   5   6   7   8   9   10
I'm still way off   Getting there   The niche has a home!

Checking in with Your Goals

Earlier you identified some long-term goals as well as some things you were willing to give up to achieve them. It is important from time to time to go back to those goals and reconfirm that the niche you are creating for your business will actually achieve what you want. Ultimately niches serve to achieve those goals and nothing else. Since it is likely the niche you are making looks different than it did when you started out with the process, you should scrutinize it carefully, ensuring that your goals and niche are on parallel courses. Inadvertently some people wind up creating niches taking them someplace they had no interest in going. You know, the bus that goes to Denver when you really wanted to go to San Francisco. Don't ever forget, you are the driver of this process; it is up to you to always keep your eye on the road ahead. Most of all, you drive the niche, not the other way around.

The Case of Multiple Niching

"Can I have more than one niche?" The question is a logical one, which I am asked regularly by people in all walks of life and in all types of businesses. They know that good nichemaking depends upon clear focus—upon an audience being able to see your product or service in a crowd and connect immediately. It is reasonable they should worry that more than one niche can cause confusion. It most likely will. Here are the rules.

It *is* possible that more than one niche product may serve your goals. A good niche allows you to develop multiple profit centers—revenue sources growing out of the basic niche but each reflecting the common niche thread. It is critical, however, that each niche audience understands what you offer. Alan, our all-over-the-mapper, sent out so many divergent signals to his various audiences, it would be impossible for any one of them to really see him as Special. Except, maybe, as an all-over-the-mapper.

Entrepreneurs typically have multiple ventures. An entrepreneur's niche might be just that—a particular approach to undertaking business enterprises. Each of those ventures may represent a niche-market activity, but the entrepreneur's overall niche may be that person's style or business system.

Most of all, your audiences must always know what you stand for. Remember, *a niche is only as good as your client's perception of it*.

If you get the right people confused about what you are up to, it won't matter how wonderful you are or how great your service is; those potential buyers will go elsewhere for the service.

And finally, it is important to remember there is only so much of you to go around! What I mean is this: You have a limited amount of time in the day to accomplish things, and your mind can hold only so much information before it will go into overload. If you take on too much, you run the risk of diluting not only your image but your energies as well. In either case, you are encouraging failure instead of success.

A Kind of Negotiation

One of my favorite ways of looking at good niching is as a kind of negotiation, or as Roger Fisher, founder of the Harvard Negotiation Project, has described it, the process of "getting to yes."* He reminds us that the key to successful negotiation is knowing what is most important to the other party. What in fact they will go to the wall for. Once you truly understand that point and have appropriate information, you are in position to create win-win situations. Thus, if you want to get your niche to yes (aka get clients or get a job) you must know what your audience really wants. Once you've done that you can create your own win-win situation. The kind that only a fool will turn down; and you aren't interested in working with or being around a fool, anyway!

---

*Fisher, Roger, and William Ury. *Getting to Yes*. New York: Penguin Books, 1991.

Summary

"Moving in with Your Customer" is more than this chapter's title. It is one of the critical themes of this book and one of the central factors influencing your success or failure in today's business world. This section has offered a range of ways to make that move—to live where your customers are. Once you master these strategies, you will be able to flexibly and quickly adjust your niche to your customer's needs. Most of all, you will ensure you have customers, and plenty of them!

5

MARKETING STRATEGIES THAT INCREASE PROFITS

All the work you've put in up until now—all the thought and decisions about what kinds of niches will work best for your business—what kinds will make your effort the most prosperous and successful possible—all that will be of no use without effectively getting the word out to the *right* people. Remember, one of the key distinctions drawn in this book between ordinary niches and those that work is that *good* niches are wanted by someone. The *right* someones! We agreed much earlier that you are not going to try to do business with everyone who walks in the door. In fact, you may wind up turning some business away because it is the *wrong* business. Thus, the *right* people have to know you exist. Call it by any name you want, the issue we are talking about here is marketing. The kind of marketing that takes your niche to the *right* customers/clients and gets them clamoring for it!

Becoming a Household Word

Interestingly, depending upon the strategies you select to get the word out about your widget, your marketing efforts can themselves be your ultimate niche. Regardless of whether your

166

niche is a tangible product or professional service, the principles guiding successful niche marketing today remain the same. The rest of this chapter offers a range of strategies you can implement to ensure that your niche becomes a household word fast. As you've probably already figured out, *household word* is a major theme of this entire book, and especially of this chapter. If you are serious about success, you must literally become part of your customer's life—well before they need or want your service. No single strategy will do the job. It is naive and nearly always a waste of money to implement one strategy without a full system in place.

Perhaps the best example of money going out the door along with hopes and dreams is when people buy that wonderful ad space in their local paper or special magazine. Too often the series produces little or no immediate results. The disappointed entrepreneurs are angry at the ad salesperson, even more frustrated with the paper, and decide no one wants their widgets. What they don't realize is that one strategy is not enough. Most importantly, you need to know what you can reasonably expect from each strategy. If you are really serious, you will have a series of strategies happening simultaneously. But the really good news is that while often overlooked, the best strategies cost the least.

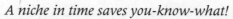

A niche in time saves you-know-what!

"Getting on with it *now*" is more than a cliché in successful business development of any kind. Once you've defined that special entity, speed is of the essence for its ultimate success. You must penetrate your intended market with the speed and accuracy of a laser. *If you don't, someone else will*. It's as simple as that. A key ingredient in effectively marketing your niche is efficiency. The strategies you select should meet that criterion at every juncture.

To be sure you are ready to move on to identifying marketing strategies, let's see how close you are to actually knowing what that business niche looks like. Test yourself by filling in the blanks that follow:

My target customers are: _____

_____

My niche is: _____

_____

You'll know you have made real niche progress when you can complete the following sentences to your satisfaction:

Here's what we do: _____

_____

And here is what's special about it: _____

_____

How is your niche so far?

Is It Marketing or Selling?

Before going any further a quick vocabulary lesson is in order. It's a lesson about two words we've heard nearly all our lives—*marketing* and *selling*. As you might have expected, the important distinctions we're going to come up with here won't be found in your local biz book or college classroom. But they may well make the difference between you or your organization having a niche that succeeds gloriously and one that fails miserably.

Over the years, as I've asked my seminar attendees to share their definitions of these two terms, two descriptions have come to be my favorites.

Throwing the Net and Catching the Fish

The first asks us to think about the difference between throwing out the net and actually catching the fish. Think about it. You don't get the fish without throwing out the net first. But you can't just throw the net anyplace. You have to think about where the fish will be at any given time. And you also have to think about how big your net holes are going to be. All this means you must be very sure you know exactly what fish you are after because if you are after herring and have a net meant for tuna, it's all over for the season!

And then there's the actual catch. The transaction between you and the consumer. The sale. A single action you hope will be repeated many times over. Obviously you don't get that single transaction without a lot of careful preparation. It's called marketing.

The Bakery or the Candy Store?

Far and away my favorite example of marketing is what I heard some time ago described as the difference between the candy store and the bakery. Think about it. You walk past a candy store. Usually there are some pretty boxes and samples in the window. If you walk inside, there will probably be some "tastes" on the glass counter. "Good," you say and perhaps buy some of the product. The concept of freebie worked. You had an experience with the product and liked it. Great. Except for one thing. A lot of people are going to have to have a lot of freebie tastes if this strategy is going to work over time.

Personally, I like the bakery metaphor. Walk within a block of your favorite bakery and fragrance wafts out to greet you— to pull you in to check out the source of that sweet smell. Your mouth is watering even before you get to the store. The power of this fragrance is so strong that the sweet-roll shop in your local mall probably paid a premium for a special fan whose primary purpose is not to keep employees cool but to push that seductive aroma throughout the mall as much as possible. Aroma that gives customers a sense of what's to come. A sense of promise. A sweet experience. Aroma out. Customers in. And no freebies involved.

The kind of marketing I encourage you to think about is *like the bakery*. Whatever your niche, you want to have a bakery kind of system working for you. A system sending the fragrance of your niche out all the time. A system designed to draw customers in rather than your having to run out after them or do giveaways forever. Most importantly, this is a system that informs people about your niche (whatever it is) so that *when they are ready,* they will know whom to call within an acceptable amount of time, which is a heartbeat or less!

Is Your Marketing for the Chickens?

Successful marketing strategies are aggressive marketing strategies. They constantly remind your audience that you are an indispensable part of their lives. Unfortunately too many people rely exclusively on the strength of their widget to promote itself. It simply won't work. The following short story makes this point all too well.

The setting is a small farm in Middle America. The family raises chickens and ducks and sells chicken eggs at market. They sell lots of chicken eggs. The young son asks his father, "Dad, I can't figure something out. We eat duck eggs and they are really good. They're bigger than chicken eggs, and it seems like the ducks lay more of them. I don't understand why other people don't eat them too. They'd like them a lot, I know. Why don't we sell duck eggs too?"

Smiling at his son, the father answered with a knowing look on his face. "Son," he said, "when the chicken lays an egg, she advertises!" So much for our duck's marketing acumen or lack thereof. The moral of this short story is pretty clear. It doesn't matter how great the product is if you don't announce it *all*

the time. While duck eggs may be bigger and better, our noisy chicken's marketing wins out.

On Selling

Contrary to popular opinion, *sell* is *not* a four-letter word. Assuming your niche has perceived value to its intended audience, *you are doing your prospective customers a favor* by calling it to their attention. If you don't sell your niche to them, they can't have it (unless they steal it). Curiously, scores of individuals and organizations alike spend huge sums of money marketing but neglect this vital step, never asking for the sale. In case your deals seem to go south just when you think they should be coming together, the following tips will help you strengthen that critical element known as "the close."

First, it's important to remember that it is up to *you* and not the customer to close the deal. After learning about the prospective client and providing all appropriate information concerning your product or services, it's up to you to ask: "Does this seem like an approach or program that would meet your needs?" or "How would you like to proceed?" or "What kind of time frame are you looking at for getting started?" or "Getting started is very simple: My retainer is X dollars. The widget requires an X-dollar deposit."

The second and extremely important thing for you to watch out for is a mistake many companies but especially young firms make all too often; that is, conveying an attitude of being too hungry—almost desperate for customers. Nothing will kill a deal faster than having a client feel you need them to get by. Think about it. If you have a big problem, you aren't likely to pick up the phone and look, much less settle, for someone you perceive as marginally successful. You want to know that whoever works with you has a track record and is likely to be around long after your issue is resolved.

What this means is that you must feel very confident about your own background and real credentials. You must convey strong belief in your own niche. If that is the case, you will demonstrate a sense of personal power and full awareness of what you stand for. You've got to be able to comfortably say, "I don't have any doubt that this is what you need" or "You called the right place" or "You're talking to the right person." Over and over again we come back to something very basic: your sense of self. And the reason is pretty simple. If you don't believe in yourself and your product, don't expect anyone else to. After all, who knows you better than you?

And finally, you will be straightforward about what your fees are and what the terms are for acquiring your services or products. You, *not* your clients, set the rules for selling your niche. Most of all, don't make it hard for the right people to have your niche.

Define Your Geographic Universe

One of the first steps you must take is carefully defining your geographic universe. How far will your niche extend? Are you going to do business exclusively in your town or city? Your region? The entire country? Perhaps all over the globe? If you are part of an economic development planning team trying to rejuvenate a dying town by niching it with a strong theme, how far do you want the message to travel? From how far away do you want visitors or customers to come to enjoy your town and products? Similarly, if you are niching a personal service business of some kind—perhaps an accounting practice—where do you want your clients to come from?

This may seem like a perfectly simple—perhaps simplistic— question, but it is a critical strategic decision. Most importantly, it's crucial to remember that with transportation and technology as they are, doing business around the globe is not a fantasy for most people—if you factor that into your plan. And contrary to popular opinion, doing business beyond your immediate environment isn't something you need to wait for either! If that's where your market is, you need to get there fast. On a regular basis, for example, I talk with clients whom I have never met face-to-face. With fax and computer we communicate about their needs and businesses. I have guided many people from the beginning of their business to its full development simply by using the gifts of Ma Bell and her relatives. If the shoe fits, you can do the same.

We all know people whose business backyards are very big. One of my lawyer clients, for example, advises U.S.-based businesspeople on how to do business in Vietnam. Using all available technology, he and his partner travel regularly to Vietnam, connecting their clients to important resources throughout the world. Phone, fax, airplane, and computer make their business niche possible.

Suzanne's Ritzy Rollups represent yet another example of a single product literally rolled out coast to coast. The key here was vision from the beginning. Understanding that she wasn't planning just to sell to her local deli, Suzanne looked for the right system to move her product out fast. She found it in the club stores such as Costco. Your success is only as large as your vision. It sets the boundaries for your success. So why put limits on something of such importance in your life?

Keeping your geographic universe possibilities in mind is important for everyone but absolutely critical if you are on the move. People subject to frequent moving for whatever reason must have businesses that are not geography-dependent. By the same token, if you are taking up residence in your dream community—a place you plan to stay for the rest of your life—the rules for success are still the same. Define your geographic universe carefully, and above all don't make the fatal error of thinking much too small when considering this question. Remember your very big backyard possibilities. The world is truly your oyster. And never forget, once you, your service, or your product are well niched, other products emanating from that core can go virtually anywhere. A tight niche will create customers who show up on your doorstep wanting to buy what you have to offer.

As a preliminary step in defining your business's geographic universe, complete the checklist below.

EXERCISE 5.1

MY BUSINESS NICHE UNIVERSE

Check off the levels indicating where you expect your niche and or niche products to go.

_____ Within my organization

_____ Local community

_____ City

_____ State

_____ Region

_____ Entire United States

_____ North America

_____ World

When you're well niched you can do business anyplace!

Stages of Innovation

Now that you have identified the major geographic areas through which you expect your niches to travel, it is important to consider the process they must go through. Following is a Stages of Innovation checklist. Researchers tell us that every new idea must go through the following stages before it is actually implemented on a serious basis by any audience.

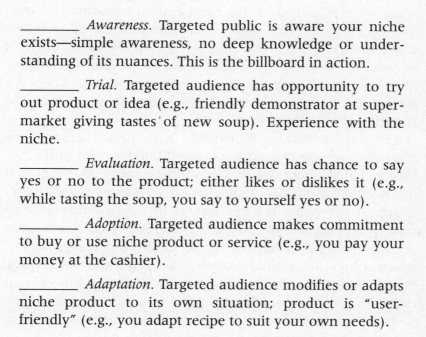

EXERCISE 5.2

STAGES OF INNOVATION CHECKLIST

Whether you are introducing a niche within your own organization, a tangible product, or a service to a world-wide constituency, your niche must pass through each of the following stages to be successful:

_____ *Awareness.* Targeted public is aware your niche exists—simple awareness, no deep knowledge or understanding of its nuances. This is the billboard in action.

_____ *Trial.* Targeted audience has opportunity to try out product or idea (e.g., friendly demonstrator at supermarket giving tastes of new soup). Experience with the niche.

_____ *Evaluation.* Targeted audience has chance to say yes or no to the product; either likes or dislikes it (e.g., while tasting the soup, you say to yourself yes or no).

_____ *Adoption.* Targeted audience makes commitment to buy or use niche product or service (e.g., you pay your money at the cashier).

_____ *Adaptation.* Targeted audience modifies or adapts niche product to its own situation; product is "user-friendly" (e.g., you adapt recipe to suit your own needs).

_____ *Maintenance.* Value-added services to clients, employee education and staff development programs. You nourish the niche.

Notice that each of these stages of innovation requires a different kind of information and experience by the user. If you have a new product (or one perceived as new) your greatest wish, of course, is to have it adopted by your target audience. Sadly, too many products and ideas never even get tried out, simply because the target audience wasn't aware they existed. A profile of one of my recent clients illustrates this point.

THE CASE OF CLIENT X

Client X is a very large and powerful statewide professional organization. Over the years it earned a national reputation for being a leader in its field. Time and again it introduced innovative programs, putting itself in the forefront for its members and other key people. Approximately ten years ago, Client X introduced one program in particular that took off like a lightning bolt; it was truly the only game in town. With Client X's extraordinary delivery system, this program was virtually a household word. Successful.

And then something happened. Other organizations, large and small, private and public, for-profit and not-for-profit, figured out that Client X had a good thing going. They got into the knockoff game. Though Client X's "market share" didn't disappear overnight, the day came when apparent interest in their widget was flat to waning. By the time Client X arrived in my office they'd decided a whole new profit center was in order. A logical conclusion, almost. Since no one was buying, they assumed no one wanted their widget any longer, that either it needed to be improved upon, overhauled, or dumped, probably the latter. And I was supposed to help them figure out what the replacement widget would be.

Fortunately, before launching a costly widget development project I asked one simple question: "Who's heard of your product?" Realizing the stakes were very high, we asked the question to association members many times and in many ways. And guess what? The answer was virtually *no one*! Client X's product had become invisible. Their target audience didn't even know the widget existed, much less what benefit it might provide. "How," I asked, "can anyone buy your service if they don't even know it exists?" I warned Client X, as I do you, not to conclude upon the success or failure of your widget *unless you have successfully addressed each of the levels of innovation*. In this case, my client had flunked on the most basic test, awareness.

Once this observation was taken seriously, we introduced a system capable of making the right people aware of my client's product. That system guaranteed that each of the six levels of innovation would be addressed individually, simultaneously, and constantly.

Memorize the six levels of innovation; then do them!

What This Means to You

Before going any farther, it's important for you to complete your own Stages of Innovation checklist. Consider each of the levels carefully, identifying strategies that will work for your own business at each stage. *Also of great importance*, consider your geographic universe when doing this exercise. Remember, each of the levels must be active throughout your prospective client or customer's universe. If that universe is your immediate neighborhood, the strategies must extend throughout the neighborhood. If it's the globe, your strategies must do the same thing. Keep in mind that these strategies must be operational *all the time*. You don't do one level. Quit. Then move on to the next. Quit. You are definitely walking, talking, and chewing gum simultaneously. Think of yourself like a juggler. You're keeping your 9 steps in motion and ensuring your levels of innovation are in action all the time as well. As your strategies are introduced you will see how they support and reinforce one another (or should!).

When you look closely at the six stages of innovation, you can understand how so many products simply never see the light of a customer's day. All too many organizations invent their widget, then jump to adoption level, Nothing happens. No one buys anything and the organization decides the effort was a failure. As we've seen, however, the real problem was a case of invisible niche.

Moral of the story? Don't plan to be a best-kept secret!

Your Aggressive Marketing Plan

Regardless of the type of niche you are making, it will not get anyplace significant on its own. The marketing system you put in place must be aggressive, ongoing—indeed, relentless. Most of all, it must be intentional just as your niche must be. Your success in spreading the word about your niche—hastening its success up steps of the innovation ladder—will be hastened by how fast you get the message to the *right* people.

The Cutty Sark story makes this point all too well. A combination of legend, rumor, and storytelling have it that somewhere in the distant annals of the thirties a marvelously long, gilded Rolls-Royce pulled up in front of one of New York's poshest nightspots. As you would expect, the door attendants rushed to offer their most gracious assistance as two elegantly dressed couples exited the extraordinary vehicle. Quietly and deftly each of the door attendants was thanked with a crisp hundred-dollar bill. Similar gratitude was extended to the maître d' for ensuring the couples the finest seats in the house.

Within moments after our couples were seated, waiters descended upon them, inquiring what they would like to drink. Without a second's delay, the host answered, "Cutty for all of us." His answer was short and definite. "I beg your pardon, sir? What was that you said?" the waiter asked. "Cutty Sark for us all," the guest repeated, this time with a note of impatience in his voice. "Of course, sir. I'll have it for you in a moment, sir. Thank you, sir," the waiter responded before rushing to the kitchen, then to the bar, and then to the maître d' and anyone else he could find who could figure out what Cutty Sark was.

As you can imagine, it was not with much excitement that our waiter returned to the table of four elegants only to report, "I'm so sorry. We don't seem to have any Cutty Sark. Could I get you something else?"

"What? No Cutty?" In unison four faces showed amazement and sheer disbelief as they rose to leave. "No Cutty? We'll just have to go elsewhere." And out they huffed into their gilded Rolls.

Story has it that this episode was repeated not more than a dozen times in the sleekest restaurants before virtually all of New York City's respectable nightspots highlighted Cutty on their bar menu. Even with the rentals on Rolls, furs, and jewels, this was probably one of the least expensive and ultimately most successful marketing campaigns in history.

Regardless of how fictionalized the account is by now, the moral(s) of our Cutty story are still relevant. Most of all, it reminds us that a key strategic decision is not just who ultimately will get the product, but who appears to have it first. If the first to have it are important enough, that alone may give critical impetus to selling your niche.

You can't be invisible if you want any business. Being successful and invisible are contradictions in terms in today's extraordinary world. As the stages of innovation showed you, and as our duck-versus-chicken story emphasized, no one can ever buy your product or service unless they have at least established some awareness of your existence. Hence, you must create systems that take your niche product into your potential clients' lives at their every turn. Following are several strategies shown to be especially powerful for delivering strong niche messages.

You must be a household word.

CONSIDER SEMINARING

Want to get out to the right people fast? Seminars can make your niche a household word almost overnight if you do them right and can be extremely powerful regardless of whether you are selling a tangible product or professional service. Here are some tips to make your seminars work:

1. Niche, niche, niche. The niche message must be totally clear. Tens of thousands of other smart nichecrafters are also going to be using seminars to spread the word about their products and services. Whatever vehicle you use for telling people about your seminar, be certain it clearly expresses the Specialness of your product.

2. Let others sponsor your programs. Identify organizations having vested interests in the same groups you do. Create win-win relationships, encouraging them to join you in reaching target audiences you both need.

3. Don't bother networking in the conventional sense. That is, forget trying to establish new networks. The key

is in identifying the best existing networks and penetrating them as rapidly as possible.

4. Give serious advance thinking to the outcomes you desire from the seminar. What do you want to have happen as a result of the event? What do you want attendees to do? How you answer these questions will strongly influence what you put into the program. If you are using seminars as marketing tools, your primary goal will probably be to convert registrants to customers.

5. Under *no circumstances* should you make your seminar technical. Your participants are not interested in becoming experts in your subject. They simply want to be more successful. Your seminar should focus on issues pertinent to them. Talk about problems first. If your participants connect with the problems, it is likely they'll connect with the solution: you.

6. Seminars intended to generate customers come out of your marketing budget. Don't even think about charging much, if anything, for your program. The issue is to get in front of as many of the right people as possible.

7. Give careful thought to your leave-behind information. You want participants to know how to reach you when they are ready for your product or service.

8. Consider a variety of formats, including mini-seminars and by-invitation-only small group previews.

9. Do not lose sight of the purpose of your program. It is *not* to make everyone there experts in the subject. It's to gain customers. It's to give them a sense of who you are, an appreciation for your expertise, and most of all a conviction that you have something they would benefit from. You do this by dealing with issues that are germane to them, not you. Problem—solution. In essence, you are giving them an experience with you, a taste of what it would be like to have your services. The point is not to give them every bit of information and solve all their problems in one short seminar. If they connect with you, they will pay you to do that.

Seminaring is the marketing vehicle I chose for myself in establishing my own business several years ago. Knowing I had to penetrate the market fast and at the lowest cost possible, I searched for the right sponsors—organizations that were already part of existing powerful networks, organizations that could take me to my audience in ways I could not do myself. So, the big question I asked myself was, "Who has a vested interest in the same audience I do?" It didn't take me long to figure out that the fine business journal that I read religiously every week targeted my prospective clients. "So why not do a deal?"

Realizing that the worst that could happen was that I'd be told no, I introduced myself to one of the most respected publishers within the then rapidly growing *American City Business Journal* chain. Mike Flynn, publisher of the *Puget Sound Business Journal,* instinctively understood the concept of niching. His paper was doing it every day. So it was that the *PSBJ* was one of the earliest sponsors of my seminar program. Because it was part of such a large and highly regarded network, I was able to move from city to city with relative ease—through an existing network. Although there were more than a few times when none of us made any money on the seminars per se, we each achieved our most important goals: the papers offered more value to their existing and potential customers, and I gained the critical visibility necessary to grow an international consulting business.

If you want to work with sponsors who can help you in a similar way, be sure you are already living and breathing Step 3, on your 9-step chart. This step is about helping your customers win. What I know for certain is that when they win, so do I.

THE RIGHT NEWSLETTER CAN DO THE JOB

The right newsletter can persuade potential clients or customers they need to pick up the phone and get hold of you, fast! So what does the right newsletter look like? First, last, and always, it's a marketing tool. Like seminars, its primary purpose is to get you more of the right customers. It's not a ponderous, jargon-filled treatise on the technical aspects of your subject. And it's certainly not some canned thing you buy and make-believe personalize by putting your company stamp or photo on it. *It comes from you, it's about you, and it's by you.*

Following are some more features of good marketing newsletters—the kind that will spread the word to the right people about your niche. Good marketing newsletters are:

1. *Journalistically written.* They are interesting and enjoyable to read. They are not full of jargon and technical language. Remember, you are the expert in your business, not the people buying your product or service. If they were the experts, they wouldn't need you.
2. *Short.* Somewhere between two and four pages at maximum in most cases.
3. *Results and outcome oriented.* They report your successes in concrete terms; case studies are frequent. If you are working with confidential information, you can create hypothetical case studies demonstrating how particular problems can be addressed without using names or data inappropriately.
4. *Problem-solution oriented.* This is an essential ingredient of all successful newsletters. It is what your clients or customers buy you for—to put them in a better place than they were before they met you or engaged your services. If they don't connect to this immediately, it's trash-can city for your precious newsletter. Two of my favorite problem-solution examples appeared in a newsletter from a neighborhood hospital and healthcare center. The headline that instantly caught my eye read, "Roping Accident Cuts off Thumb. Surgery Saves It!" Underneath the headline was a big photo of a smiling

person sitting up in a hospital bed, thumbs up. Thumbs on. A great testimonial. But a brilliant headline because it didn't launch into pedigrees of talented surgeons or latest theories of sewing on thumbs. It simply and importantly conveyed problem-solution.

The same newsletter had another article we can all learn from. "Arthritis Sufferers Don't Have to Live with Pain," it read. So why is this such a smart lead title? The fact is, many of your clients and customers don't know there is a way out of their pain or problem. In fact, they may have gotten so used to it by now they accept it as part of their lot in life and business. But we know they're wrong. There is a way out. You're it. But you have to start with their pain.

5. *Full of practical tips.* Here you offer checklists and advice to help customers or clients manage their businesses and lives better. The tip lists can be short. You want people to keep your newsletters around for a long time. Often the tip lists are the reason newsletters get posted on bulletin boards, fronts of refrigerators, and other places likely to be seen over and over again. Give people an excuse to keep the newsletter.

6. *Warm and people-focused.* They emphasize the human part of your operation, as with photos of you and/or your clients. Nothing is more powerful than a photo of a satisfied customer standing alongside you or your employees. Remember, your customers buy your success with others. Let your newsletter shout success by highlighting others who have had the pleasure of your services or enjoyed using your niche widget!

7. *Regular.* Probably published quarterly. Don't get in over your head trying to get it out every month. The point behind newsletters is becoming a regular and familiar figure in your audience's life. Since you are using this as a marketing tool, you are not charging for it. The idea is to get people buying more products and services because they receive it from you.

8. *Sent not just to the ultimate buyers of your niche but to those who influence the buyers as well.* Remember that personal

referral is one of the most powerful ways business is generated. The right newsletters sent to the right people frequently are passed along from the influence-makers to potential buyers—*with a blessing!*

 9. Focused upon your niche. Every word in your newsletter must relate in one way or another to your niche. Like spokes linking to the hub of a bicycle wheel. If it doesn't fit, it's out of there. Plain and simple.

10. *A means of introducing new products and services.* Before each issue, think carefully about your newest products and services or other items you want to highlight in your newsletter.

11. *A way to establish a personal relationship between you or your company and the intended audience.* The newsletter allows you to connect almost as if you were writing a personal letter to the reader.

12. *Opinionated!* This is a very important feature of your newsletter. You are not just reporting information, you are offering your perspective on it. This is your opportunity to let people know what you stand for in no uncertain terms. It's time to be a bit provocative. Always include a "From the Desk of" column where you offer commentary on important issues.

13. *A way to create your own mailing list.* Go back to your wish list. Identify anyone and everyone you want as your customers and clients. Their names go on the list first. Your current clients go on the list. And then another critical group—and one most often overlooked—the gatekeepers. People who influence your wish list need to be on your list. People in positions of responsibility and likely to influence your wish list should be fixtures on your mailing list.

Regardless of how strong the temptation may be to go out and buy yourself a canned list, I urge you to scrub the idea. If you do wind up buying a list or multiple lists, be prepared to develop categories very carefully. Don't turn the assignment over to someone else and just wait for the mail to come. Not if you want your niche to produce customers in the door, that is. Granted, building a good list takes time, but if you're really interested in a niche that works, time is part of the price you pay.

And, of course, niche, niche, niche.

It's important to remember that the right newsletter can be valuable regardless of what product or service you are selling. It allows you to communicate with prospective and existing clients about your business in an entirely professional but low-key manner. Customers or clients are reminded about your services or products in a highly positive way but in a manner that doesn't sound like a paid advertisement.

LET THE MEDIA SPREAD THE WORD

The media—including print, nonprint, and, increasingly, electronic—can be your best friends in promoting your business. Fortunately, some of the best media coverage doesn't have to cost you a dime. What it takes is a good niche and some thoughtful planning. Following are several suggestions for ways you can get media treatment absolutely free. Since there will be times when paid advertising may also be appropriate to promote your business, specific considerations for you to keep in mind are also provided in this media section. Now, some tips to help you get powerful *free* editorial coverage to help market your business:

1. Make up a list of the key publications (business, professional) your clients or customers read. This list might also include daily papers. If you simply don't know what trade and other key publications they read, you can do two things to find out: first and most obvious, simply call and ask them; secondly, check *Gale's Encyclopedia of Associations.* You will find *Gale's* a gold mine of information, listing every pertinent association in the country. These associations produce newsletters and other publications your prospective clients subscribe to. You can and will want to get those same publications.

2. Find out who the editors are of these relevant publications. On a regular basis call them, identify yourself, and provide them with "information of possible interest to their readers." Become a trusted and reliable source of journalistically sound information. How do you know what kind of information they would find useful? If you think about our earlier discussion of the Platinum Rule and do a "hot button" check before placing your call to the editor, you will have no problem choosing what kinds of data to pass along—and how to do it.

3. At a carefully planned time, alert specific editors about your own niche product or service. Chances are it, too, will be interesting to their readers—especially if you have made it a point to know who their readers are and what they are like. You may call them up, saying something like, "I'm doing something I think your readers may be interested in. May I tell you about it?" The key hot button here, of course, is readers. Editors have a responsibility to provide relevant information and material of interest to their readers. If they perceive that you have some, you may be onto a good piece of free press. The trick is to think out what you have and what your editor's world looks like before the call.

4. Plan to be on a first-name basis with all your key media people. You will find them appreciative that you take the time to inform them about journalistically sound happenings.

5. Once you are granted an interview with a reporter, prepare a short outline describing what it is you are up to and why you called the press, emphasizing those things about you and/or your product that are noteworthy—your niche. Think carefully about what you want to have happen as a result of the interview. Who do you want to call you? What do you want people to do? How you answer these questions will strongly influence what you say during the interview. Don't make your reporter start at square one. You should be the one setting the tone and pace. I am convinced that 99 percent of all journalists have the same high level of integrity you and I do. Their goal is to get the story right and fast. They have to deal with the information you give them. So think it through in advance and be clear in presenting it. If the final story sounds unclear and confusing, chances are pretty good you gave your reporter a story that was unclear and confusing!

6. One major caveat: Don't plan to "sell" your widget during any interview, not at least in the traditional sense. If you are being interviewed about the seminars you offer, you're not going to hard sell the ones coming up next week; instead you'll emphasize the overall benefits received by people who attend your programs.

7. Have a leverage plan in place before you ever pick up the phone. Think where you want to take the article that appears about you and your business. That will influence what you say and how you conduct the interview. You may be starting with your hometown newspaper. Once that story comes out, you can send it to a major trade or professional publication or perhaps to a national paper.

    In your cover letter, once again indicate you are "doing something you think the editor's readers may be interested in." Follow up with a courteous phone call. Be persistent. Editors are swamped with work. Their desks look as if avalanches just went through, and their phones are constantly ringing. And they are nearly *always* on deadline. If you are sensitive to those real facts of life, while remembering they are people just like you trying to do a good job, and just like you, they have their own hot buttons, you greatly increase your chances of valuable editorial coverage now!

I am constantly amazed by how many people go to all the work of getting a good story in their local paper and then stop there! Real success is achieved through leverage to the next highest levels. This requires you to think through your media plan very carefully, however.

 I find that a good number of people are embarrassed to pick up the phone and alert the press (whether local, national, or international) about what they are up to. They feel it is immodest. Forget that nonsense. Consider it a public service. If your niche is worth anything, it's worth having others know about it. Just be prepared to explain to the editor what is Special about this thing you are up to. You'll never be sorry you took the time to meet the press. Editorial coverage of what you are doing is the most valuable kind of advertising you'll ever get.

PARTNERSHIP OR ALLIANCE MARKETING

In our section on seminars I referred to partnership or alliance marketing, but this tool is so extremely important it warrants attention on its own merit! In essence I'm talking about groups having a vested interest in similar audiences.  For example, what do laptop computers, airlines, and car-rental agencies have in common? The business traveler, of course. Each has a vested interest in the same group of people. Each has its own access routes to get to that audience. It's pretty simple. By joining forces for a single marketing effort you're able to capture more customers than by going it alone. Some examples will demonstrate the point.

Consider the MCI/American Airlines/Citibank alliance. Earn frequent flyer miles any time you use MCI residential service. Earn more if you put them on your Citibank Visa. I've known more than one person who converted his/her telephone service just to collect these valuable frequent flyer miles! Although Citibank and Visa were among the earliest alliances of credit and travel-related companies, they certainly haven't been the last.

While apparently very successful, the MCI/American Airlines/ Citibank alliance has recently been overshadowed by another enormously profitable marketing relationship, between the "Kings." Burger and Lion, that is. By striking an alliance, the Disney Corporation, creator of the blockbuster movie *The Lion King*, and Burger King, the fast food giant, reported profits soaring to an all-time high. Lion King and Burger King demonstrated that by getting together, they could achieve far more than by going after the same customers independently.

Alliance marketing is especially appealing because it allows you to interact with other organizations "on call." Although you leverage each other's resources, you continue to own what belongs to you—your firm, your business, your clients. No partnerships, mergers, or changes in the form of your business are needed. Your alliance with the other guy is for one purpose only. It's to offer added value to customers, existing or potential.

The best alliances exist over time, allowing various parties to benefit from the image and success of the other. That is a key distinction between alliance marketing and the more familiar technique of offering incentive or bonus gifts to customers.

Over the years I have seen alliance marketing work for scores of clients, large and small. I have also observed a peculiar and persistent misunderstanding about this strategy. I call it the "I'm too small" syndrome. The "I'm not Disney or Burger

King" excuse. The irony is that if you are a small to mid-size business, alliance marketing is a strategy you especially should give serious consideration to. You can never be too small to benefit from this important tool. Used well it will move your niche out infinitely faster than you could do so by yourself. It will also keep it out there with nominal cost to you. Don't leave home without it.

An interesting variation on alliance marketing is what we see increasingly in bookstores. I'm talking about the coffeehouse-bookstore relationship. Realizing that it's in their interest to keep people in the stores as long as possible and that browsing leads to buying, more and more bookstores have coffee bars strategically placed inside. The vast majority of those coffee bars are not owned by the bookstores. After all, bookstores are in the book business, not the coffee business. The world-famous Powell's bookstore in Portland, Oregon, was among the earliest to take advantage of such an alliance by incorporating the Ann Hughes Coffee Shop as a fixture at its main location. The relationship is symbiotic. Both parties win. The coffee shop derives revenue from an almost captive, though appreciative audience. On the other hand, the bookstore has a vehicle for keeping people on the premises longer. And importantly, the coffee shop contributes to the overall culture of the environment, something all business owners should be concerned about.

It's clear that Powell's is more than books. It's an experience. The symbiotic relationship between the businesses helps establish and deepen each one's niche. In a sense, each becomes a member of the other's niche team.

Who's on your team?

Take your first step now in setting up an alliance that will work by asking yourself "Who has a vested interest in the same audience I do?" Your answer and the deal you put together with them may be the most important marketing you ever do. After all, it's a strategy used by Kings!

NICHE PARTNERS
---

1. In the spaces below identify groups or organizations sharing an interest in the same audience(s) you do.
2. Indicate their own specific reasons for that interest. What do they want out of the deal?
3. Then prioritize the groups, with 1 being the group you are most able to partner with and 5 being the one you are least able to work with.

RANK	GROUP OR POTENTIAL PARTNER	THEIR INTEREST
_____	_____	_____
_____	_____	_____
_____	_____	_____
_____	_____	_____
_____	_____	_____

Adding Value: The Case of the 13th Donut

The idea of adding value is really nothing new. Old-time merchants were experts at it. Perhaps the best-known example of years-gone-by value-adding was the simple baker's dozen. You went into your local bakery, bought a dozen donuts, and as a way of saying "Thank you. We appreciate your business," the baker gave you a present. A 13th donut. On the house. A personal touch. You left smiling, mouth surrounded by powdered sugar.

Today, the 13th donut is more important than ever before.

As you think about your own business's potential for adding value to your customers, consider one of the most successful efforts in recent times to provide that something more. That Special piece. I'm talking about something Nordstrom used to do as a matter of course. That is, if you needed an item immediately, the salesperson would deliver it to you personally. They would even come to your office after hours, hauling along a variety of garments for you to try on. Personal selling at its best. Granted, this took time away from the sales floor, but it definitely built Nordstrom's reputation for being client-centered. And it got return trade. Lots of it. One of the interesting things about adding value is that in some cases it doesn't just secure your niche, it becomes your niche, as with Nordstrom.

A very successful lawyer recently described his own version of the 13th donut. He'd noticed that when clients got their bills, the thing that caused them the most discomfort wasn't the professional fees (which were considerable) but—you guessed it!—the fax, phone, and courier charges. Although these were the real thorns, they were also nickels and dimes compared to the tens of thousands of dollars his clients were paying him. So what did our successful lawyer do? He 13th-donuted those charges. He absorbed them into overhead. The cost of doing business. I do the same thing in my own billings, noting "Courtesy fax, telephone charges, etc." on the client's statement.

Other examples of value-adding strategies include:

1. Offering special seminars or forums for preferred clients and wish-list customers. These do not necessarily have to be on topics immediately dealing with what you sell. The issue is getting people in your door by providing something having perceived value to them. They come to know you as a trusted resource. You are doing something for them even when you are not involved in an immediate transaction. Just one more way to become part of their team.

2. Establishing a "club" for preferred clients and/or customers. In some cases, a card acknowledging their status
   will be useful. If you wonder how many people take
   such cards seriously and question the idea's potential
   value to you, just sneak a peak inside the wallets of a
   few friends.

The opportunities for adding value are limited only by your
imagination. Whatever vehicles you choose, keep in mind that
you want to do something having a very long shelf-life.
Something whose impact will remind your appreciative customer time and again of your presence. Consider strategies that
in one way or another help your customers achieve their own
goals.

Finally, it is important to emphasize that in most cases you
are not just adding value to the product or service but to the
relationship you have with your customer. You are giving that
person one more reason to come back to you over and over
again. All things being equal, you are giving them a reason to
choose you.

Talk, Talk, Talk

One of the very best ways to get the word out about your
niche costs absolutely nothing: it's simply by talking. Not hard
sell. Just enthusiastic talking about how interesting your business is and the great response you are having from others—
from your friends and clients. I strongly discourage you from
directly hitting up friends to buy your product. Do that often
and your list of friends will dwindle fast. This doesn't mean,
however, that you should keep yourself and your products a
secret. The issue is *how* you talk about both. When people ask
what you are doing, describe your focus and what it does,
always keeping in mind who you are talking to. Be clear. Don't
waffle around. Have one short sentence describing your niche
ready to share at a moment's notice.

Think about the listener's hot buttons. Then push them.

Appropriately. Give examples of the kinds of problems your product or service solves. Consider that person's worldview, so you can frame what you do in a way that will connect with the listener. Don't be obnoxious. If you give friends good information in the right way, they will pick up on the opportunity for your service when they perceive they are ready. The point is, they have to want more if it's going to work. Whet their appetites, but don't shove the morsel down their throats. They'll throw up! If you notice you have sparked interest, you can say, "I'd be glad to make an appointment to tell you about the product/service or have someone else explain the system."

Of course, the rules are altogether different for someone who has walked into your store or called you concerning your product/service. That individual has expressed at least a minimum level of interest and should be considered a business prospect.

My preference regardless of who you are dealing with is to soft sell through enthusiasm and emphasis on other people's success with what you offer. After all, that's what people buy. Success!

Middle-Seat Marketing

I am constantly amazed by how many people totally pass up no-cost golden opportunities to market their niche. One of the most overlooked is what I've come to call middle-seat marketing. It works every time, and I guarantee it won't show up in any biz school curriculum. And of course, it's very simple. You just need a little courage (in some quarters known as chutzpah!).

The next time you get on a plane, be sure you have reserved the middle seat. If you are a frequent flyer, the customer service people will do everything in their power to keep you out of it, since most people don't want the middle seat and they will want to please you. Sometimes you will even get bumped to first class lest they displease a preferred customer by putting you in the middle. But stand your ground. Sit in the middle seat, where you have twice as much opportunity to talk to someone interesting—someone who might want your service.

Plan to carry some eye-catching items so that those on either side of you can get a glance at what you do. If they don't pick up on how intriguing your work is, gracefully drop some promotional pieces. On their lap might be a bit much, but the issue is to get the stuff out there. Too many businesspeople keep themselves and their widgets wrapped up as best-kept secrets. You've got to let people know you exist. I've met an endless number of fascinating people—and yes, significant clients—in that middle seat!

Think of Yourself as a Billboard

How many times have you gone to a meeting where even though names tags were available, half the people weren't wearing theirs? What you know about these people is that they were either naive, didn't care about their business's health, or were excessively shy. Most likely, they were naive about the missed opportunity they have every time they put on a name tag announcing who they are and what their business is. It's really awfully silly when you think about it. Many of these same people would pay money for a newspaper or radio ad. Buy a billboard. Pay for an advertising campaign. But when it comes to something that doesn't cost anything and offers an opportunity to market their niche to the right people, they blow it.

Simple as it sounds, here's what you should always do with your name tag.

1. Make sure it's clear and readable from a distance. Bring your own felt-pen. Better to have it large. Remember, a lot of us don't read phone books without glasses anymore. Don't make it hard for us to know you.
2. Have your business name as well as your own name on the tag. If it isn't on, put it there. You don't go to jail for name-tag defacement. You do lose money, though, on missed opportunities.

3. *Leave your tag on after the meeting. All the way home.* Stand outside a meeting room and watch how many people literally throw away name-familiarity opportunities by hurriedly trashing their name tags.

The point of all this is that for people to buy you or your product, they must know you. Take advantage of every opportunity to make this happen.

Beyond Networking to *Relationshipping*

Over the last several years, the virtues of networking have been more and more apparent to people seriously interested in getting their niche to the right others. It's also increasingly clear that a big difference exists between people who just network and those who are successful at it. Successful networkers typically do much more than simply meeting people, talking casually with them, and exchanging business cards. They understand the power of personal relationships and have a plan for building them. Most importantly, they understand that it takes time to create an old friend.

On the surface the difference between networking and *relationshipping* may seem so negligible as to almost be splitting hairs. I guarantee you, it's a critical hair. If you are serious about developing relationships that deliver your niche goals, you will:

1. Build into your busy schedule sufficient time to nurture personal relationships.
2. Realize that significant relationships are built on trust and respect. Those qualities are earned over time. They don't automatically happen when you trade business cards, no matter how slick your logo may be. This point was driven home to me by a young executive from an international corporation. Describing a three-day meeting with the CEO of another global organization, she said, "Saying goodbye was a lot different than the hello.

There was a bond." Networking at its best is about building that bond. The tie that binds.

3. *Do your homework.* Before going to any meeting or special gathering, find out who is likely to be there. Do some background work, finding out to the extent possible any interesting tidbits you can about key individuals. Nothing breaks ice faster than demonstrating to someone that you know of them and/or their work. Asking people about themselves and their background (e.g., "How did you get into this field?" "How do you like this area?" "Tell me about your family") is an excellent conversation starter. Plan to connect first with the human being you are meeting; technology and business will follow.

4. Don't just send your body to a meeting. Better to stay home than to isolate yourself in an unfrequented area of the room. Plan to talk. But even better, get people talking about themselves and their concerns. Their views of the world. Learn all you can about their niche or lack of it.

Research shows that the more other people talk, the smarter they think you are!

---

5. *Share.* I don't mean killing yourself by giving away free advice all the time or handing your widget out for nothing to everyone who passes by. I do mean being generous, however. Helping those who need help. Giving honestly, without the expectation of any return. Ultimately it will come back to you. Maybe not today or tomorrow, but it will come around. Ultimately people want to do business or work with those they respect and trust. If you are serious about being perceived as a person worthy of retaining as an advisor or buying a product from, your reputation as a human being is your most valuable asset. And like every other aspect of your

niche, it won't happen by accident. At least not the good part!

6. *Do a relationship inventory.* Think about phases of your life. Who you met when. If you are like most busy people, chances are you have not kept up with a lot of former friends and associates who would enjoy knowing where you are, what business you're in, and, yes, what your niche is. It's possible that some of these relationships can be enormously important resources as you shape your business. Your college relationships, regardless of when they were formed, can be especially powerful niche-building blocks. More than a few college relationships have been parlayed into successful enterprises, including Hewlett-Packard (Stanford buddies) and Ch2M-Hill (Oregon State friends). Not to be forgotten is the Webber-Rice alliance, which has produced many of the world's greatest musicals (*Jesus Christ, SuperStar* and *Phantom of the Opera*). The moral of this story is that if you haven't reviewed your university relationships lately, start now. If you're still in school, look around carefully. Your study partner today may be a niche alliance tomorrow.

Advertising: When to Buy It and How to Use It

Used in combination with other marketing vehicles, advertising may be an important resource for you. Rarely, if ever, will it be your exclusive strategy. Because this is one strategy that most often you have to pay for, I urge you not to even think about it until you have your entire niche plan developed. I have seen too many situations where hardworking, potentially successful people literally dumped precious money into ads that were premature, ill-conceived, in the wrong publication, in the wrong media, or done in a vacuum. Now, with the Internet, innocent business owners have even more opportunity to throw money away unless they create a tightly orchestrated niche plan *before* spending one dime. Having said all this, let's look at when and how advertising can be useful to your business niche.

Advertising has two basic purposes: to sell something *now* or to get and keep your name out there until the customer is ready to buy. As the seller, you have to decide what you want to achieve. The type of ad, where you place it, and how long you run it will be affected by your answer to this important question. Another very key issue that will affect the type of advertising you do, if any, is whether your niche is a professional service or tangible product. While both can advertise, the rules are very different for each.

Make certain you already know what your niche is. Don't expect the ad to answer that question. Nor should you expect the medium you choose to do that job for you. Most of all, remember, *you are only ready to advertise when you can complete the statement we presented earlier: "This is what we do, and here is what is special about it: . . . ."*

If your firm is a professional service, you are selling your information and knowledge. You must always be careful not to sound or look as if you are begging for business or selling snake oil or schlock. It's amazing how strategies used for selling cars can be killers when selling legal or other services. Professional service ads don't offer microwave ovens or free this or that. Typically the best professional service ads are those linking the service to an activity promoting education or some other public service. Perhaps your firm is involved in a seminar or special event. The issue is getting your name out there in the right way and on a regular basis.

Longer-term name familiarity can be achieved appropriately through what I call celebration advertising. When something important or special occurs in your town or city (perhaps the nation), celebrate this by taking out a display ad saying how proud you are of the major players. Congratulate them on behalf of your company. It's nothing less than virtue by association. Although many companies do run regular business card ads, I find them colorless and nondistinctive.

If your company is selling tangible widgets (fashion, autos, com-

puters), the rules are quite different. You can use strong imme-
diate-response techniques. Offer incentives—encourage time-
response (e.g., offer ends on x date), volume discounts, sale
prices, etc. Some other tips that will help you get the most for
your advertising dollar include:

1. Place ads in publications your prospective customers read.
   Research this carefully. If *you don't know* for certain, ask
   them. Get demographic and "market penetration" information from the paper. Don't be fooled by the publication's size of circulation. The issue is does it get to the
   right people. In this case, those people are your prospects.
   The question, of course, is "How well niched are they?"

2. In which section of the magazine/paper/electronic
   media will the article appear? In some cases it will be
   important to pay more to have it appear in a location
   seen by your readers. You don't want it buried in a corner irrelevant to your readership. Back pages are nearly
   always the most desirable locations. They are also much
   more expensive.

3. If you are unable to give the publication camera-ready
   ad copy, be certain you manage the ad development.
   You cannot and should not expect them to understand
   your niche and target-audience needs. It is up to you
   first, last, and always to ensure that the final product is
   consistent with where you want to go and what you
   want to say.

4. Set yourself up as an ad agency in advance and receive
   a 10 to 15 percent agency discount on your total cost.

5. In some cases you may even work a trade with the company. Do you have something that will provide them an
   important benefit? If so, submit a proposal outlining a
   mutual win-win deal, and you may wind up with a
   great ad, more customers, and *no bill!!*

6. Repetition is more important than ad size. You want
   customers to accept you as a familiar face or product in
   their world. Don't expect this to happen with one-shot
   advertising. Develop a long-term media plan.

Bundle Your Niche

Like many other good strategies, bundling is not totally new. Many highly successful companies have been using it for years. Health and beauty aids are among the most frequently bundled products. Buy toothpaste and get an introductory package of dental floss or new mouthwash free. Sort of. Chances are, you're actually paying a little more to buy both products than were you buying only one. It could be that one company is using the second product as an incentive or bonus item to encourage you to buy the main product. They know that sometimes people buy the bundle just to get the apparent give-away.

The great thing about bundling is that your product or service gets a free ride to a target audience you'd otherwise have to go after on your own. And if you've ever tried to get your product into a retail store, you know that shelf space is very expensive. In a sense, bundling is creating an alliance of sorts. By packaging together, you sell to each other's customers.

Software companies have also exploited bundling for years. Chances are excellent that when you got your last computer, it came preloaded with a bundle of software. Maybe it had Prodigy or CompuServe on it. How lucky. Ten free hours. But what afterward? Of course, the service continues after you pay. And a lot of people do. Bundling solves a huge problem for many people trying to get their niche to market. It simply puts your product in front of the right people. The tremendous power of this concept is evidenced by MicroSoft's effort to bundle its own electronic on-line communications system within Windows 95. Arguing that the bundle would give MicroSoft unfair advantage, the company's competitors asked the Justice Department to prohibit the bundle.

What does this mean for you? To effectively bundle your product or service, you should put on your alliance-marketing cap. Think about who has a vested interest in your audience and already has a system in place to get to that audience. Your product or service can help sell more of their products while moving yours to market as well. A simple win-win situation.

Making Technology Work for You

Technology offers extraordinary opportunities for making your niche even more successful. Unfortunately, however, the gifts it offers us can be very seductive and misunderstood. To ensure that you make technology work for your niche, keep the following basic rules of working with it emblazoned in a highly visible place so that you are reminded of them on a daily basis:

Rule 1: Use technology to achieve your goals, not the other way around. Whatever vehicles you choose should be consistent with those goals.

Rule 2: Don't let technology run you. It is only a means to an end. It is not the end.

Rule 3: Be sure you match your choice of technology with your wish list. Just as you would carefully research the readership of any publication in which you were considering advertising, you should pay equal attention to the fit between your niche and your high-tech or cyberspace marketing vehicle.

Rule 4: No tail wagging dog. Don't fall in love with any high-tech or cyberspace product or service. If it doesn't put your niche in a better place, either scrub it or don't use it to begin with.

Rule 5: Regardless of the vehicles you use (e.g., on-line marketing, interactive multimedia), they are not panaceas or substi-

tutes for a good niche. You can upgrade your computer until it will fly, but if you don't have a great niche you've wasted your money.

Now that we've addressed some of the basic rules, let's look briefly at some of the most exciting opportunities high tech has visited upon us.

THE INTERNET: BLACK HOLE OR GOLD MINE?

If you answered "Both" to the above question, you're absolutely right. Your business may ultimately benefit tremendously from having a web page replete with a full description of your products and services. The only problem is—and it's a pretty big problem when you really think about it—*people still have to have a reason to find you on the net.* And as if that weren't bad enough, they still have to have a reason to distinguish you from the other 10 to 30 million people estimated to be using the Internet! In a sense, the urgency of having a niche that will cause the right people to find you among all the masses is much greater than before Internet arrived. That's because the masses now include the planet. Unless you have a system giving people a reason to look for you and to recognize you when they find you on the net, you're worse off than being the small print in the Manhattan Yellow Pages. In other words, *you still need a niche.*

Notwithstanding the caveats, cybermarketing is already producing many success stories. A market that has been described as essentially invisible until now is one of the definite beneficiaries of the Internet: black businesses marketing to other black and minority-owned firms are finding appreciative consumers through the net. For example, Melanet, a service of New Perspectives Technologies (Norfolk, Virginia), describes itself as an electronic commerce, resource, and research center. It provides a place on the Internet where black businesses and services can sell to each other. Quoted in the *New York Times*, Melanet owners said their firm turned a profit just three months after it was set up. The real trick, however, will not be whether Melanet makes an ongoing profit, but whether the other businesses advertising on its service also benefit. To be successful and be chosen by the right customer from among all their good company, they must also have a you-know-what.

They need a niche.

HOME SHOPPING: LET TV HELP YOU SELL

It used to be that if you wanted to go shopping, you had to get in the car and find your way to the nearest store. And you can still do that. But now millions of people are also shopping from their living room. It's possible your niche could be one of the things they buy. Getting your widget accepted by one of the home-shopping channels could be enormously profitable for you. Just a few things to consider as you weigh this marketing option:

1. Research the various home-shopping programs carefully. Be sure you understand who they perceive their audience to be. If you have problems with this, go immediately to Step 3 on your 9-step *Nichecraft* chart. It's time to revisit the Platinum Rule.

2. Make sure you know what each program's perceived niche is. Does it match yours?
3. The advantages of hooking up with a home-shopping channel are substantial. The major one is that in a few

fell swoops you arrive in millions of homes at no significant cost to you. The home-shopping channels are like
retail stores. You sell wholesale to the channel. They take
orders and do all the fulfillment. Of course, you must be
able to handle your end of fulfillment. Before any deal is
struck, you will be required to demonstrate that you are
able to handle the orders that may pour in fast.

We noted earlier that sometimes your marketing strategy
may well become your niche. It could be that your widget is
already on the market through conventional retail channels.
Using home shopping could move it out in an entirely different
way. Or as Wee Willie Keeler reminded us earlier, "Hit 'em
where they ain't!"

MULTIMEDIA IN THE MAIL

One of the most exciting vehicles for getting the word out
about your niche is multimedia transported via CD-ROM.
Almost daily I receive a CD from someone wanting me to have
an experience with their service or widget. And an experience
is what multimedia allows me to have. At this point, a CD is
still more complex to put together than a conventional marketing piece, but its potential as a sales tool is extremely powerful. Whether your niche is a product or service, you should
definitely explore distilling its essence on disk. Though paper is
here to stay for basic marketing pieces, the bar has definitely
been raised. Even if you are not familiar with multimedia's
advantages, your customers and clients will be very soon. And
as their awareness rises, so do their expectations. If this vehicle
fits your niche, plan to get on board.

Summary

In this chapter many strategies were offered that will help get
the right people knowing and wanting your product regardless
of what it is. Strategies that will help you become a household

word efficiently and consistently. Each of these strategies (e.g., seminars, newsletters, correct use of the media, cybermarketing, talk, talk, talk) can be extremely powerful for you. But you must *never forget one thing*. And ultimately it is the very essence of this book: A strategy without a clearly defined niche is not going anyplace. The strategies by themselves are not going to do the trick. You must have articulated clearly what you are up to and use these vehicles to get the word out. Don't expect them to *invent* your niche.

6

THE GUARANTEE OF SUCCESS: NO PLAN B

You're almost there. By now you've given serious thought to what your Special business niche looks like, who's going to get it, how they're going to find out about it, what it's going to return to you for nurturing and growing it, and the solid business practices you need to implement your goals. The fact is, it's time to act. But will you? Ironically, it is at this very point where many potentially successful businesses die because of one thing only—their owner's fear of risk-taking.

Whether you are a sole entrepreneur building your dream business or orchestrating a large organization's niche, the bottom line of successful niche development requires focus, commitment, and action. In the process, it's entirely possible some feathers are going to get ruffled. Status-quo lovers may feel threatened. Valuable resources, not the least being time and money, must nearly always be allocated to achieve a new niche or enrich an existing one. All this is to say, a niche that works often tests its owner's mettle to the limit. Faint at heart need not apply.

Remember Max, who missed capitalizing upon a potentially powerful niche mainly because of personal insecurities? Up until now, much of your niche development has been intellectual—rational, that is. Now you have to put yourself on the line. And you put yourself on the line not only with others but with yourself as well. Though this fear almost never has anything to do with the niche itself, it is so inextricably linked to your success or failure I am obliged to consider the subject before sending you on your way. The topics contained in this chapter are those I have seen other businesspeople wrestle with over the years—some successfully, others less so. As you read this section, ask yourself at each juncture to what extent any of these issues apply to you.

Behold the lowly turtle.
It only gets ahead by sticking its neck out.

Risk Versus Gamble

Virtually every day of your life is filled with risk. Get up in the morning and you could trip and fall down the stairs. You risk when you drive down the street or get a flu vaccination. The outcomes of such risks are clearly not 100 percent in your favor. But if you've done everything you can—made every reasonable effort to prepare for the event or activity—your preparation is markedly different from depending on a lottery or crap table for success. You've done your homework. You're not gambling. Granted there is a chance your number won't come up. But unlike the lottery or crap table, it's not because the house odds are against you. As we proceed, keep in mind the enormous difference between risk and gamble. Additionally, it's important to keep in mind that risk is in the eye of the beholder. What's a big risk to me may not seem like such a big deal to you. In many cases the issue of risk by itself becomes less important than how we deal with it.

Risk is in the eye of the beholder.

Your Risk History

A first step in making even better
decisions involving any degree of
risk is understanding how you
have confronted risk in the past.
The following exercise will help
you gain clarity about what for so
many people is the ultimate R
word.

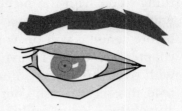

EXERCISE 6.1

YOUR RISK HISTORY

Answer the following questions as completely as you are able.

1. Thinking back over your entire life, identify the three
    biggest risks you ever faced (e.g., flying first solo).

    _____

    _____

    _____

2. Looking once again at the biggest risks you ever faced,
    describe your feelings in each situation (e.g., fear,
    exhilaration).

    _____

    _____

3. How did you respond to each of the risks you faced
    (e.g., pushed the throttle forward and moved down
    the runway with knees shaking)?

    _____

    _____

4. Now, looking back at each major risk you have just listed, identify several outcomes or consequences of having taken the course you chose (e.g., increased self-confidence).

_____

_____

Notice that the above questions asked you to respond to risks you *faced*. Many people jump automatically to the word *took*. The purpose of this exercise is to help clarify how you respond to risk generally. What you don't do is as important as what you actively do.

And now we come to probably the most important question concerning the biggest risks you faced. That is, what would your life have been like had you *not* stretched yourself? *Not* stuck your neck out. Of course you can't say with certainty, but with the advantage of a little history we can often see more clearly how pieces of our lives and business actions have built on one another. We can also see the profound truth in the old saying "No action is an action." So, how would your life be different today had you not risked yesterday? How will your business be different tomorrow if you don't risk today?

WHY IS IT IMPORTANT TO ASK "WHAT IF . . ."?

What-iffing throughout life can get us into lots of trouble. Monday-morning quarterbacking and brilliance by hindsight are cheap commodities. So why am I encouraging you to look hard at the what-ifs in your life? It's one reason only: retrospectively we can see that our choices had consequences. So did the "no action" choices. Looking back we can see how subtle, often imperceptible, decisions added up to major life and business directions. Every breath we take has a consequence to ourselves and those around us. The point is to be in charge of that direction. If you were less in charge of that direction in the past than you would like to have been, make it up by taking control of your future.

Good niches aren't luck of the draw or roll of the dice!

But risk there is! Ultimately you have to decide if your niche is worth that risk. The following exercise should assist you with that question.

RISK/OPPORTUNITY BAROMETER CHECK

Just as your niche has risk associated with it, we've also seen that it may have considerable opportunity. Think very hard about that opportunity, then mark where you think it is best described. In other words, give your niche an opportunity score; quantify the success your niche can produce. Give your niche a risk score, too. Given the information you have gathered, assuming a rational approach to implementing it, what kind of risk level is involved with your niche?

Your Barometer Check

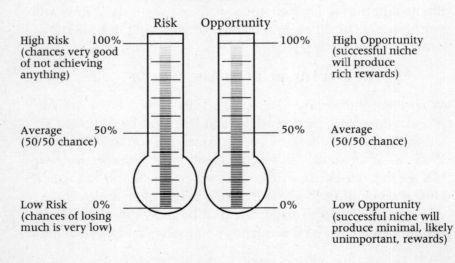

High Risk   100%
(chances very good
of not achieving
anything)

Risk   Opportunity

100%   High Opportunity
(successful niche
will produce
rich rewards)

Average   50%
(50/50 chance)

50%   Average
(50/50 chance)

Low Risk   0%
(chances of losing
much is very low)

0%   Low Opportunity
(successful niche will
produce minimal, likely
unimportant, rewards)

Your risk/opportunity score should provide important information as you continue growing and protecting your niche. It's not likely that a niche worth anything will be risk-free. Obviously, what you are looking for is a situation where your opportunity score outweighs your risk score. If your risk score is significantly high, then you will want your opportunity score to be equally high or more so. It will be up to you to decide which is a stronger need in your life or business—the opportunities inherent in your niche or the apparent security and predictability that come from avoiding any risk. This exercise should also offer you a pragmatic view of your niche. By asking yourself what its real opportunities are should it succeed, you are less likely to barrel ahead with a whimsical idea more suitable for a hobby.

Regardless of how high their score may be on the opportunity scale, some people still resist starting because of an omnipresent fear of failure. Rather than fail, they choose not to start. Gary is one of those people.

GARY'S IMPOSSIBLE DREAM

Gary made his appointment for my counsel after hearing me talk on the radio about the importance of keen focus and ensuring you truly have something perceived by others as Special. From the first time he called I thought he was onto something intriguing and potentially very lucrative. The service he wanted to offer was one I definitely wanted to buy! I had no idea most of my work with Gary would be to shove him off the dime and get him just doing his dream.

"Dr. Falkenstein, I have this idea for a business," Gary told me. As he talked he laid out in front of me pounds of papers with plans, numbers, research, names—what looked like years of homework. He went on to describe a fascinating combination of mobile car wash and high-end car valet services. Perfect, I thought, for professionals too busy to wash their own cars but still wanting them shiny and presentable.

Although I usually actively avoid judging the value of anyone's widget based upon my own interest, I found his concept so interesting I nearly signed up for it on the spot. In fact, I told him I'd be first on his list! The more interested I sounded, the more he resisted, or so it seemed.

"Dr. Falkenstein, I want to do this right. I want everyone to be satisfied. I don't want to make any mistakes." Gary explained how he wanted to do an interest survey and then a test to see if his concept was feasible before we undertook any announcement of its availability. All that sounded sensible. The only problem was that no matter how finished the survey was or how much research Gary did about possible logistics, he was never quite ready to implement either the survey or the test.

Finally, on one of his visits, I said to him, "Gary, it seems to me you are looking for excuses to *not* start. I'm wondering how much you really believe in this concept of yours. Every time we get to the edge of go you find a reason to stop and pull back."

He looked at me and smiled a gentle acknowledgment. With kind of a sheepish grin, he said, "You know, I think I'm afraid it's going to be too successful and I won't know what to do." As he spoke, I thought to myself that success *would* produce some real decisions for him. Gary already held one full-time job and owned a janitorial service he ran in his off hours. His new concept would require some definite trade-offs of time. It would have to come from somewhere.

But I didn't think that was at the heart of Gary's anxiety— the thing that was blocking him from getting on with his business concept. I sensed Gary had hit the nail squarely when he said he feared success. His fear of winning was keeping him from ever starting.

We talked for some time about Gary's lack of confidence. Like so many others around him, Gary was caught between the proverbial yin and yang. He wanted yet was afraid. All the intellectualizing in the world wasn't going to be enough. At some point, he was going to have to weigh his potential risk against his potential opportunity and get on with it. Getting on with it could very well mean doing nothing because, as we've already observed, *no action is an action* with consequences as real as overt activity.

Which direction are you leaning toward for yourself:
taking the risk or waiting it out?

Your Instinct History

Much of this book has been devoted to exploring rational approaches to creating the right niche for you and your business. There is another part of our lives and being, however, that cannot be ignored, or at least should not be dismissed. That piece is our instinct.

We all have instinct. Most often we are reminded of that instinct after the fact. You'll be talking to someone and hear yourself say, "I knew I should have done that." Or you'll be driving home thinking about a new product one of your friends has brought out and you'll say to yourself, "I knew I should have done that." Again and again, you "should have done" something. What you should have done was listen to your instinct.

All things being equal, how often do you trust your own judgment on a key decision? Just as we each have a risk history, we also have an instinct history. Trusting your own instinct in making sound business decisions is so critical, it is essential that you have a clear picture of that instinct in your life—so far.

The following exercise will help you see more clearly how you have treated your instinct in the past. It will also give you important clues to how you want to treat it in the future.

EXERCISE 6.3

YOUR INSTINCT HISTORY

In the space below, write down several times in your life when your instinct or intuition told you something very strongly. Then write down your action—how you responded to that intuition, to what your inner brain was telling you. Did you listen? Did you go against your instinct? Then, assess to what extent the action you took was detrimental or positive in both the short and long run. On balance, what role should your instinct play in making business decisions and other key choices?

Instinct	My Action	Result	Positive/Negative

Not listening to yourself is yet another risk-avoidance mechanism. You might be saying "But you said be client-centered. Now you say listen to myself? Isn't this contradictory?" Not at all. You can ask around, do all the research in the world, but if your intuitive self says something totally opposite, I'd say the safest bet is with that intuition. If you've applied the rules of nichecraft, you will have combined the rational with what you feel, having the best of all worlds at your fingertips.

The paths I've taken, and not . . .

Like most books, this one contains its share of hints about the author. While neither an intentional nor precise autobiography, *Nichecraft* is nonetheless a reflection of my experiences and lessons. This particular section is the most important to me personally. In completing these exercises myself—first in the solitude of my car (where my most creative thinking takes place)—I realized that by far the most important pieces of my life had been directly linked to those times when I had risked. The more I perceived I risked, the more I gained. In retrospect, I shudder to think what my life might have been had I not risked one step at a time.

And that's one of the interesting things I've learned about risk. That is, it's a skill that grows in increments. Like confidence. You don't get born with it. You earn it by experiencing successes. And you achieve successes by risking. You risk in small increments. Pretty soon what you risked last time doesn't even seem like a risk. It's part of your invisible arsenal of life skills.

I've also learned that like so many other important things, risk is something you can't hand off to anyone else—not if you want to enjoy the benefits. That would be a little like watching someone else exercise and expecting to reap the rewards. It just doesn't work that way.

I learned that effectively dealing with risk involves our total perspective and approach to life. It's a perspective that doesn't understand "It can't be done." Instead it starts with the opposite and energizing question, "How can we do it?"

And finally, I'm reminded of why Robert Frost remains one of my favorite American poets. He understood what so many of us have to learn through experience. Remember the lines from your high school English class? They are from "The Road Not Taken"(1916).

> *I shall be telling this with a sigh*
> *Somewhere ages and ages hence:*
> *Two roads diverged in a wood, and I—*
> *I took the one less traveled by,*
> *And that has made all the difference.*

What road are you on? And what difference is it making in your life, your business, or your organization's future?

No Plan B

"What do I do if I fail? I need a backup plan." We heard the B word in Chapter 1, from Spencer, who was so all-over-the-map. He would never be able to focus on one direction long enough to achieve real success. Perhaps you've even heard yourself say these things. If you have, read carefully. What I know for certain after years of working with people growing serious businesses is that winners don't have backup plans. They simply don't plan on failing. They know that if their concept doesn't work perfectly, they'll simply go back to the drawing board and make it work. They'll tweak and massage and revamp until it works. In many cases the final widget looks a lot different from the one they started out with, but *never, never* was failure even a possibility.

The real problem with thinking backup is that it kills your commitment level. How can you commit to something that you believe may fail? Additionally, achieving and maintaining the level of focus required for success demands your full attention. There isn't enough of you to go around for you to be doing backup or part-time anythings and everythings just in case. Remember, the whole point of *Nichecraft*'s 9-step process is to eliminate gamble. You aren't jumping off a bridge or blindly launching something crazy. By carefully going through each step, you prepare for success. *No plan B.*

Commitment Versus Contribution

As we've seen too many times, it's easy to get off the niche track, forgetting what our real core effort is about. Tail begins to wag dog and pretty soon we literally don't know which end is which. Who's driving what? If you are going to stay well niched while growing multiple profit centers, while evolving and continuing to grow, you must understand the difference between commitment and contribution.

Nothing illustrates this difference better than a simple plate of ham and eggs. It doesn't take very long to figure out where the real commitment on that plate came from and where the simple contribution was made. Indeed, the pig went the whole way while the chicken walked away. You, too, must be prepared to go the whole way with your niche commitment—but of course, don't wind up on somebody else's plate! Keep track of your niche regularly, ensuring that its focus is still clean and clear by asking one simple question:

Commitment and contribution—where are yours?

Ignoring the Distractions

 True risk avoiders have many clever strategies. They don't even recognize some for what they are. One of the most ingenious is what I call Distraction Derby syndrome. These people are similar to the all-over-the-mapper in that they have fingers in so many pies at the same time they are never in one spot long enough to really do the job. They are distracted from ever having to declare, "I commit to this project/direction and am going to give it my fullest attention." If they don't really commit, how can they lose? Sharon D. is one of those people. You might recognize her story.

THE CASE OF SHARON D.

Sharon D. is a real estate entrepreneur, though she would not acknowledge that herself. If you asked her what she does, Sharon would tell you, as she did me, "I'm a technical writer." Indeed, Sharon does do technical writing for large companies needing additional professional support in this area, but the truth is, she doesn't enjoy or want to do more technical writing on a consulting basis. What she really loves is buying and selling properties for herself. And she has acquired several of them in Hawaii, around the Northwest, in Canada. She's not done badly for a person whose professional life resembles that of a quick-change artist. During one of our meetings, Sharon was updating me on her technical writing contracts, and one firm in particular where she'd signed on for some additional work. Her face didn't suggest she was thrilled about the prospect of spending time on their needs.

"You know, I don't know why I keep taking these things on. I can't stand doing them. Yet I do. Here I'm doing well in real estate. What I really should be doing is devoting myself full time to organizing that as a serious business. But for some reason, I can't say no to these other things."

"Sharon, here's what I think," I offered. "I think these 'other things' keep you from having to seriously commit, to say flat out, 'I'm taking the risk. I'm going to do this and do it right.' If you don't take that position, you can't lose, at least on the surface. But you and I know full well that losing is a lot more than what's on the surface."

We talked about this for quite a while, and ultimately Sharon acknowledged that her technical writing was in fact a hedge against possible failure in the field she loved the most: real estate. Ultimately, though, she had to choose—and did—one over the other. I'm glad to report she chose full-scale commitment to her first love, real estate.

Dick Harvey's Deer Story

Dick Harvey is a Seattle-based management consultant. Some time ago I heard him tell a story that etched itself on my mind and has acted as a reminder not only of his professional wisdom but of the ultimate futility of succumbing to distractions, however reasonable they may seem at the time.

Dick tells the story of what at first appeared to be the mysterious death of many otherwise healthy deer. It seems that at this particular location in the Pacific Northwest, it had been the pattern for a very long time for deer to make a river crossing by swimming from one side to the other. Deer are known to be good swimmers, and when deer after deer, all ages and sizes, began showing up downstream, washed ashore rather than shaking themselves dry from the cold river water, conservationists became very concerned. It took some time—too long for many who felt pain with the death of every deer—before the mystery was solved. But when it was, the answer had meaning for each of us—as well as for the deer embarking upon their swim.

It seems that after years of simply swimming across an unobstructed stream, this season the deer found themselves having to circumvent a sizeable obstruction of logs which had found their way right into the middle of the usual route of crossing. The deer did the logical thing. What seemed to be the easy thing. They swam downstream around the logs. But instead of getting back on course and continuing across the river, the deer found themselves swept on downstream to deadly rapids, where they were smashed to death by torrents of water and razor-sharp rocks.

You may be imagining, as I did, some of your own personal experiences where the sirens of opportunity diverted your attention and thinking, about how long it took you to get back on track—to regain your focus—to shore up your self-discipline. Dick Harvey's deer story will remain with me forever as a constant reminder of the importance of staying on track, keeping focused, and always in touch with where we are going.

Worrying About What Others Think

Worrying about what others think is one of the biggest stumbling blocks for many potentially successful nichemaking efforts. What will they think of me as an individual, as a businessperson? The fact is, some people may think you are unique, different, not following the rules of convention. Maybe even eccentric. Ultimately you will stand out. You certainly won't be ordinary in their eyes. I say congratulations! This is called niche.

One of the issues you will always face as a successful nichemaker is that of being perceived among your colleagues and friends as something of a threat. After all, nichemakers set trends instead of following them. In a very real sense you are upsetting someone else's apple cart. If your way works, it's possible that theirs will have to change. And that in itself is the ultimate threat for some. As you can see, if you rely on others to tell you what you should do—whether you should risk this or that—you are likely to get some very skewed advice.

Truly successful nichemakers, then, aren't seeking approval for their actions from their neighbors and others around them. The most important approval comes from inside themselves, as does their most powerful motivation. If you find yourself constantly worried about what others are going to think, you're not ready to make a niche with impact. This applies in any area of nichemaking, and is relevant whether you're growing a healthy home-based business or a global corporation.

EXERCISE 6.4

YOUR RISK READINESS SCALE

This scale will give you a reading on your current readiness to take necessary risks to achieve your niche(s). Circle the number that most accurately expresses your feeling.

Action/Attitude		Feeling Level			
	Low			High	
1. I fully believe in my (this) niche.	1	2	3	4	5
2. I am prepared to ignore distractions and other apparent opportunities that will dilute my niche-making efforts.	1	2	3	4	5
3. I have made every reasonable effort to ensure that my niche is *Special*, thus reducing any downside that may exist.	1	2	3	4	5

4. I am listening to myself   1   2   3   4   5
   first rather than friends
   and colleagues.

   How to Score: Add up your points.
          25 = You are ready for niche success!
     23–24 = Above average but some refining needed to
              ensure maximum rewards
     21–22 = Average but vulnerable
   21 or less = You should spend more time evaluating your
              risk/opportunity barometer and explore with
              yourself why you are not yet ready to com–
              mit to this important next step: doing it!

Staying the Trendsetter

Most people follow trends. Some people set them. The people who set them are most often the ones who are successful nichemakers. By definition, a trend doesn't exist forever; hence no niche lasts forever. I'm sure you're already visualizing many examples of what I mean. Remember the wonderful retailer who was so successful ten years ago or the family-owned business that thrived for generations. It was so successful, in fact, that it never changed. It just went out of business. Died. Became a mausoleum while its owners could not acknowledge that they needed to change.

Or maybe you're thinking about larger companies such as the used-to-be Hayes "Smart" Modem. As it turned out, Hayes modems worked fine. His niche just didn't keep up with the market he created. A pioneer in modems, Dennis Hayes' name was long synonymous with the exciting technology that allowed computers to talk to one another over telephone lines. For much of the eighties his products dominated the market. Unfortunately, Hayes was too slow in responding to smaller companies that entered the market and virtually niched him to death. Following the company's 1994 filing for Chapter 11 bankruptcy, Hayes announced plans to merge with a competitor, a move that promises to give the niche-that-got-away a second chance.

Moral of the story? You can't fall asleep at the niche!

Whatever niche you are creating will have a life span of X years. A significant part of your success with it will be to accurately predict how long that span will be. One year? Five? Will it be a fad, in today and out tomorrow? However long it lasts, you should be planning for the next step—the re-niche. Remember, keeping a good niche alive requires you to always push the envelope. Plan to be ahead of the curve.

EXERCISE 6.5

YOUR NICHE'S LIFE SPAN

In the spaces below, indicate the time you will spend in each stage of niche development and the dates from beginning to end of each stage.

Start-up time/infancy: _____ months/years

from _____ to _____

Maturity: _____ months/years from _____ to _____

Transition and re-niche time: _____ months/years
    from _____ to _____

The Knockoff Artists

One of the ironies of successful niching is that as soon as you've created a good one, others are going to jump in the ring. It's common sense. Watch winners and do what they do.

The only problem is that if the winner is you and someone else is jumping in to copy you, your unique widget may be out the door. And it will be unless you are awake 24 hours a day, because knockoff artists abound.

Thus, one of the key questions becomes "What can I do to ensure my niches stay mine?" Probably the two most important things you can do are (1) to create a marketing system so powerful that it virtually puts you in your client's life on a daily basis and (2) to create a niche that has a personal identity to it. Although it may happen someday, the one thing remaining in our world yet to be cloned is personality. Yours is unique. Build upon it. Make it larger than life to your public. It is yours alone.

The Impostor Syndrome

Yes, there is one more potential glitch to get in the way of a finely executed niche! You should pay particular attention to this potential obstacle if you, rather than a tangible product, are your niche. The impostor syndrome can afflict anybody, but the irony is, it strikes when you are most successful. It may have been lurking in the bushes ready to hit all along, but it doesn't make its presence known until you have made yours known also. In essence, the impostor syndrome does what its name implies: it weakens you by causing you to feel that whatever success you have achieved with your niche couldn't in fact be real, and if it is, it surely must be by accident rather than design.

If you suffer from impostor syndrome, you are always waiting for your bubble to burst, expecting that at any minute the world will find out that you are really a fake carrying off an act, believing that success is something you get only by sham. People compliment you and you chalk it up to luck. Remember, the success produced through good niches doesn't happen through luck or lottery. It's intentional and rational. In other words, you work for it. So, when you are successful, let yourself enjoy the pleasure of that success. You earned it.

In addition to allowing you to enjoy your well-earned success, there is a very practical reason to rid yourself of impostor syndrome. That is, if you don't believe you deserve success and that you have rightfully earned what you have, you may actually sabotage your niche success. If this shoe fits even slightly, pay special attention to our next topic. It could well be you had plenty of help learning to sabotage yourself.

The "Unhelpers" in Life

On your way to growing good niches you will be confronted with an array of people offering various opinions about what you are up to. And of course, for the most part, they won't have much understanding of your perspective. It will be very important for your own success that early on you learn to distinguish your genuine support system from the sabotage crew. Based upon your own experiences, you may wish to add a few characteristics to the following descriptions, which my clients and general observations have provided me with over the years.

The genuine support system is characterized by individuals who urge you to push your skills and niche concepts as far as they will go, who respect your passion and drive to achieve that Specialness and do not feel threatened by your accomplishments. You might say this support team could qualify in any support situation, not just a nichemaking environment. That may be true. But it is essential when you are crafting Specialness. The genuine support system facilitates rather than hinders. It does not worry about understanding what you are up to but accepts and respects.

The sabotage crew is recognizable by at least the following behaviors. They love to urge you to be *satisfied* and they encourage you to *relax*. What they don't realize is that you are relaxed achieving what you have set out to do. They love to use terms such as *driven* in describing your single-mindedness—as if it were a malady rather than a gift of focus and discipline. By denigrating your energy and intensity of effort, they are compensating—

rationalizing their own lazy, nonachievement-oriented, status-quo mentalities. In their eyes you err by refusing to accept the ordinary. Don't wait for their approval; you'll never get it.

And most dangerous of all, they keep asking "What will you do if you fail?" We have already observed that this may well be the most dangerous of all questions you will ever face. The reason? You may take its implicit assumption seriously. You may believe it. When things get tricky, you may quit instead of continuing. You may say it can't be done instead of figuring out better ways to achieve your goals, instead of asking "How can I do this?"

Although most of us will never create a McDonald's Corporation, the following story reminds us that dreams mixed with a good niche can pay off. It also reminds us to put ear plugs in when faced with naysayers.

Ray Kroc wasn't born a multimillionaire. In fact, for most of his life he seemed to make one false business start after another. People called him a dreamer. Someone who wasn't very realistic. I've heard it said that people even felt sorry for his wife because she had such a peculiar person for a husband. But he persevered and stayed his course. And in 1954 he signed a franchise agreement with Dick and Mac McDonald allowing him to open his first restaurant in Des Plaines, Illinois. Ray Kroc was 52 when he signed that agreement. Imagine how our fast-food industry—indeed our lives and culture—would be different had he listened to those who told him to settle down, get ready to retire from selling malt machines, and quit trying to do it on his own terms.

Navigating the Obstacle Course

On our way to being even more successful with our lives and businesses, each of us confronts obstacles. We've just discussed a few of them that could divert or even sabotage your own nichecrafting efforts. One of the best ways to ensure you don't get sidetracked or, worse yet, totally bushwhacked by a surprise obstacle is to identify in advance the ones most likely to affect you. The following exercise will help you navigate through possible obstacles.

EXERCISE 6.6

NAVIGATING THE OBSTACLE COURSE

In the spaces below, make a careful list of the biggest potential blocks that could come between you and success in your business (e.g., fear of success, financial constraints).

_____

_____

_____

Now that you've made your list, do the following:

Prioritize the obstacles you believe are most likely to occur.
Examine each issue very carefully, identifying different ways the obstacle could be addressed should it actually arise.
Most importantly, think about ways of preventing the obstacle from becoming a blocker in the first place.

RETURN TO SENDER

Each of us has a list of possible blockers. Hopefully yours isn't too long! As you look at your list, whatever length it may be, think for a moment about the source of each of your potential

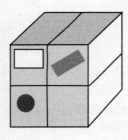

obstacles. I've found that many of my clients discover when they look closely at their biggest blocks that those blocks were put in their way by someone else. Yet they have accepted those blocks as reality for as long as they can remember. A conversation I had with Caroline illustrates this point.

At the time of our visit Caroline was 40-ish, extremely talented, and transitioning from one business enterprise to another. She had a track record of hit-and-miss entrepreneuring. She'd start a project but things never seemed to get off the ground as she'd planned.

"I'm just inept," Caroline blurted out one day.

Startled, I asked, "Where did you figure that out? Whoever told you that?"

Without any hesitation, Caroline provided a litany of support for her conclusion: "My former husband always said I was an incompetent wife, my children tell me I'm an incompetent mother, my father reminded me all the time how I basically couldn't do anything right. . . ."

Beginning with her earliest days, Caroline collected negative baggage from her father, then her husband, and finally her children. She collected so much baggage, she believed it was true. And worst of all, she had begun to act on her assumption of reality.

"Caroline," I said, "it strikes me that for whatever reasons a lot of the people you've met through life have been dumping their own problems on you, giving you responsibility for things that aren't your issues. Incompetence was *their problem*, not yours."

Then I went on, "Fortunately there is something we can do. Since the original baggage wasn't yours to begin with, we should get rid of it as fast as possible. One way to do that is to put all of it in a box marked Return to Sender." Caroline was already grinning. She knew where I was going and liked the idea. If you, as she did, have blockers that you accepted from someone else, it's time to return them. The exercise below will get you started *now*.

EXERCISE 6.7

RETURN TO SENDER

---

1. Start by listing obstacles that were "gifts" from someone else (e.g., "I'm inept," "I can't do it").

2. Now that you've made your gift list, it's time to iden-
    tify who sent you your presents. This is very impor-
    tant, so go back in your memory as far and carefully
    as you can. Then, next to each potential obstacle,
    write down the sender's name.

3. And now, the very best part of all. You are going to
    return your unasked-for gift to the original sender.
    Do this by writing a letter to the sender, spelling out
    exactly what you are returning. Go into as much
    detail as you want. Be very clear that the person
    sent you something that was definitely theirs, *not*
    yours.

4. In some cases you may actually want to mail the letter
    or, as many of my clients have done, make up an
    attractive Return to Sender box and keep it in a safe,
    accessible, though private place. Mark Return to
    Sender all over it.

The next time an obstacle begins to emerge, consider where
it came from. If you didn't create it yourself, get your pen and
paper and Return to Sender. You'll find that even though you
may never mail a scrap of your writings, the symbolic gesture
of ridding yourself of another person's problems is enormously
effective.

So, what does all this have to do with securing my own niche?

One of the most important steps in clearing the path of
blockers to good niche development is rationally understanding where these blocks came from in the first place. Whether
you are primarily concerned with a large business, an organi-
zational niche, or a smaller home-based business, it's critical
that you are always clear not just what the issues are but who
they belong to. You can't solve anyone else's problems, but if
you let them, they can wreck a potentially beautiful niche
before it ever gets off the ground.

YOUR INTENTIONAL ROLE MODEL

One of the best ways to successfully maneuver through the niche obstacle course is by carefully identifying an intentional role model. Throughout life we all have role models. Some of them are less than ideal. Most of them are *unintentional*. By identifying someone who has achieved the level of success you can see yourself achieving, you can telescope your own success path dramatically. The following tips will help you in your quest for an effective and intentional niche role model.

1. You can have more than one intentional niche role model. In some cases, one person may represent one feature and another individual may represent something else.
2. You don't need to know your role models personally. You can read about the individual or, better yet, carefully examine the visible strategies that person has implemented to develop his/her niche. In some cases, you may want to talk personally with the individual, asking "What strategies did you use to get where you are today?"
3. Looking for an intentional role model is not a personality contest. The main thing you are looking for is someone who has achieved the kind of success you envision for yourself. Once you identify the person or persons, you are simply going to "unpack" the strategies they used and do those things yourself, when appropriate!

The virtues in having intentional role models are many. By far the most important one, however, is that by watching winners you avoid needless and costly mistakes. Most of all you are reminded that winning is possible. And most of the time you'll find your role models didn't achieve their success with a lottery ticket. They did it the same way most of us achieve our goals. We sprinkle a good niche with work.

Who is your intentional role model?

Beware Gold Fever

We are in business to succeed. Most of us would like that to happen as fast as possible. On our way to success, we must be very careful, however, to avoid gold fever; that is, focusing so much on the pot of gold that we develop a Mother Lode mentality. We've all met people suffering from Mother Lode. They are always about to strike it rich. They are after the big one so much they lose sight of the process for creating a good niche. Actually, they don't really care about that niche. They want only what it can produce. They tend to flit from one pot-of-gold opportunity to another. Unfortunately, if you don't keep your eye glued to your niche, your home run can turn into a foul ball and fast. Making a good niche is rarely an overnight process. Don't ever allow yourself to be beguiled away from your precious core by the promise of a fast buck or that famous home run. By itself, gold fever doesn't get you where you want to go. Good niche does.

Your Business Is Getting Unniched When . . .

Once you believe you have satisfactorily created whatever kind of niche you set out to make, you must guard that niche with vigilance, always watching for clues that the initial Specialness you created is slipping. Ordinariness is an amazing phenomenon. If you are not careful it can creep up on you before you know it. Following is a list of indicators that hint your niche is slipping:

1. You hear yourself saying such things as "So-and-so is doing the same thing I am."
2. Others can't tell what your product or service stands for.
3. You are following instead of setting trends.
4. You're losing your focus, being tempted by those sirens of opportunity.
5. You're finding yourself worried about market share instead of strengthening and/or reshaping your own unique niche.

6. You have too much to do and not enough time to do anything right.
7. You feel frazzled—at loose ends.
8. You keep adding products and services, thinking each new item may be the cure to your ills.
9. You can't decide which of your several different business cards to give out to people you meet.
10. You feel as if you're herding a roomful of cats.
11. You're chasing the bucks.

Plan to take Your Business Niche Self-Test (Exercise 1.2) at least every three months to ensure you are retaining that special edge called niche. You should also plan to ask that "friendly stranger" (see Chapter 2) to assist with Exercise 2.15 again. Remember, it's not just what you perceive your niche to be but also what the ultimate consumer believes.

Your Entrepreneurial Scorecard

Throughout this book you have been challenged to examine many of your own personal features and assess their relationship to your business niche. Yet one more area requires careful attention, and that is your "entrepreneurial quotient." Following is a list of characteristics and behaviors successful entrepreneurs report as most important in helping them achieve their goals. If this is your first independent business activity or if you are transitioning from conventional employment to entrepreneurship, this section will be especially important for you.

EXERCISE 6.8

YOUR ENTREPRENEURIAL SCORECARD

---

1. Highly focused, single-minded drive, and strong goal orientation are reported as the major features motivating successful entrepreneurs. While earning money

and achieving a satisfying career are important, they don't rank at the top of the list.

Is this you?   Yes   No

2. Walking, talking, and chewing gum at the same time are prerequisites for successful entrepreneuring. Working lockstep on one project, one task at a time, and completing one thing before thinking about another matter are not facts of life for a successful business owner. You become a champion juggler. Murphy's Law prevails here: If you are working on a critical project and cannot be interrupted to think about anything else, you will be.

Is this you?   Yes   No

3. Successful entrepreneurs are skilled at transforming lemons into lemonade. They are not overwhelmed by apparent setbacks. They build on past experiences instead of being their prisoner. The lessons of their experiences become the keys to their future successes.

Is this you?   Yes   No

4. Living with their work is characteristic of most successful entrepreneurs. They rarely separate what they do from who they are. While their lives have other dimensions, they do not need to go to the beach to relax. They enjoy what they do and can do it anyplace.

Is this you?   Yes   No

5. Successful business owners know a well-niched product or service isn't dependent upon the external economy and are willing to launch their enterprise any time in the traditional business cycle. They know that if they are truly well niched, they are recession-proof.

Is this you?   Yes   No

6. Successful entrepreneurs know they must have many customers or clients. Regardless of how large any sin-

gle client may be, it is dangerous to cater to one at the cost of others. You should be building a well-rounded clientele that will not be vulnerable should one or two customers find refuge with another vendor.

Is this you?   Yes   No

7. Time off during your business's early years is a luxury few successful entrepreneurs allow themselves. Successful business owners have made conscious decisions about what they are willing to give up to get where they want to go.

Is this you?   Yes   No

8. Complacency never afflicts the successful business owner. Even if your business turns a great profit and is experiencing much success, you must still be thinking ahead, perhaps preparing to re-niche. You are willing to return most of your profits to the business to ensure its continued health and growth. You know that business failure is never more than a smug grin away.

Is this you?   Yes   No

9. Successful business owners are totally committed to maintaining the health and growth of their enterprise. Not unlike the rearing of a child, they take it from infancy through its various stages of development. Even when it appears able to stand on its own, the most successful entrepreneurs are looking for ways to make their healthy business even healthier.

Is this you?   Yes   No

10. Successful business owners are able to articulate to themselves and others what is truly Special about their business. They understand the concept of niche so intuitively, it is part of their being. (They carry copies of *Nichecraft*'s 9 steps with them all the time.)

How to Score: Add up the yeses.

    10 = Excellent. You were born to be a successful business owner.

    9 = OK. You have a strong entrepreneurial bent but need to do some work in key areas to ensure your success.

    5–8 = You have potential and can achieve success but should pay keen attention to the areas where you collected nos.

    4 = Marginal possibilities. Are you sure you want to go it alone?

    3 or less = Face it: Traditional employment is your cup of tea.

Your Own Private and Quiet Space

As many businesses grow successful, a particularly ironic problem emerges for their owners. I hear it said over and over again. "I don't have any time for myself! I'm buried in paperwork. I have so much to do, I can't even think anymore." If this sounds familiar, you are close to big trouble, if not already in the middle of it.

Chances are very good that whatever idea you originally parlayed into a great niche grew out of some quiet, creative space in your head. As your business grows, demanding more and more of you, there may be little of you left for you. To keep your business niche healthy, *you* must stay healthy.

One of the best ways to do this is to plan regular retreats for yourself and other principals in the business. It is imperative that you take yourself *away* from the actual business site. You must be far enough removed that phones and fax can't reach you, except for emergencies. You must be far enough away to regain the rich sense of perspective and creative energies that allowed you to be successful in the first place.

Of all the advice I give, I confess this is the hardest for me to follow faithfully. Notebook computers, cell phones, and all those wonderful office-on-the-run conveniences just add to the temptation to take my work with me. It's only with monumental mustering that I take myself away someplace very special, preserving and nourishing a quiet bubble of precious personal space and privacy. I'm always glad and can't figure out why I didn't do it earlier. I suggest you do the same, only sooner.

Off to Court We Go!

From this book's earliest pages I have warned against thinking of our subject matter as simplistic or, as some misguided souls may naively believe, trendy. Should you meet anyone who still doubts the importance of making a good niche in today's world—indeed, one belonging to you, alone—you may now advise them that the concept has established itself firmly enough in our lives to increasingly be called upon in court! The following case, in which I appeared as an expert witness, illustrates the growing significance of niche in our lives and business.

It was a few years ago that I first received the call from Ms. X's lawyer. Ms. X is a retailer located in a large city in the Pacific Northwest. Her store, Seaside Gifts,* is located at a popular marina frequented by locals and tourists alike. In naming her store, Ms. X took into consideration its unique waterfront location. While products similar to those she carries may be found in other stores in the area, her seaside location cannot be duplicated anywhere else in town.

Ms. X's problem and the reason her lawyer called me was that Ms. X's lease was about to expire. For a host of reasons her landlord did not want to renew the lease. Her landlord contended Ms. X could take her store anyplace else in the city and do just as well. Ms. X did not want to relocate. Among other things, her lawyer contended:

1. If she moved, the name of her shop, Seaside Gifts, would be irrelevant. The shop's location distinguished her from all the other retailers in the city who carried similar products. The shop's name was so intimately related to

---

*Specifics of this particular case have been altered to protect the confidentiality of the situation and client.

the location that the two features in combination added up to—you guessed it—a niche! Take this away from Ms. X and you would take away her business.

2. Secondly, and of enormous importance in the legal arguments presented, was the assertion that the local market was saturated with like products. Her counsel effectively argued (and I concurred) that Ms. X's chances of succeeding if she moved from her present location would be nil. She would essentially be starting a whole new business, creating a new name for her store, and entering a market filled with like products. Once again, the thing that distinguished her from all the other retailers in town selling similar merchandise was her location, which was closely linked to the name of her store.

Thus we see that Ms. X's store became a destination. People were drawn to it because of the larger setting, which was the real niche. Take that away and you would take away Ms. X's livelihood. This, in essence, was her lawyer's argument. The judge ultimately agreed, and Ms. X and her store are prosperous ever after in their seaside location—oops, I mean *niche*.

As you would imagine, this case was neither as short nor as simple as I've just described it. The lesson we learn from it, though, however abbreviated the version, is that niching is no laughing matter. And it certainly is not an option. For those of us seriously interested in doing more than surviving in the nineties and beyond, distinguishing ourselves from everyone else is imperative. It is also called niche.

And finally, this story reminds us that the niche we make for ourselves must be strong enough to stand up in no less a place than a court of law. If tested in court today, how would your own niche stand up?

Revisiting *Nichecraft*'s Basic Steps

As we move toward the conclusion of your initial *Nichecraft* experience, it will be interesting for you to take your basic

Business Niche Self-Test again right now. Turn back to Exercise 1.2, answer each of the questions, and score yourself. Has your score changed? If so, how and why? What kinds of things do you still need to do before that score will totally satisfy you?

Niche Summary Test

Throughout this book you have been presented with a variety of strategies to assess how closely on target you are with creating niches that will do what you want them to; that is, make you and your business even more successful. Although it will be important for you to review each of the exercises from time to time, following is a summary test you should use as a niche checkup on at least a monthly basis. I encourage you to take and retake your test. If you find your score slipping, slow down, perhaps even stop if necessary. Most of all, identify where the slippage is coming from and shore up the score. Remember, good niches depend upon you.

EXERCISE 6.9

NICHE SUMMARY TEST

Read each of the following statements carefully. Then circle the number indicating your present niche score.

1. My niche meets tests of *Specialness* (e.g., unique, only game in town, one of a kind, singular) (100 points)

   0   20   40   60   80   100

2. I know who my niche audience is.

   0   10   20   30   40   50

3. I know who my niche audience isn't.

   0   10   20   30   40   50

4. I have carefully thought through what I'm willing to give up to achieve what I want.

    0   10   20   30   40   50

5. I am implementing #4 above.

    0   10   20   30   40   50

6. I have strong support rather than a sabotage crew lurking behind me.

    0   10   20   30   40   50

7. My niche is constructed with a built-in system of evolution protecting it from ossification and *dinosauritis*.

    0   10   20   30   40   50

8. I know exactly where my niche is in relation to its life cycle.

    0   10   20   30   40   50

9. I know exactly what my niche stands for and what it doesn't stand for.

    0   10   20   30   40   50

10. I practice client-centered niching and remind myself about the Platinum Rule frequently.

    0   10   20   30   40   50

11. I have identified my wish list of niche consumers.

    0   10   20   30   40   50

12. I have carefully identified "hot buttons" that my niche consumers will resonate to.

    0   10   20   30   40   50

13. Consistency is visible in all my niche-related activities.

    0   10   20   30   40   50

14. My niche achieves my short-term goals.

    0   10   20   30   40   50

15. The niche will achieve my long-term goals.

    0   10   20   30   40   50

16. This niche meets the criteria of a *good* niche.

    0   10   20   30   40   50

17. I am implementing a niche marketing plan that will take the niche through the stages of innovation required to get to my wish list.

    0   10   20   30   40   50

18. My niche marketing plan is intentional, tight, and exciting.

    0   10   20   30   40   50

19. I regularly assess the niche's risk/opportunity score, and if opportunity appears to be dropping I readjust the plan.

    0   10   20   30   40   50

20. I am on guard at all times for clues indicating that the niche may be on the verge of becoming ordinary or nonexistent.

    0   10   20   30   40   50

How to Score

1045–1050 = Excellent but don't become complacent. As you know, the price of a successful niche is constant vigilance.

1035–1044 = You are definitely on the right track but need to watch every move carefully.

1025–1034 = OK, but your niche status is a candidate for a quiet takeover by creeping mediocrity. Better speed(re-)read this book and

get an aggressive plan in place. Join a
Nichecraft Group.

1015–1024 = Ordinariness has taken its toll already. You
need to seriously revamp your approach
to niching and do it now.

1023 or less = Start a Nichecraft Group. You need all the
support and constructive assistance possible!

Form a *Nichecraft* Group

For a host of reasons, a Nichecraft Group may prove an
important vehicle for refining, protecting, and maximizing the
niches you work so hard to create. I have found nothing better
to help people clarify their niche situation than other people
seeking similar goals. It makes sense. As in a support group of
any kind, individuals have at least a nominally shared frame of
reference, an understanding of the overall goal. To create a
Nichecraft Group* that works, do the following:

1. Identify individuals you know who are themselves try-
    ing to create true niches in their business or profession.
2. Limit your group to a maximum of 15 or 20 people.

*To learn more about forming your own Nichecraft Group, call or write:
Dr. Lynda Falkenstein, 1800 SW First, Room 605, Portland, OR 97201;
503-228-6776 or FAX 503-228-7898 or e-mail Dr Niche@aol.com.

3. Try to have a variety of people in the group—from a range of walks of life and points of view.
4. On a regular basis meet to individually and collectively review the exercises and ideas in this book.
5. Work in groups of two or three people, listening to and challenging each other's focus. Insist that what you hear be clear and consistent. Most of all, make certain that it meets all the criteria for good niching.
6. From time to time, invite in "niche winners," people who have created niches that have taken them where they wanted to go in business. Have them explain the process in detail. How did they know when they had arrived at that special moment, the Aha! time?

As your group continues to meet, you will establish a pattern of review and evaluation of members' niches. As simple as this process sounds, you may well find that it is one of the most effective ways of ensuring your long-term success. Instead of operating in a vacuum, the team of people evaluating your moves are all playing with the same rule book as you.

Your Plan for Action

Congratulations. You've done your basic nichecraft training. You've "unpacked" yourself. You've thought about what you and your business bring to the table, who your customers are and what their world looks like. You've considered whether there is a fit between what you are offering and what your wish list wants to buy. You have weighed your tentative niche against the criteria of a good niche. No niche from hell for you. You have market tested your product or service and are confident buyers await. Most importantly, you have designed a marketing system that will shoot your widget out fast, making it a household word on a consistent basis. You are not taking it for granted that your niche will sell itself and you certainly aren't going to let it become invisible. You are so close to getting started that you are already thinking seriously about your re-niche.

Your *Nichecraft* Pledge

In this book I have tried to give you a host of safeguards—ways not only of growing but also of protecting whatever niches you create. Yet another device is the one that follows. It is your Nichecraft pledge. This section differs from those preceding in one way: it calls for your commitment—your absolute promise to yourself. Without that ingredient, you might as well forget the subject. Good niches simply won't happen by themselves. They need you from beginning to end.

My *Nichecraft* Pledge

I will not just talk about being *Special* but will distinguish what the *Specialness* looks like.

I will never be content with the ordinary.

I will remember that *good* niches are not sacred in themselves but for what they achieve in my business, profession, or personal life.

I will plan for the healthy evolution of the niches I create, protecting them from ossification and death at an early age.

I will practice *nichethink* all the time, constantly challenging my niche to ensure that it is still alive and well.

I will get on with it now, remembering that *no* decision *is* a decision. It is time to commit and do it.

_____

Your signature and date

7

THE CRAFT IN SUMMARY

And so we come to the close of this basic guide for growing a successful business by making niches that work. In many ways this book—and the entire 9-step process on which it is based—may seem very simple. And in many ways they are. But don't be misled. The essence of successful niche creation is understanding the process conceptually. Once you have done that, you can apply the idea to virtually any aspect of your business.

As your guide to and through nichecraft, I hope, of course, that you remember every word and exclamation point. If, however, you incline to forget some of the lesser details, I urge you to remember the few key ideas. They have been in my mind at all times while writing about this process. The first, of course, has to do with growing Specialness. Good niches are always beyond ordinary. Beyond excellent. Beyond good. They are Special. Singular. Unique. One of a kind.

Secondly, and of great importance, no single niche panacea exists for every person, business, or organization. There are many roads to a good niche. You must choose the one that will work best for you. To do that, however, you must also be aware of the various options, and then you must shape and massage them until they fit your needs perfectly. One size definitely does not fit all in this case.

Thirdly, this process is never done. Or shouldn't be. No tidy bows exist if you are serious about achieving the right niche. Regardless of what kind you are making, if it is a good one, it

will also be dynamic, growing, and renewing—truly an unfin-
ished curriculum!

And as you've discovered, we've been talking about a whole
new way of thinking. You are done thinking about competing
with anyone else. From now on, you're achieving the *niche
advantage*. You're also aware that even after you identify a
clean, narrow niche, a focus with infinite promise, the real
work is in keeping that niche together. In not allowing it to get
all over the map, becoming an unidentifiable mess. What we
know is that niche messes come in all sizes. You can never be
too small or too large to fall victim to the mythologies of days
gone by. Days gone by that said big was better. Instead, your
new language for success teaches you to think small and deep.
Stay focused on your core. Eyes on the prize.

Most of all, I hope you have come to see the process of creating good niches as something over which you have influence
and control. The process requires your skill, knowledge, intuition, and savvy. The process is truly a craft. By applying the 9-
step *Nichecraft* system to your business development, you ensure
intentionality, consistency, and customers.

And finally, the kind of focus we've been talking about cannot be handed off to someone else. It requires your attention
and full commitment. It requires your *doing* it. Acting upon it. I
am certainly not the first nor will I be the last to urge you to
seize the moment. To not waste time by inaction. More than a
hundred years ago, the great writer Goethe said the same thing
his way. He reminded us:

> Until one is committed, there is a hesitancy, the chance to draw
> back, always ineffectiveness, concerning all acts of initiative and
> creation. There is one elementary truth, the ignorance of which
> kills countless ideas and splendid plans: that the moment one
> definitely commits oneself, then providence moves too. All sorts
> of things occur to help one that would never otherwise have
> occurred. A whole stream of events issues from the decision,
> raising in one's favour all manner of unforeseen incidents and
> meetings and material assistance which no one could have
> dreamed would have come their way. What ever you can do or

dream you can, begin it. Boldness has genius, power and magic in it. *Begin it now.*

And so it is time for me to say good-bye for now, wishing you the best and always urging you, as Goethe did, to go for it! And of course, *good niche.*

Appendix

NICHECRAFT'S MOST FREQUENTLY ASKED QUESTIONS (AND ANSWERS!)

One of the distinct advantages of writing this new edition of *Nichecraft* is that time has allowed me to see my system applied firsthand. As indicated earlier, since the book's first printing I have been fortunate enough to hear from scores of readers all over the country. They have provided enormous support for and testimony to the value of this simple system. They have also asked important questions, which have been invaluable in helping me clarify specific ways nichecraft can be used to achieve our most important goals. The following section is a collection of some of the questions most frequently raised by others concerned about creating the kind of niche that works.

NOTE: Several of the following questions have appeared in my "Niche Doctor" column, which is carried by a host of daily papers across the country. Special thanks to the many loyal readers who have helped me understand even more the power of achieving that Special focus I call niche.

Q: How is niche really pronounced?
A: Pronouncing niche "right" appears to be a function of what side of the Mississippi River you live on. East of the Mississippi you are probably saying niche as in quiche. If you live west of the Mississippi, it's more likely you talk about niches as in itches. It's important to remember that regardless of which side of the great river you live on and no matter what inflection you apply to the word, the ultimate significance of the word

niche remains the same. It may well be the single most important factor influencing your success or failure in the nineties.

**Q: Why did you title your book *Nichecraft* instead of
something straightforward like *Nichemaking*?**
A: I selected the title *Nichecraft* very intentionally after realizing
there is a world of difference between making just any niche
(and who wants to do that?) and the process of making a good
one. And that's what *Nichecraft* is about—making niches that
work for you. By applying the word *craft* to *niche*, we join the
idea of singularity, one of a kind, to a process described as both
an art and a skill. What I have tried to show in the book is the
process for achieving the niches that work for you whether your
goal is to create them in your business, career, or profession.

**Q: Isn't *nichecraft* just another gimmicky term to use
instead of the word *marketing*?**
A: Definitely not! While marketing is an important feature of
the overall nichecraft process, it is only one part of the much
larger story. After all, you can market virtually anything,
though you have no assurance anyone will ever buy or even
want the product in question. Nichecraft is much larger than
marketing. You create entities that are perceived as Special in
your ultimate consumer's eyes, not just your own. Most of all,
it is a vehicle for developing good niches, which can take you
or your business where you want to go.

Q: What are a niche's most important features?
A: Far and away the most important distinguishing feature of
a niche of any ilk is its uniqueness, singularity, or only-game-
in-town character. But remember, there is more to the story
than making just any niche. *Good* niches are your goal, and
those are crafted with skill and sensitivity. Once again, the
moral of the story is that it is not enough to make just any
niche. You only want niches that fit into your overall plan.

**Q: Does everyone have a niche? What if there simply
isn't one for me or my organization?**
A: This is a troublesome question and one I hear people ask
very frequently. It is troublesome because of a highly vulnera-

ble assumption implicit in the question. The assumption is that we inherently have niches—that they are sitting around ready for our discovery—that a game of some kind exists and if we play it right we'll find the magic or elusive niche. Nothing could be further from the truth. We all have many opportunities to make good niches. A major key is in being able to distinguish between nice niches, which you should reserve for hobbies and less-than-earthshaking matters, and the kinds of niches that serve particular ends. It is critical to remember that a niche by itself is just one part of the entire story. What you do with the niche is an equally important chapter!

Q: If it's a good niche, how soon will I see profit? When do the bucks flow in?
A: Although this is a frequent and to-be-expected question, there is no way of saying exactly how long it will take before profits accrue to your bank account from good niche development. What I can tell you is that without the niche, there is little or no chance of your business going anyplace you would ever be glad about.

Q: Is niching the same as positioning or target marketing?
A: This is an extremely important question because it reflects one of the most common and potentially serious misunderstandings about nichecrafting. While positioning, or target marketing, is a part of what we are up to, the complete nichecraft process involves far more. By employing the nichecraft process you reduce the likelihood of creating widgets that have no hope of being appreciated by any kind of serious market. Nichecraft requires that before you ever go to market you determine to the extent possible that you are not trying to be all things to all people—that you make fundamental decisions about who you are and who you are not. The truth is, nichecraft is even more than a process, it is an entire system.

Q: After you've determined the niche, should you have a strategic marketing plan?
A: No. You don't have the plan after the niche. You have it before and during the nichecrafting process. To wait until you

are done is too late. This is an activity where being able to balance five acts at once is essential to your ultimate success. Remember, however, that whatever plan you put in place is going to go beyond conventional definitions of *strategic*—it will, instead, be client-centered, making the fit between what you want to sell and what someone else wants to buy.

Q: How long will I have to work on my niche?
A: Forever. Crafting good niches is a continuous process. Don't even start if you expect to reach niche nirvana, take a sabbatical from the whole affair, and come back and see your niche chirping along in great shape. Good niches require constant vigilance and nurturing. As soon as you think you've made it, it's time to start all over again.

Q: If what I think I'm good at is satisfying to me, shouldn't I be able to make money at it?
A: Not at all. One has almost nothing to do with the other. Granted you should be able to enjoy what you are doing, and most of the time if you are good at something you are going to enjoy that particular activity. But financial return is virtually always a function of someone else also enjoying or wanting the fruits of your labor. It is not enough for you to love what you do. Someone else also has to feel that way! That's what nichecraft is about.

Q: Can I have more than one niche?
A: Because your niche is carefully identified with a specific audience, you must be very careful that any one niche activity does not confuse another niche audience. While it is possible for you to successfully manage several niches in succession, it is next to impossible for most businesses to maneuver through them simultaneously.

The answer is the same concerning niching and your personal life. You may have many interests, but if you are serious about developing something causing others to take you seriously—then you must carefully focus. If you are all over the map personally, no one will ever be able to identify you with any particular approach, position, or strength. Your personal niche can be crafted with the same discipline and rational process you apply to niches in your business and professional life.

In sum, then, while multiple niches are possible, most people and businesses will find they have all they can do to fully develop good niches one at a time.

Q: Is niching more applicable to certain industries than others?
A: A resounding no! Making good niches is imperative regardless of what kind of business or industry you are in. While the 1980s were characterized by people talking about the need to find a niche, the 1990s are a decade of action—actually making those niches. Hopefully they will be good ones.

Q: What if the niche I want doesn't seem to be wanted by anyone else?
A: If you've already manipulated the variables, massaged them as much as possible, checked out potential audiences, reread the *Nichecraft* guidelines, and nobody matches up to your desired niche, there is only one option. Get a new one. Put the old niche someplace where you can't get hurt. Make it a hobby, give it to someone else. Most of all, don't give it priority standing. Check it out from time to time. Maybe you are too early or too late, or maybe it will never work. For now, however, move on to another niche option.

Q: Why do you make such a thing out of making instead of finding niches?
A: The reason I emphasize this point to the extent some people feel is ad nauseam is because the whole concept of *finding* is rife with a seriously misleading assumption. If people go along thinking getting to good niches is a matter of luck or simply working hard or determination, they are in for disappointment at best. So what I say is, let's understand the idea from the beginning. Good niches simply don't happen by accident any more than do successful lives. The central issue is understanding what goes into them and then knowing the appropriate steps that will get you where you want to go—as fast as possible!

Q: If I'm going to find a niche, should I look in certain kinds of markets?

A: Once again, let me emphasize that you are very unlikely to "find" any niche simply by happenstance, much less one that is worth much. Any niche likely to do the job you want, whether in personal or professional aspects of your life, is going to be highly intentional and always rational. It will deliver emotional and irrational joys because of its success, but don't plan to have those unless you put the blueprint in place yourself.

Now that I have given that tirade again, it's important to emphasize that one of the joys of niching is that when you are effective in the niching process you no longer have to search out markets. The fact is, you *make* them. You don't share your pie with anyone. You make a new one, and it's all yours! That's the idea behind niching to begin with. You are creating something that is singular, unique, one of a kind. All yours. By going through the entire nichecraft process, you create the market you otherwise hope to stumble upon by accident.

Q: How does nichecraft apply to long-established organizations?

A: Nichecraft may well be the answer to these kinds of organizations surviving in the nineties. Many companies that built themselves into tremendous successes through nichemaking as recently as this last decade now find themselves threatened by competition and diminishing returns. How can this be? They created niches. They became household words. They did so many things right. Except for one thing, they could still be on top of the heap. They either became complacent, fell in love with their niche, or simply refused to re-niche. They ignored the reality that every niche has an effective life cycle. Like the lonely dinosaur you met earlier in the book, these companies essentially put themselves out of business because they refused to take charge of change. In their cases, they were either unaware or refused to accept the aphorism that *no* decision *is* a decision.

Q: How can niching apply to everyone and everything?

A: This is an entirely reasonable question. To answer it I offer you an analogy between the rules of good nutrition and most living creatures. Granted, the specific ingredients making up the diet differ from species to species, but the overall framework and purpose of taking in nutrition to produce energy remain the same. Architectural blueprints differ depending upon the structure's specific purpose, but the principles of sound building design remain the same whether you are engaged in a futuristic concept or one highly traditional in form. So it is with making good niches. While the manifestations—the outward applications—will be individual, the process for getting there will be shared by all making good niches.

Q: Is there a formula I can work through to get my niche?

A: To ensure you have created the right niche for yourself or business, you will want to use the entire 9-step process described in *Nichecraft* and apply the various formulas within it. Keep the book with you as a basic reference. You may find yourself reflecting about a particular direction you are tempted to take. Just pull out your *Nichecraft* handbook, turn to the appropriate matrix or set of guidelines, and give yourself an on-target score. This process will lead you to creating good niches and to maintaining them as well.

Q: I'm the all-over-the-mapper you talk about in *Nichecraft*. The problem is I'm afraid to let any activities go because they fill in the "shoulder" seasons. You know, the times when business is a lot slower but you still need revenue to function. While what you say makes sense to me intellectually, my irrational side tells me I need the diversity to maintain a secure business. What do I do?

A: Your question raises several points that need to be addressed. First, the idea of shoulder seasons. You must reteach yourself that one of the reasons for niching in the first place is to eliminate shoulder seasons. By creating Special entities you are able to develop a host of products delivering the essence of your niche. The term is *multiple profit centers*. You are able to create a host of revenue streams all related to the niche. In fact, they strengthen the niche position because each stream markets the other. A central key here, of course, is making certain the various streams are all tightly related to your core niche. They must simply be different vehicles for delivering the overall concept—not new niches confusing your existing audience.

And finally, the issue you raise about being afraid to let go. This certainly has to be one of the most powerful issues individuals and large organizations confront almost daily. Bottom line, the answer lies—I believe—in having confidence in what you are up to and realizing that you are not playing craps in Las Vegas with the odds loaded against you, nor are you playing a national lottery. The fact is, if you carefully work through the good niche process, your chances of achieving success are very high. The flip side of my statement of confidence is that you have to do it!

Q: What are the biggest errors people make when working on this niche process?
A: Unfortunately, the biggest errors people make in the nichecrafting process are also the errors most frequently made! Combine frequency with a considerable level of severity and you can understand why so many niches just don't happen, especially good ones. Following are some of those most frequently made niche errors:

1. Far and away the biggest error I see is confusion between a clear and Special niche and a larger, much more innocuous field. Even the brightest individuals seem to have a short memory when it comes to challenging their own focus to ensure that it is clearly definable within a larger field.

2. Too many people get so wrapped up in what they want to sell, they forget the potential niche receiver. They ignore what the customer/client wants to possess or buy. They practice egocentric instead of client-centered marketing (or fail to follow the Platinum Rule).

3. These same people tend to forget that nichecrafting is a process involving many different strategies or avenues to good niches. What works for your neighbor down the

street may not be what is best for you and vice versa. Crafting that right niche for your business or profession may well be a function of many different approaches.

4. Not surprisingly the very people practicing egocentric marketing with respect to niche development often forget that they must employ an aggressive and simultaneous system to get the niche message out to potential consumers. They naively assume it will magically arrive on the right customer's doorstep simply on its own merits. When it doesn't, they give the potential niche an F, say it was not a workable idea from the beginning, and move on to another concept, which has equally little chance of finding its way to any audience.

5. Yet another pervasive and always undermining error occurs with shocking frequency. The error ranges from narrowness to total lack of vision concerning the implications or possibilities associated with whatever niche is being developed. Good niches can be pushed beyond their starting points. They can spin off into products and services and a host of relevant activities all adding satisfaction and profit to your life and/or business. As you craft those good niches, stretch and challenge your vision for what can be. There is no need to settle for what is.

6. And finally, the saddest of all niche failures arises when those in charge shut their eyes to creeping ordinariness. Ordinariness (as you've heard over and over again in this book) is the bane of any successful niche. It is always around the corner ready to pop its head up. Get complacent, forget the concept of Specialness and all it entails, and you might as well say good-bye to any semblance of niche.

Q: I think the idea of getting niched is great. But how do I do it? It's very frustrating to know the thing is important and not have the foggiest idea how to get on with it!

A: Getting a good niche requires that you check out the potential niches already within you—niches ready to be exploited at

a moment's notice (see Chapter 2). One powerful way of
extracting a niche is asking yourself what your maverick is.
What unique spin do you put on an otherwise ordinary way of
doing something? Remember, a niche serves to distinguish you
from everyone else who is also good at what they do. By defining your maverick, you will ultimately come up with something that is truly singular, unique, one of a kind, the only
game in town. A niche! One caveat. If you are serious about
getting niched, be prepared to be different. To stand out.
Conformity gets you zero on the niching scale. A real niche
stands out in a crowd and proudly protects its identity. So,
what's your maverick?

**Q: I'm a financial planner and know that to be really
successful with my business I must be more outgoing. I
should be showing up at various networking groups,
talking to small audiences, and generally getting myself
in front of more people. My problem is every time I
even think about meeting someone new, I always wind
up wondering why anyone would want to buy from me
when there are so many other experts out there to
choose from. I guess it's fair to say I just hate selling
myself. I hide my fear so most people don't know how I
feel, but it really gets in my way. Sometimes I wonder if
I shouldn't become a computer nerd and hide in my
basement sending signals to customers via modem.
What do you think?**

A: I think that in addition to seeking career advice, you may
want to check with a professional who can help you ferret out
what demolished your confidence factor. Sounds like you got
hit with a Sherman Tank–size negative experience along the
way. Any career you seriously pursue will, in one way or
another, require a degree of personal sales. It sounds to me as
if *you* are the resistant buyer. Obviously if you don't believe in
you, you can't expect anyone else to.

In addition to checking out the source(s) of your self-doubt,
you need to get your feet wetter with those get-to-meet-new-
people kinds of situations. Plan to bite off small, safe chunks of
these kinds of meetings. Identify at least one new situation a

week in which you can participate. Then, plan to get others to talk about themselves. Ask people you meet about themselves, about their families, about things they do, about their opinions, about their goals, and other basic pieces of our lives. You'll see how fast people smile and open up when you encourage them to talk about themselves. The savvy person will soon turn the table and ask you similar questions. This is the time for you to begin sharing what you do for a living. You are not going to try to sell your product then and there. You have taken the first step, however. You have established a personal relationship with another human being.

Q: I am starting a new business after a messy business breakup with a long-time friend, or so I thought. It turned out that my partner, whom I trusted more than anyone, betrayed me. He funneled customers off to a competitor and has since gone into business with that person. Because of his crookedness I was left with bills, anger, embarrassment, and confusion about which direction to turn. I've been going through my healing now for two years and am ready to get on with things. The problem is I still get so angry at my former partner whenever I think about what he did, my blood boils and I want to scream. Any suggestions about how to scream once and for all and get the past behind me?

A: Yes. It's simple. Decide to be *successful*. That truly is the best revenge. When you spend time mucking around in the past, regardless of how much you got ripped off or how bad the other guy was, you basically lose. You are taking precious time away from focus instead of getting on with your life. Once you decide to become really *successful*, you channel energies into your own niche development. You figure out what it will take for you to win. And then you do.

Q: have developed a product I believe has great retail potential! With the help of my husband and son, I have worked out most of the manufacturing problems and have refined the product to a sophisticated level. But I do not have the slightest idea how to market my prod-

uct. My attempts to get the product into the stores and mail-order catalogs have been rejected or have led to poor sales. I have found my niche, but I do not know how to make it work for me. How does a person develop marketing skills after the product has been developed?

A: Thanks for your letter raising the important question, "What happens to the better mousetrap?" Unfortunately, the predicament you find yourself in is not uncommon. All too many people invent the product before checking out, much less making, a market for their widget. They wind up with white elephants, Chapter 11s, and frustration with the entrepreneurial process. This doesn't have to be the case. Consider the following observations:

First, based on your letter I don't have any indication that you have created a true niche; that is, something perceived by your target audience as Special, singular, unique, one of a kind. Do you?

Secondly, and most importantly, who is that target audience? How much information do you have about them? If you are to be truly successful in exchanging your widget for their cash, you must know their innermost wants and wishes. If you are trying to get your product into catalogs and mail-order systems, you must know precisely who their target audience is. You must be able to complete the following statement: I have a product that may be of interest to your audience and the reason I think the product is special is the following:_____. Even though you are going about the process backwards, it's not too late if you clarify who that audience is and how your widget meets their perceived needs.

Another strategy you may want to explore is what I call alliance marketing. Identify a company or organization with a vested interest in the same target audience you are shooting for. Perhaps they can use your product as a value-added offering or incentive gift to their customers. While I wish you had asked your question before you launched into product development, it is *not too late* if you begin now by ensuring that you have a niche someone else wants. Your first step will be getting inside your customers' heads, thinking about what they want to buy, not just what you want to sell!

Q: My wife has a niche but won't do anything about it. Our children are grown and she has time now to turn this thing into a real business, but I can't get her to move. Everyone comes to her for this particular product. (If I said what her product is, she might read this and know I wrote to you.) My question is, How do I get her off the dime to take advantage of the opportunity in front of her? If it were me, I'd have done this thing years ago and we'd be sitting pretty by now.

A: Probably you don't. Harnessing a niche is a very personal thing. I don't know why your wife is sitting on hers. Maybe it's a rational, sound reason. Maybe she doesn't want to commercialize something she enjoys. But maybe she's scared. Maybe she doesn't want to be pushed. Maybe her confidence and self-esteem levels are low. Maybe she's afraid of failure. Whatever "maybe" fits, it's unlikely you can do anything about it other than at an appropriate time discuss the subject with her, trying to understand the genuine, most underlying reason for her inaction, which obviously is an action. Beyond that point, you're going to have to simply accept her decision. The fact is, she's *not* you and she doesn't seem to have asked your opinion. Difficult though it may be to digest, this niche (for better, for worse, or not at all) is hers, not yours.

Q: I've got a real problem and the truth is I don't know where to turn. It's my significant other. He doesn't like the business I'm trying to create. I think it threatens him in lots of ways beyond my control. This business endeavor is more than just money to me. It's a vital part of my life. I receive tremendous personal reward and can see great things ahead. The stress I am feeling right now from his negative support is getting to me, but the thought of having to quit the business is more than I can bear. Any suggestions?

A: Ouch! You are experiencing one of the thorniest niche problems around. You need to determine something very important: Is your significant other really on your side? Does this person really want you to win by achieving goals important to you? If the answer is yes, do everything you can to educate him about what you are doing. Sometimes feelings of isolation and lack of information are underlying reasons for a person's apparent negativism. If, however, you answer no, please accept my sympathy because your significant other is a full-fledged member of your sabotage crew instead of the vital support system you need. Sabotage crews make you choose one or the other—your niche or them. My hunch is you're headed toward that uncomfortable decision.

Q: You're always talking about how if we set up our business right, we will be recession-proof. This sounds like one of those too-good-to-be-true kinds of statements. We're a medium-size management consulting firm and have tried every trick in the book to even out the peaks and valleys (more like abysses) which strike all of us in consulting. What's the magic answer you have in mind?

A: No magic. Just be unique and focused enough so that you can roll out several profit centers from your single niche. Different profit centers doesn't mean diluting your niche message; it means delivering it in multiple ways. It means several revenue streams at once. Each revenue stream supports the other but is a legitimate and serious profit center by itself. And secondly—when you are truly niched, you are perceived as the only game in town, which means you are the only one delivering your service. When hard times come you don't share the pie with anyone else; you own the whole pie! In essence you are indispensable, since if someone needs your service there's only one place to go. *You!*

Q: How will I know if I'm really well niched?

A: You'll know because the right people will find you. In other words, your wish list of employers, clients, customers will be able to tell you apart from everyone else out there. Remember, the whole point of a good niche is so that the right others can distinguish you from the masses of other good people out there.

Q: I own a small public relations firm and know I need to get a niche, but something is always getting in the way. The "things" include such items as:

1. **In the last year my husband walked out and decided he didn't want to be married anymore!**
2. **A key client I was banking on started going through his own financial duress.**
3. **I have two children who need to eat and a mortgage that needs to be paid and a debt service of several thousand a month.**

Although I know I need to spend time working on my niche, there is only so much time in the day and I'm spending time running from client to client to keep the cash flow coming in. I know about time management and make lists till I'm dizzy. When do I get time to get niched?

A: What you do is *get started* one niche step at a time. Your issues are very real but so is the need to get on with your life and get control of it. Every day you wait to get your niche together, you are pushing success away in exponential proportions. One of the biggest mistakes many people make is thinking they have to do the whole thing today. They look at the task ahead and gag. A little like swallowing an elephant (whose gestation period, by the way, is 11 months, which is another way of saying big things don't happen overnight). Get started by making a *plan* for the next year. Leave a portion of each day to you and your niche development. That time should be inviolate. You don't have time *not* to niche.

Q: I just entered the field of real estate and have become a partner in a small firm in this area. Our goal is to make a name and niche for ourselves that get us recognized as serious players. We don't plan on being weekend salespeople. This is our business and we want to make it work. What's our first step in getting a niche that's worth something?

A: The first thing is figuring out who your target audience is and who it isn't. You can't be all things to all people, so decide now who you are not going after as clients. Simultaneously,

decide what is going to distinguish you from everyone else in
your burgeoning field. Remember, in the nineties a niche that
means anything goes beyond excellence and good customer
service. It is a feature that causes you to be perceived as
beyond the ordinary. You must be perceived by your target
audience as Special, singular, unique, one of a kind. It matters
little that you think you are special. Your potential customers
are the ones who must be able to tell you apart from everyone
else in your field. Most of all, you are not like pasteurized milk,
bland, homogeneous, indistinguishable from the masses. In the
words of songwriters Aaron Tippen and Buddy Brock, "You've
got to stand for something. . . ."

**Q: I'm 57, male, and a top manager of a nationally
known manufacturing firm. With the option of early
retirement approaching I am seriously thinking about
transitioning out, perhaps establishing my own consulting practice, something you commented on a few weeks
ago. The major thing holding me back is my concern
about selling myself. I don't have the slightest doubt
that I can help my customers with just about any problem, but I feel strange about the prospect of selling
myself. What do you think?**
A: What I know is you have legions of great company. Among
all the issues people have transitioning to a consulting practice,
selling themselves is a frequent and paramount concern. I have
several suggestions. First, you're on the right track acknowledging your high level of competence. After all, if you don't
believe in you, don't expect anyone else to!

Secondly, it's important to recognize that selling your services will be very different from selling other products. As a
professional, for example, you won't be having fire sales. Nor
will you give volume discounts or microwave ovens to entice
the right clients. You will convey your expertise through a
range of powerful strategies including seminars, newsletters,
speaking, and a host of other proven vehicles.

And finally, a little "attitude adjustment" may be in order
concerning your feeling about sales in general. Too many people look down their noses at selling, which is an important

profession unto itself. If you have a quality product (which you admit to), you are, in essence, doing your public a service by making that product available! Look forward to sharing your knowledge and important lessons gained over your years of experience with appreciative clients!

Q: I am a general partner in a small law firm in this area. In order to survive we offer a broad range of services. Because of our size, however, we are simply unable to really compete against the larger firms which control the market here. Basically we are getting demolished with no change in sight. We read your column regularly and would appreciate any suggestion you might make about how to successfully compete against giants with mega millions of dollars and huge clients.

A: Thanks for your important question. Of all the questions I hear, this one certainly is among the most frequent. Interestingly, I hear it from firms of all sizes. Big firms say they can't compete against the hundreds of smaller companies nibbling away at them, and the little firms say they can't survive in the face of the big guys. So what's the answer?

First of all, quit blaming size for your success or failure. Instead of focusing on what others are like and what they do, think first about your own niche in relation to your prospective clients. Secondly, rid yourself of the notion of competing against anyone because you can't win with that approach. You win today by being perceived as Special. You do that by identifying a tight focus that makes sense to your clients and staying on course.

Most of all, you win by addressing your customers' perceived issues, *not your own.* All too often I talk with clients who have given little or no thought to what the world looks like through their customers' eyes. It's critical that you carefully identify and be consistently sensitive to what your clients perceive as "pains." Once you do that, you are in position to frame your services as solutions to problems they perceive as real.

And finally, consider turning your size into an asset. Instead of complaining about what you *can't* do, think about what you *can* do. Smaller means you can respond quickly to customers' needs, you are able to offer very personal service, clients don't have to go through layers of personnel to get to you, etc. In your case, small can definitely be beautiful.

Q: I enjoy your column very much and read it regularly. One thing, however, bothers me and I hope you will clarify or comment on it. It seems you emphasize entrepreneurism as the only hope for anyone who wants to get niched. What does that leave for those of us who don't want to go into business for ourselves? What about those of us who are happy helping others achieve their goals? Are we up creeks without you-know-whats?

A: I am asked this so often I am particularly happy to respond to your question. First, it is important for me to clarify that I view entrepreneurism as a vital approach—a perspective you can employ whether you start your own business or are employed by someone else. Being an entrepreneur means that you look for opportunities, you don't wait for them. You identify problems to solve before they are dropped in your lap. You think about trends and predict needs that you can help fill. You know that if a product is going to be successful in the market, it must be visible. Hence you have an ongoing campaign to inform your audience that you are alive, prosperous, and ready to help make their lives better. Most of all, you are proactive. Entrepreneurs don't sit back waiting for the world to happen to them; they make it happen.

Q: I just sold my store after 35 years in retail. I was extremely successful in the business and am well regarded in my industry, so I'm thinking about doing consulting and helping others who want to do as well as I did. My problem is that I'm 69 years old and my daughter tells me I should slow down and spend time with the family. She says my grandchildren need me and that it's time to share myself and cookies with the kids. While I do love my family, I don't want to stop and head for the rocking chair. What do you think I should do?

A: First, let me say your problem is not your age but your daughter! You are more ready than ever to take your knowledge and experience to market. With all that you know you can be extremely valuable to others and get paid well at the same time. You are facing what increasing numbers of women nearing "retirement" age experience. Families often pressure them to slow down, to give up what they loved to do, in favor of baking cookies and acting like a grandmother. I urge you to do what is right for you. Whatever your decision, your daughter will love you all the same.

Q: I want to go into business for myself but am scared that I can't compete with the big guys and that I'm barking up the wrong tree. What do you think? Can I compete against them? Should I stay where I am and at least know what the next paycheck will say?

A: *No, you can't compete* against big guys or small ones. In the nineties, you can't compete against anyone and win. You can't compete against people and businesses according to the old rules. Rules that said if you worked hard, made a good product, and gave excellent customer service, you would win. Today you win by being Special. These features are no longer special. *Everyone* claims to have them. So, if you want to win against small, big, or in-between you must distinguish yourself from everyone else. Once you do that you eliminate your competition (without bloodshed)!

And about the second half of your question, should you stay where you are, only you can answer that. I will say, however, that if you're banking on security from conventional employment, you may be deluding yourself. Paychecks that 25-year-veteran employees "banked" on coming till they retired have been stopping with increasing and frightening abruptness. If you want real security, plan to make your own widget, not someone else's.

Q: I'm beginning to think I'm the kiss of death for companies I go to work for. Each of the last three jobs I've had disappeared within a year because the companies folded. Although things seem OK right now at the place I'm currently employed, I'm paranoid, afraid the rug might get pulled out from under me any day. Am I a Typhoid Mary of sorts or just a bad judge of employers?

A: Definitely not and probably not. Most likely you've been thinking about your own niche and overlooked assessing how well niched the companies are that you are working for. In the nineties it's all too clear that businesses that don't get themselves niched don't get customers. Not enough customers means you're out on the street taking it personally when the real culprit is probably a management team still playing by obsolete rules. You know, the ones saying that if you made an excellent product and gave the best customer service in town you'd surely succeed. So much for history! Today, businesses that thrive even in recessionary times (and a lot do!) have created the kind of Specialness that distinguishes them from everyone else. The moral of this story is that if you really want to be with a firm with staying power, find one that practices survival of the nichest!

Q: We own a retail store in a small town. Our fate was sealed a few years ago when the freeway shifted the traffic pattern away from the core area where we are located and put it closer to the mall several miles away. Since the freeway and mall have gone in, our customer base has dwindled to the point where we are just a few months from having to liquidate. We are not alone in this predicament. Most other shop owners here are also on the verge of going out of business because there is no way we can compete with the big guys who build malls with huge advertising budgets. We have tried everything but nothing seems to work. Any last-ditch ideas you have would be greatly appreciated.

A: While not a panacea, I do have some suggestions for you that could make a difference in your staying power. They include:

1. You are right. You can't compete against the big guys. So don't even try. Instead think about creating a niche that will cause customers to drive out of their way to find you. Think Special. Think "destination" shopping.

2. Work with other shop owners to identify a special theme or unifying thread defining your town (or neighborhood). It's important that you work with others because the issue is bigger than a single store. You must create a unified presence.

3. Recognize that since you are not going to compete, you will be different from the stores in the mall. Consider capitalizing on your town or neighborhood's history or interesting cultural background.

4. Most of all, remember that once you do create a genuine identity targeting a specific audience, people will drive miles out of their way. They will even get on planes and travel across the planet to find you. They will cart their kids and fight traffic and do all this in the face of uncertain economic times. If you don't believe me, check with anyone who's been to Disney World lately!

Q: I'm 48, female, and have been professionally and financially successful for many years. I have a business that is a model for others in the industry. I've been able to enjoy my work and have a good family life at the same time. "So what's the problem," you ask? It's this: I'm told increasingly that I intimidate people. Recently a client of mine told me that another person he'd spoken with was too intimidated to call me directly to examine my product line. The irony is *I don't even know that person.* We've never met! This may not sound like much of a problem, but if I'm intimidating people who don't even know me I wonder if I'm losing business which could make me even more successful. At this rate, I might ultimately fail because I'm too successful!

A: Although you think this is a peculiar question, let me assure you I've heard it more than a few times. Unfortunately, I don't think there's much you can do about it, because the problem isn't yours, it's the other person's, and fixing other people's problems isn't something you've any control over. Sometimes people who feel inadequate or less than successful themselves are put off by the thought of being in the presence of someone they perceive to be more successful than they are. You can't fix their feelings.

What you can do, however, is arrange informal settings where people can meet you in less than imposing circumstances. Let them know you as a real person, not just a successful professional. If you want people beyond your immediate area to get the message that you are approachable, think about communicating that attitude in your various promotional vehicles. In addition to helping others know you better, you are likely to find your own support system and relationship base deeper and richer than ever before.

Most importantly, you need to remember that you can't do business with everyone nor do you want to. It's entirely possible that the people you are speaking about should not be your customers in the first place. People needing significant personal bolstering to benefit from, much less seek, your services require an additional level of attention. If that's the type of clientele or customer base you want to acquire, then your concern is warranted. If it isn't, accept the fact that well-niched professionals and other successful people know who their audience is and who it is not, and they don't spin their wheels and resources rounding up the latter.

Q: I am just completing my degree in clinical psychology. I am also a mom and wife and I don't want to give those roles up. My husband makes a very good salary and any income I make is strictly extra spending money. Although I'm seriously interested in developing my psychology practice, I'm concerned that it will require me to work 60 hours a week. Do you think I can possibly devote 20 hours to the business and plan on having it just be supplemental income instead of the main course?
A: Yes and no. You can devote whatever amount of time you want to your practice. The real question is your level of commitment or seriousness of purpose. I am very concerned about your use of the term *supplemental*. Oftentimes I hear people using this term as a defense mechanism so they don't have to commit to what they're doing. As you well know, the flip side of commitment is risk. The problem with *supplemental* is that it allows you to just dabble, which is OK if that's what you really want. Dabbling has a role in our lives. But dabbling, by definition, doesn't have to go anyplace. It has no direction. No purpose. It usually requires little investment of time or money. It

requires that you give up little to get where you want to go. You don't have to prioritize and make hard decisions about what's really important to you in the long run. And unless you take yourself seriously, it's going to be very hard to get others to do the same.

Now that I've said that, I need to emphasize that you *can* develop a very healthy practice without working 60 hours a week, without abandoning your family, and without giving up vital balance in your life. A successful business is less a function of the number of hours you put in than of what you do when you're there. Your attitude and focus are what make the difference. You need to define your niche and be very specific about your goals. Then create a business plan that will deliver those goals. Only you know what level of commitment you bring to your new career. For you, I hope it's a serious one.

Q: A while ago I was working with a person who allegedly was going to develop some materials with me, which we in turn would use for training within his industry. He was developing the materials based on a program I created. Shortly after we began our work together, he dropped out of the picture. I had invested several hours going over my program, working up possible outlines for the new joint venture. We even had a title selected, again based on my program.

Lo and behold! After many months of not a word from or about my "friend," I heard through a mutual business associate that "friend" was conducting exactly the program he and I had worked on together. It sounds as if he has stolen parts of my material or at least adapted them for his own use. We didn't have a written agreement at the time we worked together, but the understanding was we would have a mutual copyright on the new product.

I feel ripped off and angry. Since we didn't have a prior written agreement, I'm uncertain what recourse, if any, I have. Your suggestions would be much appreciated.

A: I suggest you find an excellent lawyer whose niche is intellectual property and/or copyright protection. It sounds to me as if your "friend" is making hay out of your hard work. Unfortunately the situation you describe is all too common. As one who makes my living writing about ideas and creating products around those ideas, I empathize with your disappointment, frustration, and even anger at the situation. I also know that the issue is far too important to just drop. If you don't act now, you set yourself up for every opportunist in town to capitalize on your hard work without ever having to work up a sweat themselves. Moral of the story once again: Get thee to a lawyer!

Q: I'm a recent entry into the commercial real estate industry. Some of my friends say I'm crazy because the business is so competitive. They also say the industry is changing so much I'll never really get a handle on what's going on. It also seems to be boom or bust. From my vantage point, however, it appears to be very interesting and potentially lucrative, if I do things right, so I've decided to give it a go. Any suggestions you have for making sure I am successful will be very much appreciated.

A: The suggestions I have for you apply to virtually anyone else seriously interested in succeeding in today's rapidly changing business world, especially those of us selling professional services. Some of my priority recommendations include:

1. Worry less about how rapidly changing your own industry is and *focus* on change in your clients' industry. For you to be truly successful you must understand every nuance of your clients' worldview, including their pains, their goals, and their perceived needs. Once you do that, you are in a position to describe how your service will help them achieve their own priorities. It is *critical* to understand that your widget (real estate) is only a vehicle for your clients to achieve their goals; it is rarely a goal in itself.

2. Forget about competing against anyone else. Yes, you read the sentence right! Forget about competing. It won't work. You can't win anymore by competing against anyone else in the same field. Instead, you win

today by distinguishing yourself from everyone else. By being perceived as Special, singular, unique, one of a kind. Only game in town. Niched. When you are truly niched, you *have* no competition. It's a contradiction in terms. You are in a perfect position just entering the field to shape a niche for yourself that is truly intentional and powerful. Most of all, don't allow yourself to fall into the trap of thinking about or blaming competition. Concern yourself with what you stand for and what *others* perceive that you stand for. By the way, what is your niche?

3. Don't allow yourself to fall into the trap so many other hardworking but naive people have tripped into; that is, trying to be all things to all people. Especially when you are entering a field for the first time, unestablished, and with no clients, it's tempting to take anything that comes in the door. Do this now, however, and I guarantee you it will be short-term gain and long-term loss. Who you do business with today strongly influences who you work with five years from now. You must begin *now* choosing who your clients will be and who they *won't be.*

Q: When you talk about niching something, I'm wondering if the same rules apply to all the "widgets" to which you refer. That is, are the rules the same for niching a professional service as they are if I am selling washing machines?

A: An important question. Thank you. While the basic niching steps apply to professional services and tangible widgets, there are some key differences, which you must keep in mind if you are serious about your niche success in a professional service. They include the following:

1. For starters, in the professional services the primary thing you are selling is *you.* I don't care what the field is—law, insurance, real estate, it doesn't matter. While you must focus in on a specific area, your real niche is *you.* What you bring to the table. Your way of doing business. Your approach. Your reputation, which distin-

guishes you from everyone else in your field. You must begin to think of yourself as bigger than any industry and certainly bigger than whatever technology you are dealing with. A person to be reckoned with. Someone who makes an impact wherever you go.

You are helping clients address very big issues in their personal and/or business lives. The bigger the issue, the less important money is in determining who a person chooses to perform a professional service. In issues of huge consequence, people choose other people who they perceive can make a difference. And that's why your primary concern should be developing a reputation as a person of consequence in your field and all the way around!

2. Once you understand how important *you* are in niching a professional service, you understand better why our marketing strategies are so important in conveying just the right tone and message. Strategies such as cold calling give off messages of desperation and begging instead of developing a sense of respect for your capabilities and presence.

3. And not the least important difference between developing a professional service niche and one related to tangible products is that your professional service doesn't go on sale. If you are a surgeon, you don't give volume discounts for appendectomies and cut-rate prices if business is slow. At least not if you want to grow a serious business. People buy other people they perceive to be already successful. Begging through cold calls and slashing prices rarely conveys a tone of self-confidence and success. Regardless of what service you are selling, think of yourself as the "surgeon" of your industry. No fire sales needed. Your reputation speaks for itself. That's called being niched.

Q: I have followed your column for a long time now and enjoy it very much. In my business we do a lot of cold calls, which I understand you frown upon. I would appreciate your comments about cold calling and how to maximize the strategy if I'm actually going to use it.

A: First off, I need to clarify. I don't have anything against pre-qualified telephone calling—the kind where you have reason to believe the person you're calling may be interested in what you have to offer. Where you have done your homework and have a personal referral or some specific, legitimate reason to talk to the person at the other end. Where you are able to say, "I'm doing something with some of your colleagues that I thought you might be interested in. May I take just a moment to tell you about it?"

The cold calls I love to hate are ones that go something like this: The caller starts out referring to me by my first name as if we are long-lost friends notwithstanding that he/she sounds prepubescent. The spiel gets launched without the caller ever asking the most basic questions: (1) "Is this a good time to talk—are you in a meeting right now?" (2) "Do you have an interest in hearing about my product/service?" By the time these callers get into their monologue, it's clear they don't have the remotest idea about what I do for a living, what size my business is, how many employees—if any—I have, or if their product is appropriate for my needs. About the only thing they know for sure is that I have a phone that works.

Finally, the thing that makes an already awful cold call a total disaster is having it made by an intermediary. For example, I just received such a call. It went something like this: "Hello, Lynda?" (another old friend, I assumed). "My name is Becky and I'm calling for Fred X from XX insurance company." My first thoughts, of course, were Who's Fred? Have I met him before? Why isn't Fred calling me himself? I wonder if Fred is mad at me that he has to have someone else call me. If personal relationships have anything to do with getting business these days, it occurs to me that Fred is doing everything he can to avoid establishing one with me.

Cold calling doesn't have to fall into the fiasco category I just described. It's just that most do. If you are using cold calls and you are serious about your business, plan to do homework about the person or company you're calling *before you ever pick up the phone*. Most of all, figure out in advance how you are going to begin establishing a relationship—that is, how you are going to connect to the person at the other end of the phone. That connection has to be more than a technological process. Cold calls that work connect people, not just plastic machines and microchips.

Q: I am working for a large company that is always talking about getting the "competitive advantage." Isn't this what you're talking about with getting niched?
A: Thanks for your important question. The answer is *no*. I'm talking about going *beyond* competing to creating something perceived as truly Special, singular, unique, one of a kind. When you compete, you compete against someone else. When you are well niched, you are the only game in town to your intended audience. Mr. Webster reminds us that, by definition, a niche is one thing at a time! In other words, niching and competing are contradictions in terms. This is a critical distinction because, in today's world, it is clear you can't win by competing against anyone else; you win by distinguishing yourself from them, by creating that niche which is perceived as truly Special. NicheThink is a very different way of looking at the world than the compete mentality. Though no less aggressive and altogether intentional, the big difference is that you worry less about what the other guy is doing and focus more on accentuating that which distinguishes you from the rest of the pack. The nice thing about this approach is you don't get into the syndrome of trying to beat someone else down so you can win. The moral of this story, then, is: If you are serious about achieving success, forget competing, it's the niche advantage you're really after.

Q: We are a large real estate company with offices in several areas across the country. The office I manage is in what should be an excellent location. I say "should be" because in the last few years we have been losing our market share to other smaller companies that seem to be coming in and picking our clients away like cherries on a tree. We spend a lot of money advertising and sending out expensive slick mailers so people will know we're here, but it doesn't seem to be enough. Got any ideas?

A: Thank you for the very important question, which relates to businesspeople in virtually every field of endeavor, especially the professional services. I have several things for you to consider.

Before going one more step, you must ask why you are losing your existing clients. The answer most often goes far deeper than simply someone else entering the game. If they are getting picked off like cherries, my hunch is you're leaving the ladder around for someone else to use. More specifically, you may be committing the all-too-frequent sin of getting the client and running to your next possibility. Selling without serving is what I mean. A national study I recently conducted to identify how people choose one commercial real estate provider over another supports this conclusion many times over. Responses to one particular question were especially revealing. The question? "How many times have you seen or heard from your broker since your deal was completed?" The vast majority of interviewees couldn't remember when or if they had talked with the broker who did their deal!

What we know for sure is that it's much more expensive to get a client than to keep one. At least five times more expensive! Instead of running from one new opportunity to the next we should be taking very good care of those we have, figuring out ways to become even more indispensable, creating more value in their eyes. Not to do this reflects short-term thinking and creates long-term loss. Lawyers who communicate with their clients only when the client calls with a problem, or real estate brokers who wait until their tickler file says a lease is coming up for renewal, are headed for a rude awakening. Clients go where they feel their best interests are served. They want to know they can trust you with their important needs. If you just show up when it's money in your pocket, plan to have an empty pocket.

The moral of this story is that in addition to an aggressive marketing system for capturing new clients, it's even more important for you to have a serious commitment to serving and communicating with your existing clients, if you want to keep them, that is.

Q: I want to take big issue with a recent column you did on cold calling. You made it sound as if all cold calls are a worthless waste of time for everyone involved. I am in a business where we have a set number of calls to make every day and from there we get our appointments. The numbers game does work, I guarantee it.

A: OK. I grant you, enough calls can get you appointments. They can also get you appointments with the wrong people and be very labor-intensive. People who are successful using cold calls nearly always know how to qualify their prospects and have done homework before picking up the phone. All too often I get calls from some otherwise nice-sounding person who says, "Hello, Dr. Falkenstein, I'm so-and-so, and I recently sent you a letter describing a service which I'd like to tell you more about." The problem is that the service is totally inappropriate for me or my business. When I ask, "Do you know what I do?" the person usually pauses, and replies with another question, "No, what *do* you do?" The problem here is pretty obvious. I'm not about to do business with someone who doesn't know me and hasn't taken the time to find out anything about me before taking my time on the phone. Unfortunately, that is how cold calls are usually handled.

Though telephoning can work when done professionally, I still urge you to implement other marketing strategies which encourage clients to call you, instead of the other way around.

Q: I work for a well-respected company in this region. We have an aggressive marketing department and for the most part have been very successful. Here's the problem. Recently we introduced a new product. Unlike other products that we've brought to market, we brought this one out because it would allow us to be more profitable, which is something we have to do if the company is to sustain itself. In other words, it's a product the company needs. Unfortunately, our customers don't feel they do at this moment. All our marketing efforts to convert customers to this new feature have been major fizzles, at least so far. Any thoughts you have on the subject will be greatly appreciated.

A: An interesting question and kind of a backward way of product development. Backward, at least, if you have success uppermost in mind. It appears you have a few very big issues to deal with. First, if your customer base is very satisfied with its level of service and/or widget, it will be harder to budge them to your new product. Virtually every respectable piece of research suggests people must experience some level of dissatisfaction or have another level of expectation if they are to change products. If I am using your widget now and like the situation, why should I change, especially if it will mean learning something new or, worse yet, paying more? If you are serious about getting me to change widgets, you must be very clear what benefit will accrue to me for doing so. What opportunity will I lose if I don't make the change? And don't expect me to figure out the opportunity myself. Your marketing strategies must persuasively help me understand how your new widget will help me achieve even more success.

Now, of course, we come to what may well be your biggest problem. You said the new product/service was created primarily to address your company's need, *not* necessarily in response to perceived customer desire. If the company is really serious about long-term success with this new widget, I suggest you all sit down at the drawing board very fast and do an honest, perhaps painful assessment of where the new widget really fits into your customers' lives. If you can't confidently relate what its existence means to your customer's success, I'd hit new drawing boards fast. In other words, scrub.

Q: I am a trainer here in the area. I write materials that I use with business and industry. Recently I talked to an organization about my program. My goal was to sell them my services and materials. In the course of our conversation, the person I was talking with expressed lukewarm interest, mainly because, as she said, "we already use a part of it in our training program." I was aghast because I hadn't sold them any books nor had I trained anyone from their organization to use the system I spent time and money creating. Bottom line is they decided not to buy because they have my materials

from someone else, which they have adapted to their needs. Have you ever heard of such chutzpah?

A: Yes. I've heard about it so much, however, I've decided to call it something else. Stealing. Against the law. As you know, I'm not a lawyer, but I sure know where to go to get a good one. I suggest you do the same thing. Fast.

Q: I've been practicing law in this region for several years and have never gotten accustomed to talking fees with my clients. I find myself apologizing for having to bill them, and when I do send out statements, it takes forever for me to get paid. Can you suggest an easy way around this issue?

A: There is only one easy way to deal with fees. It's called being straightforward with no mixed messages. My hunch is that the one who has problems with your fees is you, not your clients. I have yet to see a serious client with any kind of significant issue who expects to have a professional work for free or even give cut-rate fees. I further suspect that you don't realize how truly valuable you are in the lives and eyes of your clients. The fact is, they *need* you. But if you apologize and waffle around about costing money, don't expect your clients to take you seriously, because it's pretty obvious you have doubts about yourself.

Although you doubtless have a letter of agreement that goes out to your clients summarizing the terms of your work together, you may want to consider a preliminary step, which involves having your client complete a client registration form similar to the kind you get when going into a medical office. In the form you can state your professional fees and ask how your client wishes to be billed. Don't forget Visa and MasterCard, since many people find these convenient options for paying professional fees. By far the single most important step in getting your clients to take your fees seriously, however, is for you to do the same!

Q: I am a college professor and have been doing some moonlight consulting to a high-tech company in the East. When I started working with this company nearly 10

years ago, they had more business than they could handle. In the last few years, however, things have gone from slowdown to near grinding halt. Personally I can live without the extra work, but it seems a shame to see the whole business go down the drain. The owner doesn't seem to know what to do to get things moving again. I think they're going in all directions except ahead. Any ideas you have will be much appreciated.

A: Unfortunately, your situation is all too familiar. Companies that were raging successes a decade ago often spent so much time and energy just doing, they lost sight of what made them a success. In most cases, it was creating a niche for themselves that they could plumb to rewarding depths. Too often they forgot or simply didn't know that a healthy niche doesn't stay in the same place any more than a healthy person does. It must be nurtured and grown, hopefully intentionally, so it goes in the direction you want it to. The last thing you need is a monster niche. Something that takes you or your business in a direction opposite to your goals and ambitions—or simply dies of starvation and lack of focus.

If the company's owner is looking for an easy answer or refuses to confront what appears to be his organization's nichelessness, I suggest you find another company to associate yourself with because this one is dead in the water. If, on the other hand, the owner really wants to re-niche and is truly committed to again growing a successful business, there are several things that can be done to move ahead fast. They include:

1. Figure out what customers have been asking you for in recent years. Is it different from when the company started? In some cases the new niche might be in the free advice existing customers have been asking for. In all cases, your customers know what their perceived needs are. Step l, then, is asking them.

2. Most importantly, the company principals must take time out and away from the pressure of daily operations to reflect, commit, and plan. For most entrepreneurs, this is easier said than done, but without this kind of time there is little chance that good decisions will be

made about the company's future. Urge the owner to
pack his bags and invite everyone key to the organization to a weekend retreat someplace. In most cases, it
was creative genius that contributed to the company's
initial success. Now you need to structure an environment that will allow that creative process to bubble up
once again.

ABOUT DR. LYNDA C. FALKENSTEIN AND FALKENSTEIN LEARNING CORPORATION

Dr. Lynda C. Falkenstein is President of Falkenstein Learning Corporation, a national seminar, training, and consulting organization. The company's clients include small to mid-size businesses as well as Fortune 500s. Dr. Falkenstein's Consulting for Profit and Nichecraft seminars, which are sponsored by major trade and professional associations, universities, corporations, and respected newspapers, have been attended by more than fifty thousand people nationwide.

In addition, Dr. Falkenstein writes two important columns, including "Niche Doctor" and "Consulting to Professionals," which appear in respected papers throughout the country.

Prior to entering private practice, Dr. Falkenstein was a university professor. Before that she served on the national staff of the American Bar Association. Her doctoral work at Stanford University focused on the "diffusion of innovations" (If you invent a better mousetrap, how do you sell it?). Today, years after her dissertation signoff, she knows the real answer to the mousetrap question. It's called "nichecraft."

If you have found your experience with this nichecraft primer valuable and would like more information about other products, professional services, or independent trainer and corporate certification opportunities offered through Falkenstein Learning Corporation, call (503) 228-6776 or fax (503) 228-7898 or e-mail DrNiche@aol.com. or write Dr. Lynda C. Falkenstein, 1800 SW First, Room 605, Portland, Oregon 97201.